182-185

THE
BIOLOGICAL BASIS
OF
MENTAL ACTIVITY

THE BIOLOGICAL BASIS OF MENTAL ACTIVITY

JOHN I. HUBBARD

Professor of Neurophysiology
University of Otago Medical School, New Zealand

Formerly Professor of Biological Sciences
Northwestern University

 ADDISON-WESLEY PUBLISHING COMPANY

Reading, Massachusetts • Menlo Park, California
London • Amsterdam • Don Mills, Ontario • Sydney

This book is in the
ADDISON-WESLEY SERIES IN THE LIFE SCIENCES

Johns Hopkins III
Consulting Editor

ISNB 0-201-03086-1
ABCDEFGHIJ-MA-798765

PREFACE

It is no accident that you are reading this book. All over the world, among educated men, the belief is growing that the study of life (biology) is now the important frontier in the search for new knowledge. Biology, like every branch of science, has its big questions. Perhaps the biggest is "What is mind?" or, as many would phrase it, "What is the biological basis of mental activity?" Many scientists feel this question may be answered in this century by experiments on the nervous system. Famous molecular biologists such as Crick, a Nobel prize winner for his part in the discovery of the structure of the genetic material, have abandoned the study of genes and of protein synthesis because they feel that the big questions have been solved in that field. Such men are now working on nervous systems hoping that the approaches which made them so successful in molecular biology will be equally successful in this new field. Some of the scientists' excitement is even percolating down to undergraduates. On many campuses there are more biology majors than physics or chemistry majors. There are many reasons for this of course, but one is certainly the feeling that it is in biology, and particularly in the study of nervous systems, that the next big advances in human understanding will come.

What is the ground of this confidence? I think it comes from the many exciting but as yet fragmentary developments arising from research into the workings of the nervous systems of men and animals. Some of these, such as the study of sleep and dreams and the effects of mind-changing drugs, are the stuff of Sunday papers. Other equally exciting developments are as yet known only to specialists. It is the aim of this book to give an account of these discoveries in a form suited to non-specialists. Such different questions as whether there are ghosts, why asthmatics get attacks in the early hours of the morning, how strong is mind power, how good are memory pills, can a blind man be made to see, have all been the object of scientific investigation.

Before you can appreciate the answers to these questions, you will have to know something about the working of the nervous system and its relationship to mental activity and, in the process, form your own opinion about the difference between men and other animals, the connection between the mind and the brain, the nature of thought, and the basis of memory. You will also learn how drugs are thought to affect the working of the nervous system. You will then be in a position to judge how well present-day biologists can answer the age-old question, "What is mind?" — which is to say, "What is man?"

Dunedin, New Zealand   J.I.H.
January 1975

CONTENTS

INTRODUCTION TO THE NERVOUS SYSTEM

1

The biological basis of mental activity may in one sense be described as the whole body with all its parts working harmoniously together. The Apostle Paul, writing in the first century A.D. said, "If one member suffers, all other members [of the body] suffer with it,"[1] a view which would be strongly echoed by anyone with a pain in his big toe. Indeed, pain in any part of the body is a solvent which can dissolve the most profound thought. The nervous system, however, is commonly, and rightly, thought of as the part of the body having the most to do with mental activity because it receives and stores information from the outside world and, by its connections, enables the rest of the body to take appropriate action.

The elements of any nervous system are nerve cells or neurons. Like every cell of the body, each neuron contains special machinery for energy production and for making fats, carbohydrates, and proteins. Indeed, neuron protein-making machinery is the most active and best developed of its type in the body. The limiting membrane of neurons, too, is specialized, for these cells can both receive and transmit information by receiving and producing electrical signals.

As Fig. 1.1 shows, neurons have a body, the widest part of the cell, which contains a nucleus and all the usual cell machinery. Unlike any other cell type, the body is drawn into extensions called *processes*, thick near the body and thinning out at their extremities. One set, of one or more branches, receives information from other cells or from the environment. The members of this set are known as *dendrites*. Information from other cells is also received by the cell body. The other set consists usually of only one process, the *axon*. Axons arise, as Fig. 1.1(a) indicates, at a thickened portion of the neuron body known as the *axon hillock*. Axons terminate by dividing into numerous axon terminals, each of which has a knob-like thickening at its end known as a "bouton" (Fig. 1.1b). Boutons are found

---

[1] Phillips' translation of the First Epistle to the Corinthians, 12, 26.

1

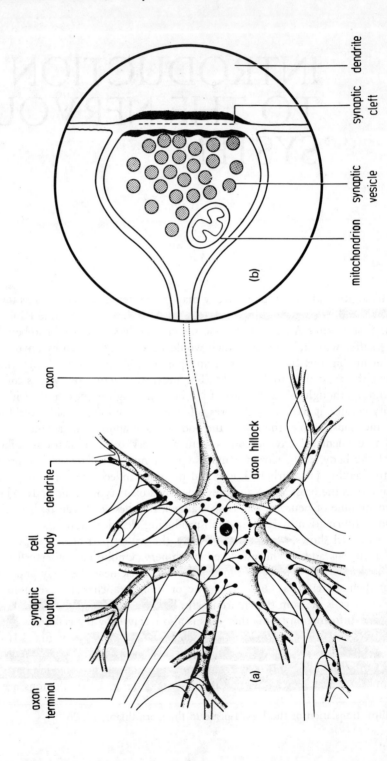

Fig. 1.1 A neuron (a) and a synaptic bouton (b) highly magnified to show a synapse.

scattered thickly over the dendrites, body, and axon hillock of most neurons. As Fig. 1.1(b) indicates, these regions of contact have a specialized structure and are known as *synapses* (from the Greek "to clasp").

Corresponding to the different anatomical parts of a neuron are found different functional properties. At the receiving parts of the cell, *synaptic potentials* can be recorded; at axons, *action potentials;* and at synapses, a short-range secretory process, *neurosecretion,* is found.

It should be noted too that the action potentials set up in response to signals as diverse as hearing an opera singer's aria or chalk squeaking across the blackboard, smelling a rose or a dead rat, feeling sand or silk, are all the same. Merely by inspection of action potentials or synaptic potentials one could not deduce anything about the original stimulus. All nervous systems (insect, mouse, or man) are composed of similar elements with the same functional capabilities. The only fundamental differences are in the number of neurons and in the number of their connections.

These facts raise fundamental problems. In one sense it is not surprising that all nerve cells are the same. They are all, after all, expressions of the same set of hereditary factors (genome) and, in the same way as all lung or all liver cells are much the same, we would expect neurons to be similar in basic structure and function. Yet we know that our nervous systems are involved in very diverse activities. It is not difficult to imagine how nerve cells could be arranged to make muscles contract or glands secrete. It is difficult to imagine how the same elements could be arranged so that we could appreciate a beautiful scene, or compose the *Missa Solemnis* without being able to hear its parts, as Beethoven did in his later years.

Aesthetic appreciation is only one aspect of a complex of functions—memory, attention, perception, vigilance, etc.—all of which are aspects of what is known as conscious life. Being conscious is a state which is difficult to define. It has been variously described as awareness of the environment and "one's self" (Cobb, 1958) and "a private perceptual space time system" (Kuhlenbeck, 1959). Consciousness is clearly a complex process which includes awareness of one's own identity and one's past as well as all aspects of the present situation.

There is abundant evidence that consciousness is dependent on the activity of nerve cells. We are all aware of the effects of strokes, anaesthetics, and epileptic seizures. There is a tendency, however, to think that "something more" than nerve cells must be required for the incredible richness and diversity of conscious life. Yet we would admit that the external world is not in our heads. Events must be represented in some way for us to be conscious of them. It is known that external events only influence us if they are detected by the receptor organs in our skin or by our distant receptors (eyes, ears, olfactory organs, etc.). Furthermore the result of detection of an external event is received by the rest of the nervous system in the form of action potentials. At their entry to the nervous system then, *events are represented by action potentials carried in defined paths,* that is, the specific connections of neurons define a potential event, action potentials in this path signal its realization.

The working hypothesis of most investigators of the nervous system is that the same representation is employed throughout the nervous system, that complex performances are possible because of the vast number of specifically connected neurons, and, finally, that the complexities of neuronal connections are sufficient to explain consciousness. The French physiologist Jouvet (1969), for instance, defined consciousness as "the central nervous system process" which gives significance to a stimulus from the external environment.

This viewpoint has arisen from studies of the structure and function of neurons (how the basic building blocks operate) and from the study of nervous systems (how the building blocks are fitted together). The rest of this chapter gives a brief outline of these matters, together with an outline of how the nervous system controls the rest of the body. It is agreed by all investigators that this controlling function can be fully explained in terms of action potentials in specific axons, that is, in terms of neuron connections. This chapter then lays the basis for understanding the application of neuronal connection theory to higher function.

I. NEURON ANATOMY

If one looks only at their shapes, there appear to be an amazing variety of neurons. On anatomical and functional grounds, however, they can all be classified into three types—receptors, effectors, and connectors.

The neuron shown diagramatically in Fig. 1.1 would belong to the largest class of neurons—connectors or interneurons—if it lay entirely within the nervous system. No one drawing can do justice to the varied appearance of such cells. Most have many branching dendrites, like the neuron illustrated in Fig. 1.1, and a single axon. This axon often branches twice, once near the cell body and again near its termination.

Effector neurons have axons which leave the central nervous system to go to muscles or peripheral neurons (ganglia). Effector neurons passing to muscles are commonly called motor neurons (motoneurons). Like interneurons, such cells have many dendrites connected at synapses, with branches of the axons from as many as a thousand other neurons.

Receptor neurons may have a single dendrite and axon. Such bipolar cells are found in the retina, olfactory epithelium, and in the auditory and vestibular systems. Unipolar receptor neurons are found in the sensory ganglia of the spinal and cranial nerves. One branch of their single process, which will be termed an axon, is specialized to respond to a certain property of the environment—it has a receptor function. As Fig. 1.5(a) indicates, there may be a specialized structure surrounding the nerve terminal. The other branches go into the brain or spinal cord and there divide repeatedly to connect with dendrites of other neurons. These are sites of connection (synapses) only in a functional sense. There is a minute (20–40 nm) gap between the axon terminal and the dendrite membranes.

Another cell type, the *glial* cell, is always found associated with nerve cells. Glial cells provide sheaths for dendrites and axons, thus insulating them from each other. Glial cells also separate the many synapses made by axon terminals with the dendrites or the bodies of neurons. In general, the glial cells have a supporting and insulating function (see Question 1.1).

II. NEURON PHYSIOLOGY

As Fig. 1.2(b) indicates, it is possible to insert fine-tipped glass needles (micro-electrodes) filled with a conducting salt solution into neurons and, by means of appropriate connections with the electrode, record any electrical events which occur. It is found that, as a neuron membrane is pierced, the recording device indicates a potential difference (membrane potential) between the inside of the neuron and the reference (ground) potential (Fig. 1.2b). The inside of a neuron is at a potential *below* ground. The membrane potential is thus negative. For convenience, membrane potentials are usually measured in thousandths of a volt (millivolt = mV). A neuron may have a membrane potential anywhere between −50 and −100 mV. It is convenient to refer to a reduction in membrane potential (lesser negativity, e.g., from −90 mV to −50 mV) as a *depolarization*, and an increase in the membrane potential (greater negativity, e.g., from −90 to −100) as a *hyperpolarization*.

As recording continues, it is found that two types of membrane potential *variation* are detected. One type consists of small, rapidly rising and exponentially declining events, known as excitatory postsynaptic potentials (EPSPs) when they are depolarizing events (Fig. 1.2b) and as inhibitory postsynaptic potentials (IPSPs) when they are hyperpolarizing events (Fig. 1.2c).

The other type, arising from EPSPs, but much more rapid in time course, are known as action potentials (Fig. 1.2b). Like EPSPs, action potentials are potential swings in the direction of reduced negativity; indeed, at the peak of an action potential the membrane potential is positive. These transient variations of membrane potential give neurons unique properties. The basis for these variations is the neuron membrane.

A. The neuron membrane

The composition of all cells differs from that of the medium in which they lie. For instance, in neuronal cytoplasm, potassium (K^+) is the chief ion. The anions, which balance the change on cations, are mostly organic molecules, principally proteins and phosphoric esters. Chloride (Cl^-) and sodium (Na^+) ions are also present but in lower concentration. In the extracellular fluid Na^+ Cl^- and HCO_3^- are the dominant ions. K^+, Ca^{2+}, and Mg^{2+} are also present in much smaller, al-

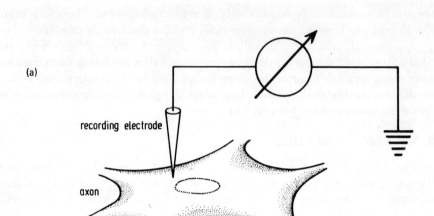

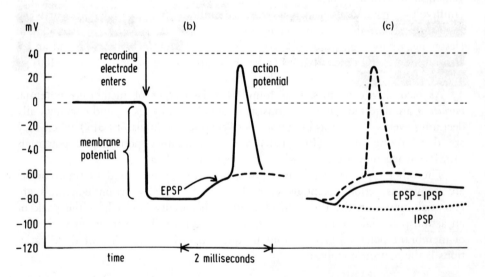

Fig. 1.2 Electrical signals recorded from a neuron. (a) A neuron about to be penetrated by a recording electrode. (b) and (c) indicate typical potential changes recorded by an electrode of the type shown in (a). Area (b) illustrates the membrane potential and a depolarizing potential (EPSP) which reaches the threshold potential for an initiation of an action potential. (c) An IPSP widens the gap between the cell's internal potential and the firing threshold. Thus, if a cell is simultaneously subjected to both excitatory and inhibitory stimulation, the IPSP is subtracted from the EPSP and no action potential occurs if the IPSP is of sufficient magnitude. (b, c, based on Eccles, 1965).

though biologically important, concentrations. These composition differences are thought to be produced and maintained by the activity of the cell membrane.

The membrane of neurons is the same as that of other cells in that it consists of two layers of lipids with their water-soluble ends (circles in inner layer in Fig. 1.3b) facing outward and their hydrophobic ends facing each other in the middle of the membrane. On the inner and outer surfaces of this layer lie protein molecules.

The special properties of neuron membranes arise from the presence of special protein molecules. In Fig. 1.3, some of the protein molecules are labeled R; these are receptors, i.e., molecules which combine with chemical substances to produce a physiological response. Such substances as hormones (Section IV-B, this chapter), transmitters (Section II-E, this chapter) and drugs (Chapter 4, V) may all produce their actions by combination with receptors.

The membrane specialization which allows combination of a chemical with a receptor to be followed by a response is ill understood. Figure 1.3 illustrates one possible mechanism. In this case the receptor molecules occupy the full width of the cell membrane. Upon combination with a molecule of acetylcholine (ACh in Fig. 1.3), the receptors are thought to change their shape (conformation) allowing a pore to open so that diffusable substances can move across the membrane.

B. Transmembrane fluxes and their energy requirements

Cell membranes separate solutions of differing ionic composition. Only if membranes did not allow passage of ions could this condition be maintained without the use of energy. The basically lipid structure of membranes certainly suggests that only lipid-soluble material could cross cell membranes. Experimentally however, it is found that ions do cross cell membranes in small but measurable quantities, probably through water-filled pores between the lipid molecules.

Ions would be expected to move, by diffusion, from regions of higher concentration to regions of lower concentration. Thus Na^+ ions should diffuse into cells and K^+ ions diffuse outward. Such a process would occur spontaneously and require no energy beyond the potential energy of the gradient of concentration. Such movements of ions are said to be "passive."

It is convenient to use the term "flux" for the amount of substance moved across a unit area of membrane in unit time. Ion fluxes have not been measured directly in neurons. In muscles, however, the membranes of which have similar properties, this has been done. The inward Na^+ flux across the frog muscle membrane is 3.5×10^{-12} moles/cm^2/sec while the outward K^+ flux (8.8×10^{-12} moles/cm^2/sec) is more than twice as great (Hodgkin and Horowitz, 1959), largely because the permeability of muscle (and nerve) membranes to K^+ ions is some one hundred times higher than their permeability to Na^+ ions. Permeability coefficients specify the rate of transfer of a substance across a membrane for a unit

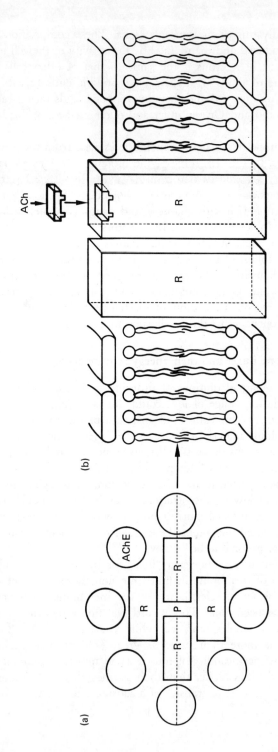

Fig. 1.3 (a) Membrane containing an ACh receptor seen from the surface; (b) Membrane and ACh receptor as seen in section indicated by dotted line and arrow in (a). R = subunits of assumed tetrameric receptor shown in (b) traversing the membrane and forming the walls of a pore (P) in (a). It is presumed that combination of ACh with site on R shown in (b), allows ions to move through pores. One of four subunits of an enzyme molecule which destroys ACh (AChE) is shown in close relation to receptor subunits.

difference in concentration between the inside and outside of the membrane. For frog muscle the permeability coefficient for K^+ efflux is 6.2×10^{-7} cm/sec while that for Na^+ influx is 7.9×10^{-9} cm/sec (Katz, 1966, p. 61).

Despite the influx of Na^+ ions and efflux of K^+ ions, intracellular ionic levels of Na^+ and K^+ are maintained within narrow limits. In frog muscle the internal (Na^+) remains at 9.2 mM compared with 120 mM outside, while the internal (K^+) remains at 140 mM compared with 2.5 mM outside.

The primary reason why cells do not continually lose K^+ ions and gain Na^+ ions has been explained as a result of experiments on frog muscle and squid giant axons. Balancing the inward diffusional flux of Na^+ in these tissues there is an outward flux of identical magnitude. This flux cannot be diffusional because it runs against the concentration gradient. Similarly, an inward K^+ flux balances the outward K^+ flux.

Studies of these fluxes are normally carried out by using radioactive Na^+ and K^+ ions. The influx of K^+ ions can be followed by bathing the tissue of interest in a medium containing labelled K^+ ions and noting the increase in radioactivity of the tissue with time. Efflux of Na^+ ions can likewise be observed by preloading of the tissue of interest with Na^+ ions and observing their appearance in the bathing fluid.

Such experiments have revealed two interesting characteristics of the Na^+ efflux (Hodgkin and Keynes, 1955). Firstly, it is dependent on a supply of metabolic energy. Exposure of squid giant axons to cyanide, for instance, stops Na^+ efflux, but the effects of cyanide can be overcome by injecting the axon with adenosine triphosphate (ATP). In contrast to the passive diffusional influx then, the outward movement of Na^+ ions is an "active" process. Secondly, the efflux of Na^+ ions is greatly reduced or stopped by removal of K^+ ions from the bathing medium. Thus in many tissues the Na^+ efflux is apparently coupled to the K^+ influx.

The mysterious mechanism involved in expelling Na^+ ions is generally known as the *sodium pump*. In some tissues there is evidence that a specific membrane-bound enzyme, the Na-K activated ATP-ase, splits ATP and with the energy so obtained expels Na^+ ions across the membrane and takes K^+ ions into the cell. If for each Na^+ ion expelled a K^+ ion is taken up, the pump is said to be electrically neutral. In some tissues more Na^+ ions are expelled than K^+ ions taken up. Such pumps change the electrical state of cells and are said to be electrogenic.

Cell ionic composition is thus maintained in what is termed a *steady state*. There is not an equilibrium but a dynamic balance between the inward and outward fluxes.

C. Membrane potential

The resting membrane potential (Fig. 1.2b) is generally thought to be a type of diffusion potential, set up mainly by K^+ ions diffusing out of neurons because of the large concentration gradient between their cytoplasm and the extracellular fluid. As the resting membrane is some 100 times more permeable to K^+ ions than to Na$^+$ ions, the potential across it arises largely from this outward K$^+$ diffusion; in fact, an approximation to the resting potential can be obtained on the assumption that the neuron membrane is solely permeable to K$^+$. On this basis every K$^+$ ion diffusing out of the cell down its large concentration gradient would carry a unit of positive charge. As this process continued, a difference of potential would be built up across the membrane, making it more difficult for further K$^+$ ions to leave. Finally, this potential difference would become large enough to balance the concentration gradient, and an influx of K$^+$ ions down the potential gradient would balance efflux down the concentration gradient. This potential difference is known as the equilibrium potential (E_K, for K$^+$ ions). Generally this is

$$E_K = \frac{RT}{F} \ln \frac{K_o}{K_i}, \tag{1}$$

where R is the gas constant, T is absolute temperature, and F the Faraday constant. For frog muscle at 18°C:

$$E_K = 58 \log \frac{2.5}{140}$$
$$= -102 \text{ mV}.$$

This is a little larger than the measured resting potential (approximately -90 mV). Inward diffusion of Na$^+$ ions carrying positive charge into the fiber makes the resting potential less negative than the equilibrium potential calculated for K$^+$ ions, and if this is allowed for, excellent agreement between observation and theory is obtained.

Because the resting potential is reduced from the K$^+$ equilibrium potential, the cell is continually losing K$^+$ ions. This loss and the gain of Na$^+$ ions is continuously counteracted by the sodium pump so that the neuron remains in a steady state.

The signals which neurons generate are all produced by allowing the membrane permeability to ions to vary. This allows either Na$^+$ and/or K$^+$ or Cl$^-$ to run down their concentration gradients, resulting in the transient membrane potential variations (*action* and *synaptic potentials*) shown in Fig. 1.2.

An intuitive appreciation of the direction and magnitude of these potential changes can be obtained by consideration of Eq. (1). As has been pointed out, if Na$^+$ ions are neglected, the equation predicts a slightly more negative potential than is in fact found. Increasing K$^+$ permeability would make K$^+$ even more dominant as the membrane potential would reach the level predicted by the equation. Chloride distributions are the inverse of K$^+$. Indeed changes in K$^+$ and Cl$^-$ permeability generally occur together and have the same effect—a small hyperpolarization.

In contrast, if a neuron membrane were made more permeable to Na$^+$, the membrane potential would become less negative (depolarized). The highest Na$^+$

ion concentration is outside and there would be net inward Na^+ flux. If the Na^+ permeability became large, the membrane potential (E_r) would be set by Na^+ ions, i.e.:

$$E_r = E_{Na} = \frac{RT}{F} \ln \frac{Na_o}{Na_i}. \qquad (2)$$

The ratio Na_o/Na_i is between 10 and 13 for nerve and muscle, so Eq. (2) predicts a positive membrane potential that is, inside *positive* to outside.

D. Action potentials

Neurons (and some muscle cells) possess a specialization of parts of their membranes by which their *permeability to Na^+ is suddenly increased enormously if the membrane potential is reduced to a preset threshold level.* The voltage-sensitive molecules have not yet been identified, although electrical signs of their movement have recently been detected.

An increased Na^+ permeability will of course lead to movement of Na^+ ions down their concentration gradients into neurons, and the membrane of the neuron will of course depolarize (see Eq. (2), previous section). The whole process is said to be regenerative, or an example of positive feedback. The permeability to Na^+ ions increases as the membrane potential falls, and the membrane potential falls as Na^+ ions enter.

Considered at one particular area of a neuron, the process is self-limiting. There are two reasons for this. First, as the membrane potential falls, the K^+ permeability also increases so that K^+ ions tend to run down their concentration gradient, i.e., to leave the neuron as Na^+ ions enter. Second, the Na^+ entry process is not regenerative but self-limiting, i.e., after a certain period of time it turns itself off. For a brief period it cannot be reexcited and is said to be *refractory*. A net efflux of K^+ ions now returns the membrane potential toward its resting value. The whole series of permeability and potential changes (reduction of membrane potential and recovery) takes about one millisec (msec). At the peak of an action potential the membrane potential, as Figs. 1.2(b) and 1.4 show, actually becomes inside positive. The action potential is thus an intensive but brief reversal of the membrane potential, brought about by changes in permeability to Na^+ ions and K^+ ions triggered by a fall in membrane potential.

After an action potential, the cytoplasm is depleted of K^+ ions and has gained some Na^+ ions. The sodium pump removes the excess Na^+ ions while simultaneously taking up K^+ ions. Action potentials do not depend directly upon metabolism, for the store of intracellular K^+ in most cells will allow several hundred action potentials to take place in the absence of any restoration of cell composition.

As Fig. 1.4(a), (b) shows, an action potential occurs in space as well as time. At any particular time there is a region in which Na influx and K efflux are going

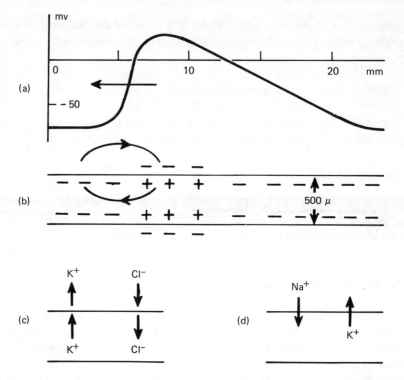

Fig. 1.4 Propagation of an action potential. (a) Spatial variation of an action potential at a fixed time. Ordinate, transmembrane potential; abscissa, distance along fibre shown in (b). The action potential is propagating at a speed of 20 meters per second to the left, as shown by the arrow crossing its upstroke. Note that the upstroke is much steeper than the downstroke. (b) Unmyelinated nerve fibre. Plus and minus signs represent approximately the transmembrane voltage given accurately in (a); distance scale of (a) applies. Diameter of cell is grossly exaggerated with respect to length as shown. Arrows represent current flow in a local circuit or loop due to the difference in transmembrane potential caused by the different properties of the membrane; highly permeable to K+ on left and right even more highly permeable to Na+ in central regions. Local circuit flow acts to reduce charge in inactive regions but has much less effect on charge in active regions because of high Na+ permeability. Propagation is achieved by depolarizing action of local current flow. (c) Capacitive current flow across a membrane. (d) Ohmic current flow across a membrane. (a & b with permission from J. W. Woodbury, in *Neurophysiology,* T. C. Ruch, H. D. Patton, J. W. Woodbury and A. L. Towe, Eds. W. B. Saunders Co., Philadelphia, 1965.)

on (Fig. 1.4b, inside +), while ahead lie regions (Fig. 1.4b, inside −) in which this process has not yet started. There is a potential difference between active (+) and inactive (−) regions.

The cytoplasm of neurons and the extracellular fluid are both conducting solutions so that current flows between regions of different potential. These currents, known as local circuit currents (arrows in Fig. 1.4b), flow from areas surrounding and ahead of the active area, into the active area. In the process these surrounding areas are themselves discharged sufficiently to initiate action potentials. Current flow in the active region is largely *ohmic*, i.e., carried across the membrane by ions (Fig. 1.4d). The local circuit current is largely *capacitive*, i.e., ions do not actually cross the membrane but they discharge its capacity. This process can be understood by considering Fig. 1.4(c). Note that a K^+ ion approaches the internal surface of the membrane and neutralizes negatively charged anions (species unspecified). This allows a Na^+ ion or K^+ ion to leave the vicinity of the exterior of the membrane. Similarly, a Cl^- ion may approach the membrane neutralizing a cation and allowing a Cl^- ion to leave the internal surface.

The travelling nature of an action potential can also be explained in chemical terms because biological electricity is carried by ions, chiefly Na^+, K^+, and Cl^-. A collection of ions has both a concentration and a charge. In chemical terms, because at one point on an axon a K^+ ion leaves and a Na^+ ion enters, there will be a local internal depletion of K^+ ions and external depletion of Na^+ ions. K^+ ions and Na^+ ions from more distant regions, now of higher concentration, will diffuse into the depleted areas simultaneously depleting their own areas. As the membrane potential is a function of the local K^+ ion concentration, this diffusion will reduce the membrane potential in areas adjacent to the area in which there is an action potential. Indeed, enough K^+ is lost in areas surrounding the active area to reduce the membrane potential to a level at which the explosive entry of Na^+ ions begins and an action potential is initiated.

An action potential is then a change of membrane potential some five to six times larger than the threshold depolarization which is able to excite adjacent resting membrane and thus propagate. It is found that action potentials in vertebrate nerve fibres 20 μm in diameter propagate at 100 m/sec. The largest invertebrate nerve fibres, the giant axons of the squid, 500 μm in diameter, conduct action potentials at only 25 m/sec. This apparent paradox is explained by the presence, on vertebrate axons greater than about 2 μm in diameter, of an insulating sheath, interrupted at 1-mm intervals by gaps known as nodes of Ranvier. This sheath, known as *"myelin,"* is the membrane of special glial cells—Schwann cells—in the peripheral nervous system and neuroglia in the central nervous system, which wrap themselves around axons.

During action potential generation in myelinated fibres the local currents are concentrated at the nodes. Action potentials are then generated not at immediately adjacent regions of the axon but at nodes. The action potential propagates from node to node, i.e., apparently discontinuously so that this form of conduction is known as "saltatory" conduction.

There are two other important features of action potentials. First, they are said to be *all or none*. What this means is that if the threshold value of membrane potential is reached (Fig. 1.2, dotted line) an action potential will be generated and its characteristics are not related in any way to the method of reduction in membrane potential. Second, action potentials are said to be *nondecremental*. Once generated, an action potential runs from the neuron body to the end of the axon, even if this involves going from the spinal cord to the big toe, without any variation in its essential properties.

Before the processes which are responsible for action potential generation were discovered (see Question 1.2), axons were known to conduct a brief electrical pulse which was known as the nerve impulse. This term is now used interchangeably with the term action potential to denote the travelling change of membrane potential which is the carrier of information in the nervous system.

E. Synaptic transmission

Neurons are separate entities with a small but definite gap between them. How do signals jump the gap?

1. Electrical transmission

In many invertebrates and some vertebrates, adjoining neurons may have small regions in which their membranes appear very close. Electron microscopy of such regions shows only a narrow 2-nm gap. It appears that in living cells there may be actual connections in the form of narrow channels between cells where small molecules such as Na^+, K^+, and Cl^- could easily pass from cell to cell. Naturally an electrical transient (action potential or synaptic potential) applied to one neuron under these conditions will be detectable in the joined cell. The junctional region is called an electrical synapse, and electrical transients spread from one cell to the other by local circuit currents in the same way an action potential reduces the membrane potential of adjoining regions (Fig. 1.4).

An important function of electrical transmission is synchronization of neuronal discharge. The tail flip of some fishes which enables them to escape quickly from a dangerous situation is initiated by synchronous action of a number of electrically connected neurons. Electrical synapses are not yet known with certainty in man although appropriate anatomical structures have been found. In view of the detection of electrical synapses in other vertebrates (see Question 1.3) it seems probable that such synapses exist also in the human nervous system.

2. Chemical transmission

Most vertebrate synapses are thought to be of this type. Electron microscopy of axon terminals and the dendrite or body of the contacted neuron shows specialization of the axon terminal and of the opposed membranes (Fig. 1.1b). In the terminal bouton, small spherical structures some 40–50 nm in diameter, known as synaptic vesicles, are seen. Several types of vesicles can be distinguished in an electron microscope and it seems probable that these morphological and staining differences can be correlated with the different content of the vesicles. The vesicles are arranged in close proximity to the densely staining areas of the axon terminal membrane adjacent to the gap. The gap itself is about 20–40 nm wide and not much structure can be seen. There is evidence that the *synaptic cleft,* as the gap is called, allows the passage of small molecules. The contacted neuronal membrane may also show densely staining areas (Fig. 1.1b). The terminal, gap, and contacted area make up the "synapse." It is convenient to refer to the terminal as the *presynaptic* side and the contacted cell as the *postsynaptic* side of the synapse.

Such a synapse is a chemical booster mechanism for electrical signals. Action potentials, when they reach an axon terminal, bring about the release of chemicals stored in the synaptic vesicles (Fig. 1.1b). It seems likely that nerve terminals have specialized membranes containing voltage-sensitive molecules controlling the entry of Ca^{2+} ions.

Ca entry into nerve terminals in some way induces the vesicles closest to the presynaptic membrane to fuse with it. The vesicles and membrane then open to the cleft. The chemicals inside—known as transmitters because they transmit a signal across the cleft—diffuse across the synaptic cleft and combine with special sites (receptors) perhaps indicated by the densities (Fig. 1.1b) in the postsynaptic membrane.

Transmitters are quite small molecules. Two are well established, acetylcholine (see Question 1.4) and norepinephrine, and there are several other suspected transmitters. In later chapters it will be shown that drugs which affect brain function may exert their effect by interfering with the action of transmitters. Transmitter action is terminated by removal of the transmitter. In some instances (acetylcholine) this involves degradation to an inert molecule by an enzyme situated close to the receptor (Fig. 1.3a, AChE); in other cases (norepinephrine) the transmitter is reabsorbed for further use by a special enzymatic process in the axon terminal.

Two types of permeability change occur as the result of transmitter action. One type is an increase of permeability to Na^+. This results in a reduction in membrane potential and the potential change is termed an *excitatory* postsynaptic potential (EPSP) because the membrane potential is brought closer to the level at which action potentials are evoked. Figure 1.2(b) shows the time course of an EPSP and its role in setting up action potentials.

The other type of permeability change has a diametrically opposed function. The result of transmitter-receptor combination is an increase in permeability to K^+ or Cl^-. As pointed out previously, a loss of K^+ or gain of Cl^- will result in a local increase in membrane potential, known as an inhibitory postsynaptic potential (IPSP). Figure 1.2(c) (IPSP) shows the time course of such a potential and its role in preventing the setting up of an action potential.

3. *Electrical vs. chemical transmission*

In addition to the electron microscopic differences between the two types of synapse, there are gross differences at the light microscope level. Electrical synapses in general have equally matched pre- and postsynaptic portions. They resemble the two parts of a sectioned nerve.

Chemical synapses, in contrast, are mismatched. The presynaptic terminal at a nerve muscle junction, for instance, is small compared with the large muscle cell. The booster function of chemical synapses, already referred to, is a specialization which, at a nerve muscle junction, enables a signal to be passed across the junction despite the size disparity.

The other great advantage of chemical transmission is the generation of IPSPs by means of the appropriate transmitter. Electrically produced inhibition is known but the mechanism is clumsy and appears an evolutionary curiosity.

Recording of postsynaptic potentials at electrical and chemical synapses reveals other differences. The time between the arrival of the nerve impulse in the nerve terminal and the recording of a postsynaptic potential (latency) is negligible at an electrical synapse, for the postsynaptic potential is an electrotonic derivative of the action potential. In contrast, at chemical synapses there is a finite, temperature-dependent interval (minimum about 0.20 msec) reflecting the various chemical and diffusional processes concerned in transmitter release and diffusion across the synaptic cleft. Much of the latency appears to be due to intraterminal events of unknown nature. Speed of transmission then is an advantage of electrical synapses.

A further point of difference concerns the amplitude of postsynaptic potentials. If the amplitude of the action potential invading the presynaptic terminal is invariant, then at electrical synapses the postsynaptic potential amplitude is also invariant. At a chemical synapse this is not true. The action potential increases the probability of release of a fluctuating number of packets of transmitter. The resulting postsynaptic potentials thus vary measurably in amplitude. One consequence of the coupling of action potential amplitude and magnitude of transmitter release is taken advantage of by the nervous system. Small variations in action potential amplitude can bring about large changes in transmitter release (see Chapter 2, I-D, surround inhibition).

4. Integration

All neurons, as Fig. 1.1(a) indicates, have many synapses, both excitatory and inhibitory in nature. The result of synaptic activity, as Fig. 1.2(b) indicates, is either an action potential (excitation) or no action potential (inhibition).

Many brain cells are continually generating action potentials because an ever-changing number of the tremendous total of synapses on them is always active. Under these circumstances, *inhibition* is detected as a fall in the action potential frequency and *excitation* as an increase in the frequency.

An action potential which travels along an axon to influence other neurons is usually generated at the axon hillock (Fig. 1.1a). This region has a lower threshold; that is, a smaller reduction of membrane potential is enough to set off an explosive increase in Na^+ permeability. An action potential is generated here if the algebraic summation of IPSPs and EPSPs (Fig. 1.2c) results in a reduction of membrane potential to the threshold level. It is now believed that action potentials may also be generated in dendrites and travel toward the soma, although such action potentials do not usually propagate over the soma and down the axon.

A neuron integrates converging excitation and inhibition in both space and time. An excitatory synaptic potential set up by the transmitter molecules released from *one* bouton is far too small to generate an action potential. The cooperative action of the transmitters released from at least 100 terminals seems to be required, all the effects adding together in a short space of time. Setting up of nerve impulses by synaptic transmission thus requires summation of excitatory action. IPSPs can also be summated in the same way as EPSPs.

Spatial summation.   Many neurons have inhibitory synapses preferentially aggregated on the soma and proximal parts of dendrites. Obviously this is a very favorable region for hyperpolarizing an axon hillock. Excitatory synapses from different sources are likewise grouped on particular dendritic branches. Dendritic branches are often extensive. Some motor neurons in the spinal cord, for instance, have dendritic branches which penetrate the whole cross-section of the cord.

Excitatory synapses far out on dendrites might seem to have little chance of producing a depolarization of an axon hillock. Recent investigations however suggest that the electrical characteristics of dendrites allow spread of depolarization to the soma more effectively than would be predicted from the properties of peripheral nerves. Furthermore, if action potentials are generated on distal dendrites and propagate toward the soma, they will depolarize the soma as they approach it. Such action potentials must invade larger and larger areas of membrane as they propagate toward the soma. The probability that any small area will be depolarized sufficiently to reach threshold becomes progressively less. The enormous increase in membrane area faced by such an impulse if it actually reaches the soma usually results in its blockage at that point. Lesser degrees of difficulty are provided by points of branching, and there is some evidence that such points of branching provide an opportunity for subtle forms of integration.

For instance, if an action potential is propagating up to a branching point and the branch and the trunk ahead are already depolarized, then the probability of onward propagation is greatly increased. Concurrent excitation then of synapses on two dendritic branches may lead to greater excitation of the soma than would be expected from arithmetic addition of the effects of each one alone.

Temporal summation.   Since every EPSP or IPSP has a time course of some 15 msec, presynaptic action potentials at frequencies greater than 50–60/sec generate potentials which summate. The summation of IPSPs and EPSPs is not a simple algebraic addition. Indeed an IPSP is increased in amplitude if set up together with an EPSP.

F. Generator potentials

Students often ask how action potentials start. One answer is that, as has just been considered, action potentials are started by other action potentials and by excitatory

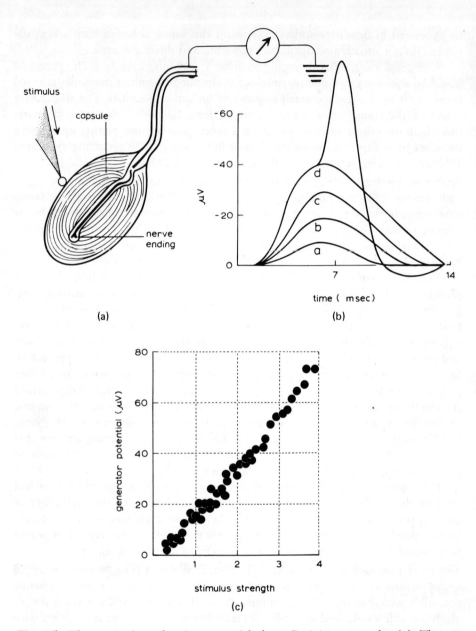

(a)

(b)

(c)

Fig. 1.5 The generation of action potentials by a Pacinian corpuscle. (a) The corpuscle stimulated by a probe. (b) The receptor potential recorded in response to pressure of increasing strength, *a–d*. Note highest pressure evokes an action potential, *d*. (With permission from "Biological Transducers" by Werner R. Loewenstein copyright © 1960 *Scientific American,* Inc. All rights reserved.) (c) The relationship between generator potential amplitude and stimulus strength based on records of the type shown

synaptic action. The final answer however is that action potentials begin in the receptor part of the axon of receptor neurons as the final response to receptor activation (see Question 1.5).

A receptor may be just a bare nerve terminal. The structural basis of the specialization, which it obviously has, to do its job, is presently beyond our limits of magnification. Some receptors, such as the Pacinian corpuscle shown in Fig. 1.5(a), have associated structures which are so large as to be visible to the naked eye.

Such associated structures may serve as part of the receptor mechanism. In the case of the Pacinian corpuscle, the capsule acts as a mechanical filter such that only transient disturbances are transmitted to the terminal. Further, there is some evidence that the associated structure may determine the particular class of stimuli for which a terminal will develop a receptor ability. After nerve transection, for instance, the terminals of regenerated nerves become vibration sensitive only when they grow into the previously denervated Pacinian corpuscles.

Receptors can be classified by the stimuli they "detect." Mechanoreceptors detect touch, pressure, and sound. Other receptors detect light, specific chemicals, temperature changes, or electricity. Men have all these types, except for electrical receptors which are confined to some fish species. Some of our receptors are obvious, particularly the great distance receptors—the eyes, the ears, and the chemical sensors in the nose (smell) and mouth (taste). Everyone is aware too of the contact sensors of the skin—for pain, cold, warmth, touch and pressure. Often forgotten, however, are the internal sensors. One great group monitors the blood. Blood pressure, volume, acidity, oxygen, and carbon dioxide levels are all continuously recorded by the nervous system. Another important group is concerned with movement. They record muscle tension and length and joint movement. The balance organs in our vestibular apparatus signal displacement from, and our position in relation to, the earth's surface.

In all types of receptors the important event is a transduction; that is, *the energy for which the receptor is specialized, is converted (transduced) into a reduction of the membrane potential of a nerve terminal.* This reduction of membrane potential is called a *generator* potential because, if it is large enough, such a potential will serve to initiate action potentials in the adjacent parts of the nerve.

The generator potentials shown in Fig. 1.5(b) were produced in response to increasing pressure with the probe shown in Fig. 1.5(a). As Fig. 1.5(c) shows, the amplitude of the generator potential is a function of the stimulus strength. At a certain stimulus strength, generator potentials are large enough to elicit an action potential (Fig. 1.5b). A larger stimulus may excite two or three action potentials. This occurs because the generator potential outlasts one action potential and will

in (b). (With permission from W. R. Loewenstein, *et al.,* "Separation of Transducer and Impulse-Generating Processes in Sensory Receptors. *Science,* Vol. 142, pp. 1180–81, Nov. 1963. Copyright © 1963 by the American Association for the Advancement of Science.)

be able to evoke further action potentials as the nerve recovers from its refractory state.

Like the initiation of a nerve impulse, the initiation of a generator potential is brought about by a change in permeability of a neuronal membrane. In the few receptors which have been investigated, such as the Pacinian corpuscle (Fig. 1.5a), there is an increase in permeability to Na^+, brought about, not by a drop in membrane potential, but by the specific energy of the initiating event. In the case of mechanoreceptors such as pressure or touch receptors, it may be a mechanical deformation of a receptor membrane that increases permeability to Na^+. The permeability change is reversible, for when the initiating stimulus is withdrawn (probe in Fig. 1.5a), the membrane potential returns to its resting level (Fig. 1.5b), signifying the return to a resting level of membrane permeability.

III. NERVOUS SYSTEMS

In all animals with backbones like ours, and in the more coordinated animals without backbones such as insects, neuron bodies are gathered together in small groups known as ganglia and found in association with organs such as the heart and the viscera. Groups of ganglia are also found collected together in the heads of animals, in connection with the eyes in invertebrates, and with the ears and nose as well in vertebrates, to form a central nervous system. The term "nucleus" rather than "ganglion" is usually applied to a group of neuron bodies in a central nervous system. Axons passing together between one nucleus and another are known as a tract, and much of the volume of the nervous system is taken up by these tracts. In sections of nervous tissue such regions appear white, while regions rich in neurons appear grey.

The central nervous system is linked with peripheral ganglia and with receptors and effectors (muscles and glands) by nerves which consist of the axons of the effector and receptor neurons. A cut across such a nerve shows that it resembles a telephone cable, consisting of an outer surrounding sheath and many smaller cables, each with its own sheath; each of these cables is an axon.

Animals with backbones have their central nervous system lying dorsal to the gut. Insects, however, have their central nervous systems ventral to the gut, except for the portion posterior to the eyes, which is connected with the rest of the central nervous system by loops around both sides of the gut. The insect gut is thus surrounded by a collar of nervous tissue, which has led generations of lecturers to amuse their students with the tale that during growth these animals are faced with the embarrassing problem of either increasing their brain size and restricting their meals, or increasing their meals and restricting the use of their brains.

As Fig. 1.6 shows, our central nervous system is divided into a brain and a spinal cord, organs which most of us never see, unless we are doctors or biologists. The brain is hidden away inside the skull, which has an opening, the great hole or foramen magnum below, where the brain is continuous with the spinal cord.

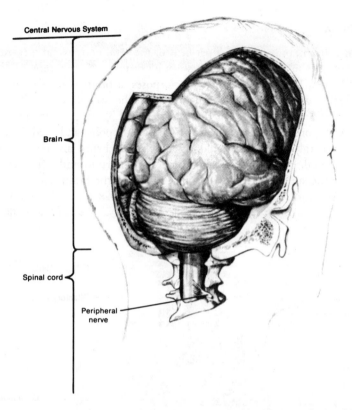

Fig. 1.6 The major components of the central nervous system in relationship to the head and neck. (With permission from Curtis, *et al., An Introduction to the Neurosciences,* W. B. Saunders Co., Philadelphia, 1972.)

The spinal cord lies in the spinal canal formed by the vertebrae. *It is the brain with which mental activity is associated.* A man's mental abilities are unchanged if his spinal cord is severed from his brain, although the parts of his body served by the spinal cord below the lesion will be paralyzed.

A. The spinal cord

The spinal cord contains an inner core of neurons (gray matter) and an outer layer of axons, either descending from the brain or ascending to the brain from receptor neurons (white matter). In the gray matter lie many interneurons and the motoneurons whose axons pass out of the spinal cord in nerves and finally reach the muscles of the trunks and limbs with which they form neuromuscular junctions. In ganglia adjacent to the spinal cord lie the receptor neurons. Their axons enter the spinal cord and branch to form ascending tracts and make local connections with motoneurons and interneurons.

B. The brain

The human brain, only about 2.5 per cent of the total body weight, consumes 20 to 25 per cent of the total oxygen intake and receives 15 per cent of the cardiac output (Purves, 1972). For descriptive purposes, a brain is divided into three regions—the brainstem (continuous below with the spinal cord), the cerebellum, and cerebrum. From the base of the brain (Fig. 1.7), the cerebellum can be seen together with portions of the brainstem (midbrain, pons, and medulla oblongata). The two cerebral hemispheres making up the cerebrum are represented by the temporal, frontal, parietal and occipital lobes of the right and left cerebral cortices which form the surface of the cerebrum and enfold the brainstem and cerebellum.

The cerebellum, though it forms about one-third of the brain volume, need not concern us further. Its neurons are involved in ensuring that movements are made

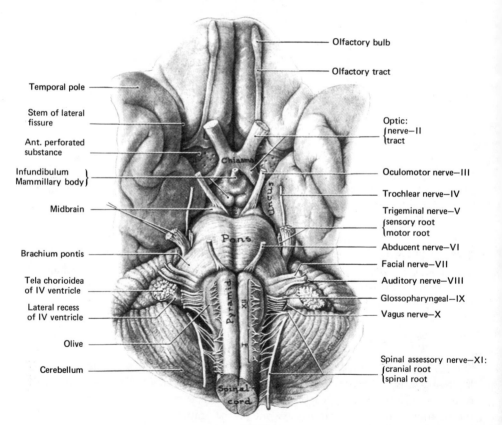

Fig. 1.7 A human brain as it appears from below. Note the cranial nerves and the midbrain, pons, medulla, and spinal cord. Further description in the text. (Reproduction by permission from J. C. B. Grant, *An Atlas of Anatomy,* 6th edition. Copyright © 1972, The Williams & Wilkins Company.)

smoothly and accurately with appropriate speed and direction. People with lesions of the cerebellum alone do not have impaired mental abilities although they may have difficulty in expressing themselves orally, manually, and bodily (speech, writing, crafts, dance, athletics). The cerebrum, in contrast, is of supreme importance. It is generally agreed that its integrity is essential for normal conscious life. The brainstem, linking the spinal cord below with the cerebrum above, has an importance transcending its linking functions, for its neurons too play a part in the maintenance of consciousness.

1. The brainstem

In Fig. 1.8, the four divisions of the brainstem are revealed by removal of one cerebral hemisphere. From below upward they are: the medulla oblongata, pons, midbrain, and diencephalon (which in some texts is included with the cerebrum). The left diencephalon is shown in diagrammatic form facing out of the picture. As Figs. 1.7 and 1.8 indicate, there are ten nerves arising from the brainstem which, together with the optic and olfactory nerves, are known as the cranial nerves.

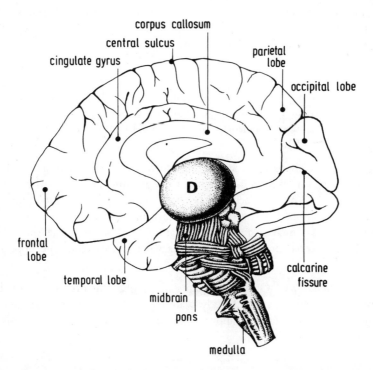

Fig. 1.8   The diencephalon (D) shown in relationship to a hemisected cerebrum. The brainstem has not been dissected (redrawn from Curtis *et al.*, in *An Introduction to the Neurosciences*. W. B. Saunders Co., Philadelphia, 1972.)

(a) *The medulla oblongata.* Like the spinal cord which it adjoins, this region contains ascending and descending tracts, interneurons, and the motoneurons for the nerves supplying the throat, neck, and mouth. In addition, there are nuclei serving integrative functions for the respiratory and cardiovascular systems. For instance, the rhythm of inspiration and expiration is generated here.

(b) *The pons.* Ascending and descending tracts continue through the pons which, in addition, contains receptor and motoneurons for the cranial nerves serving the face. The big bulge of the pons is made by the large fibre tracts entering the pons from the cerebral cortex and passing to the cerebellar cortex.

(c) *The midbrain.* This small region contains, in addition to the ascending and descending tracts, the motoneurons of the nerves controlling eye muscles and therefore eye movements.

(d) *The brainstem reticular formation.* In the midbrain, pons, and medulla, are scattered small nuclei, known collectively as the reticular formation, which have important functions in maintaining the wakefulness and sleep cycle. These nuclei lie centrally, being surrounded by ascending and descending tracts. The term "reticular" means "netlike" and refers to the microscopic appearance of a diffuse aggregation of neuron bodies of different shapes and sizes, separated by axons apparently passing in all directions.

2. *The diencephalon*

As Fig. 1.8 indicates, this is a paired organ, each half being connected with the appropriate half of the cerebrum. Two great collections of nuclei are found in this area, the thalamus more superiorly and the hypothalamus inferiorly at the base of the brain (Fig. 1.9).

(a) *The thalamus.* Separate nuclei are found here for every sensory modality except smell. These nuclei serve as relay and integrating stations on the way to the cerebrum. Pain and crude touch can be "felt" as a result of stimulation of these neurons. A peculiar fact is that the axons carrying impulses representing all the sensory modalities which relay in the thalamus *cross over* in the spinal cord or brainstem. Each cerebrum then receives nerve impulses from the opposite side of the body.

(b) *The hypothalamus.* Only four grams in weight, this organ controls homeostatic functions (maintenance of body water, glucose, blood pressure, heart rate, temperature, etc.) and initiates appropriate behavior patterns in situations where homeostasis is threatened.

3. *The cerebrum*

As Figs. 1.8 and 1.9 indicate, the cerebrum consists of the two cerebral hemispheres. Each hemisphere, as Fig. 1.9 indicates, consists of an outer layer of gray matter

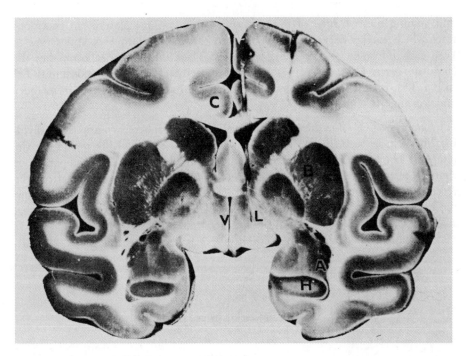

Fig. 1.9 Coronal section of monkey brain showing basal ganglia (B), cingulate gyrus (C), hippocampus (H) and amygdaloid complex of nuclei (A). The monkey was subjected to implantation of electrodes for fifteen months. One electrode tract can be seen terminating in the left lateral hypothalamus (L). The lateral ventricles (unmarked) and third ventricle (V) can also be seen. (With permission from J. M. R. Delgado and D. Mir, "Fragmented Organization of Emotional Behavior in the Monkey Brain," *N. Y. Acad. Sci. 159*, 737, 1969.

(nerve cells) known as the cerebral cortex and an inner layer of white matter (axons) in which is embedded further gray matter—the basal ganglia (B in Fig. 1.9) and hippocampus (H in Fig. 1.9). The cortex is much folded, the folds being known as sulci (valleys) and gyri (ridges). Some important landmarks can be recognized by examination of the surface of the hemispheres.

(a) *The base of the brain.* The longitudinal fissure can be seen separating the two hemispheres, and just below this lie the optic nerves, which decussate at this point (the fibers from the nasal half of each retina cross to the opposite side), forming the optic chiasm (Fig. 1.7). Just below the chiasm lies the hypophysis (pituitary) gland arising from a stalk (Fig. 1.7, infundibulum) in the hypothalamic area.

(b) *Medial surface.* Three important features should be noted (Fig. 1.8): first is the calcarine fissure in the occipital lobe, around which lies the primary visual cortex; surrounding areas are also involved in interpreting visual sensations. Second, joining the two sides of the cerebrum is the corpus callosum, an enormous tract which carries nerve impulses between the two hemispheres and serves to keep each informed of the other's activities. Third, above the callosum lies the cingulate gyrus (Fig. 1.9). This functions, together with the hippocampus (H in Fig. 1.9), in emotional responses (see Chapter 2) and also has a role in memory and learning (Chapter 3).

(c) *Lateral surface.* On the lateral surface of the hemisphere two important dividing lines can be seen. First, there is the lateral fissure (Fig. 1.10) separating the temporal lobe below from the frontal and parietal lobes above. The temporal lobe contains primary auditory cortex where nerve impulses reach the cortex from the receptors in the inner ear. Second, the central sulcus can be seen running from the medial surface over the hemisphere to the lateral fissure. In front of the central sulcus lies the frontal lobe, behind the parietal lobe.

Immediately in front of the central sulcus is the precentral gyrus—the pri-

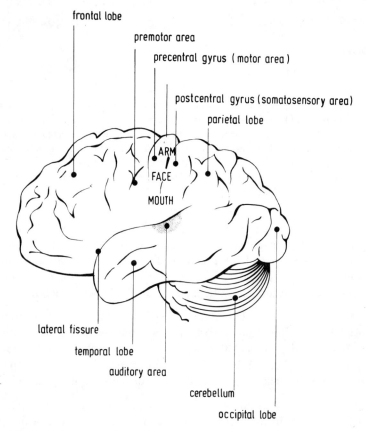

Fig. 1.10 The left lateral surface of a human brain.

mary motor cortex where lie neurons whose axons run down through the brain-stem to the spinal cord to control motoneurons which in turn control skeletal muscles. This motor area, as Fig. 1.10 indicates, is organized so that neurons in a particular part (e.g., Fig. 1.10 arm area) are connected to the group of muscles which control movement round a particular joint. For instance, a group of cells controlling shoulder movement are found in the arm area. The movement produced by motor area stimulation is a well-coordinated movement around a joint, for instance, in grasping, arm lifting, etc. The cortex through the motor areas sends appropriate signals to all the neurons in the spinal cord controlling the muscles concerned in particular movements. This in itself is quite a big order. Simple observations of, for instance, dorsiflection of the hand at the wrist will show that while muscles on the dorsum of the arm contract, muscles on the ventral surface of the arm relax. At the same time, muscle groups inserted on either side of the wrist contract slightly so that the hand does not wobble to one side or the other as it is bent upward.

In front of the precentral gyrus lies an area known as the premotor cortex, which is important in control of complex motor movements such as those involved in speech. Finally, the anterior and inferior parts of the frontal lobe appear to be involved in control of emotional behavior, particularly the inhibition of inappropriate behavior. Persons who have suffered removal of this area (prefrontal leucotomy) are not concerned by social blunders.

In the parietal lobe, immediately behind the central sulcus, lies the postcentral gyrus, containing somatosensory cortex, where nerve impulses from skin, joint, and muscle receptors reach cortex. Like the motor area, each small area in the gyrus is related to a particular part of the body. Note that the leg area is on the medial side of the cortex.

More posteriorly lies the occipital lobe, most of which lies on the medial side of the cerebrum.

4. Within the cerebrum

(a) *Cerebrospinal fluid and the ventricular system.*   Our central nervous system developed as a tube and the remnants of the lumen of the tube still remain. The spinal cord contains a tiny canal, and, as Fig. 1.11 shows, this widens out in the medulla forming the fourth ventricle, which communicates below the cerebellum with the outer surface of the brainstem. A narrow channel (the cerebral aqueduct) through the midbrain connects the fourth with the third ventricle deep within the diencephalon. From the third ventricle, which separates the right and left thalamic nuclei (Fig. 1.9), a narrow connection on each side passes to the lateral ventricles, which in turn pass forward, upward, and back in a U shape inside the cerebral hemispheres (Fig. 1.11). This system is filled with a cell-free fluid derived from the blood by filtration and secretion and known as cerebrospinal fluid (C.S.F.). The same fluid bathes the surface of the brain, passing out from the fourth ventricle around the brainstem. The fluid circulates from its site of

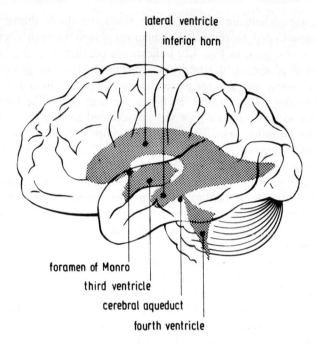

lateral ventricle
inferior horn

foramen of Monro
third ventricle
cerebral aqueduct
fourth ventricle

Fig. 1.11 The ventricular system of the human brain. (Redrawn with permission from Curtis, *et al.,* in *An Introduction to the Neurosciences.* W. B. Saunders Co., Philadelphia, 1972.

production in the roof of the third, fourth, and lateral ventricles to its site of absorption by the veins of the membranes covering the cerebrum.

(b) *Basal ganglia and hippocampus.* A number of large nuclei lie inside the hemispheres in relation to the lateral ventricles. In the lateral part of the floor of the central part of each lateral ventricle lies the caudate nucleus, one of the basal ganglia which has a long tail curving back to run forward in the roof of the inferior horn (Fig. 1.11). Rostral to the tail of the inferior horn lies the amygdaloid complex of nuclei (A in Fig. 1.9), while the entire length of the floor of the inferior horn is formed by the hippocampus (H in Fig. 1.9).

The caudate nuclei and certain other large nuclei which lie more laterally in the white matter are known collectively as the basal ganglia (B in Fig. 1.9). These nuclei are, like the cerebellum, involved in the control of movement and will not be further discussed.

5. *Two hemispheres*

While each hemisphere receives information from and controls the muscles of the opposite side of the body, there are indications of functional specialization of each hemisphere. In most persons, if part of the *left* temporal lobe or the *left* premotor area is destroyed, a severe disturbance of function follows. In the case of the temporal lobe, there is an inability to interpret sounds as words, in the case of the premotor area an inability to combine sounds into words. Similar effects are not observed following damage of the same areas on the right side. A few people have these functions localized on the right side and are then immune to left-sided brain lesions. Similar dominance of motor functions is involved in being right- or left-handed. Some 10 to 15 per cent of students today are left-handed (Hubbard, 1971). It should be noted that handedness does not necessarily correlate with brain dominance. Most left-handed persons have the dominant speech area also on the left (Roberts, 1955). Brain dominance apparently develops during childhood. Children who have unilateral damage to the left premotor area make a complete recovery, apparently because the uninjured right side takes over the integrative functions.

IV. BRAIN PHYSIOLOGY

A. Investigation

Knowledge of brain function is obtained in four ways—stimulation, recording, studying of planned injuries in animals other than man, and studying the effects of disease of the brain in man and laboratory animals. A living brain can be touched, cut, penetrated with wires, or have electrical currents passed through it without its owner feeling any pain or indeed any sensation localized to the brain.

Anatomical studies are often required to verify the site of stimulation or recording or to examine the extent of lesions or diseases. Biochemical investigations can also complement physiological studies. For instance, if certain brain pathways were thought to use norepinephrine as their transmitter, these pathways could be stimulated and the norepinephrine content of the stimulated area assayed. Depletion of norepinephrine after stimulation would support the hypothesis.

1. Stimulation

In an earlier part of this chapter, stimulation was the term used to imply setting up of nerve impulses in receptor organs by the appropriate energy—light for the eyes, sound for the ears, etc. Neurons can also be said to be stimulated by the electrical currents set up by synaptic action. Electric currents may also be applied directly by investigators and may depolarize neuron bodies or processes and cause them to generate nerve impulses. It should be noted that the results of stimulating a given brain area with electrical currents are generally rather variable. The variability is thought to arise because multiple pathways exist over which nerve impulses may spread after stimulation of one particular set of neurons. Events in the brain, apart from stimulation, may cause a particular pathway to be more easily excited at one time and a different path at another time. Furthermore, the stimulating current may be more effective at some times than others. This is because the membrane potential reduction produced by the experimenter will combine with any reduction of the membrane potential produced by activity at synapses.

Sometimes the neurons one wishes to stimulate are located far from the surface, for instance in the hypothalamus. The animal (cat, rat, monkey, man) is then anesthetized and its head placed in a stereotaxic instrument. This instrument takes advantage of the fact that an animal's brain bears a fairly constant relationship to places on its skull, such as an ear hole and particular teeth. The animal's head is clamped with reference to such places. Each point in the brain can be represented by a system of three numbers which gives the distance in three dimensions from the particular point, say an ear hole, when the head is held in the given position, for instance, by clamping the top incisor teeth. With the animal in the instrument the scalp is cut open and the skull exposed. A small hole is drilled into the skull for the insertion of an electrode or cannula which can be accurately positioned along the three coordinates. Cannulas are narrow tubes, often sawed-off hypodermic needles, used to inject drugs into the brain. Electrodes are short lengths of thin wire made of something which does not react much with brain tissues, like stainless steel or platinum. Electrodes are used to record neuronal activity or to stimulate nerve cell bodies and their processes by the passage of electric currents. Such electrodes are coated up to the tip with insulating material. Current passed through the electrode now passes out only at the tip which has been stereotactically placed in the desired position. The electrode or a cannula is then fastened to the skull by dental cement and/or screws, the scalp sewn up, and the animal removed from the clamp. When it has recovered from the anesthetic, the effects of injections through the cannula or stimulation of the electrode can be observed by the experimenter.

2. Recording

It is also possible to put recording electrodes on the scalp and record the summed activity of parts of the brain (Gloor, 1969). These records are known as the electro-encephalogram (EEG). For research use, systems have been developed which enable recording with only a sliding contact with the scalp. Such systems have been fitted inside football players' or air force pilots' helmets. Small radio telemetry units can be arranged so that no wire connection is necessary and the recorded potentials can be broadcast to an appropriate receiver. The records are produced by a mixture of action potentials and excitatory and inhibitory synaptic potentials. Because these electrical transients are recorded from many thousands of cells at a time, the wave forms are complex and often difficult to interpret.

Records from electrodes inserted into the brain substance often yield more definite information because records can be made from single neurons identified by their connections. When such records are made from an electrode outside the neuron, usually only action potentials can be recorded. Using salt-filled glass needles with very fine (1μ) tips known as microelectrodes, it is possible to penetrate a neuronal membrane and record from the intracellular position. Such records enable both membrane transients (action potentials, synaptic potentials) and slower shifts of the membrane potential to be recorded.

3. *Lesions*

In lesion studies, a part of the brain is sectioned or removed and animal function after the lesion is compared with the functioning of a normal animal. Diseases may produce lesions in men and animals and the symptoms and signs of the disease can be compared with the brain damage at postmortem. A disease which has given much insight into the brain function is epilepsy. Epilepsy is due to the overactivity of groups of neurons which spreads to the neurons controlling muscles, thus giving rise to what is referred to as a "fit." The initial activity may give rise to a particular hallucination, known as the aura, which commonly precedes an epileptic fit. An aura signals that a particular part of the brain is active. At postmortem or surgery the damaged brain area can be correlated with the form of the aura.

B. Control of body functions

Structural and functional studies have shown that there are two components of the nervous system, each with appropriate receptors and effectors, the joint action of which is the basis of conscious life. These components can be designated the somatic and autonomic systems.

1. *The somatic system*

The receptors of this system are the great distance receptors—ear, eye, nose—together with the skin receptors and muscle and joint receptors which signal the position of limbs. The detailed pathway by which each receptor projects to the cortex is of course slightly different for each receptor modality. The same general principles, however, apply to them all, and Fig. 1.12 may be taken as a representative example. When the receptor axon enters the spinal cord or brainstem, it divides. Some branches make synapses with interneurons involved in local reflexes, others synapse with interneurons whose axons go on to higher centers. Such interneurons may lie in a nucleus close to the point of entry or, as in Fig. 1.12, higher up in the spinal cord or brainstem (Fig. 1.12 nuclei gracilis and cuneatus). This is the first relay and the axons of the relay cells form the second-order fibres. Second-order fibres synapse after crossing, if they have not already crossed, to the opposite side of the brain. Thalamic axons are third-order fibres, passing to specific cortical areas.

It is important to remember that each cerebral hemisphere receives information primarily from the opposite half of the body. The motor systems are likewise controlled from the cortex of the opposite side. Thus, sensations from the left half of the body and movement of the left half are functions of the right cerebral hemisphere, and vice versa. The visual system is likewise crossed, and vision to

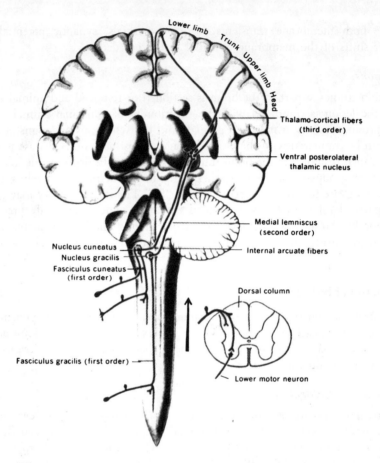

Fig. 1.12 The somatic sensory pathway for touch. This pathway is comprised of (1) neurons of the first order with cell bodies in the dorsal root ganglia and with axons that ascend in the dorsal column to the nuclei gracilis and cuneatus; (2) neurons of the second order with cell bodies in the nuclei gracilis and cuneatus and with axons that decussate as the internal arcuate fibres in the lower medulla and ascend in the medial lemniscus to the thalamus; and (3) neurons of the third order with cell bodies in the thalamus and with axons that project to the cerebral cortex (postcentral gyrus). Collateral branches of the neurons of the first order pass to the dorsal horn, the ventral horn and the dorsal column; the latter are descending association fibres. Interneurons are located within the relay nuclei. (From *The Human Nervous System: Basic Elements of Structure and Function* by C. R. Noback and R. J. Demarest. Copyright 1967, McGraw-Hill, Inc. Used with permission of McGraw-Hill Book Company.)

the right of the fixation point is served by the left side of the brain, and vice versa. Similar crossing is found in the auditory system.

The somatic effector neurons are found in the spinal cord and brainstem. Anatomists have shown that the axons of the neurons of the motor area pass from the cerebral hemispheres right down through the brainstem and spinal cord to make synapses on interneurons and motoneurons (Fig. 1.13 corticospinal tract). As Fig. 1.13 indicates, the corticospinal tract also contains axons from neurons in other cortical regions. Physiologists recording from motoneurons and stimulating the largest cortical cells in the motor area (Betz cells) have found that the synaptic contact is very powerful in the sense that only a few repetitive impulses from such cells set up such large EPSPs that a motoneuron action potential is initiated.

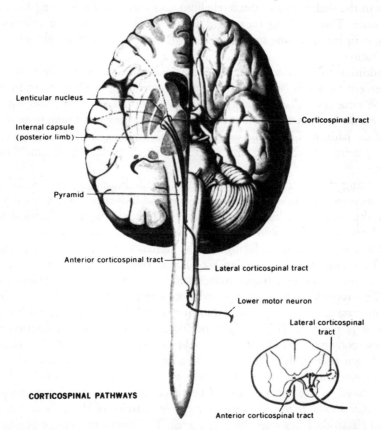

Lenticular nucleus

Internal capsule
(posterior limb)

Corticospinal tract

Pyramid

Anterior corticospinal tract

Lateral corticospinal tract

Lower motor neuron

Lateral corticospinal
tract

CORTICOSPINAL PATHWAYS

Anterior corticospinal tract

Fig. 1.13 Corticospinal pathways. These pathways are comprised of descending fibres that originate from wide areas of the cerebral cortex and pass through the posterior limb (anterior aspect) of the internal capsule, cerebral peduncle, pons proper, pyramid, and spinal cord. Most of these fibres terminate upon spinal interneurons that, in turn, synapse with motoneurons. Some fibres terminate directly upon motoneurons. The lateral corticospinal tract crosses over at the lowest medulla as the pyramidal decussation and the ventral tract crosses over in the upper spinal cord levels. (From *The Human Nervous System: Basic Elements of Structural Function* by C. R. Noback and R. J. Demarest. Copyright 1967, McGraw-Hill, Inc. Used with permission of McGraw-Hill Book company.)

Much analysis of movement control has been made using monkeys (Evarts, 1972). These animals can be trained to make specific hand movements in response to a brief stimulus such as a flash of light. These monkeys can even make the movements after their skulls have been opened and electrodes have been inserted into their motor areas to record activity of Betz cells. It is found that about 100 msec before the movement (but 100 msec after the initiating flash), Betz cells in the hand area begin to increase their firing frequency. Other experiments show that neurons in the thalamus and the cerebellum also show increased firing frequencies at this time. The resulting movement is time locked to the Betz cell response. Variations in reaction time to the stimulus all prolonged the time before the Betz cell excitation.

In addition to the time relationship, it is also possible to investigate the aspect of movement to which Betz cell discharge is correlated. Monkeys were trained to make the same joint displacement, regardless of the load, which either facilitated or opposed the movement. The output of the motor cortex was found to be coded in terms of the pattern of muscular contraction with the magnitude of action potential frequency being related to the force exerted rather than joint displacement or joint position.

Recording the summed electrical activity of the brain during a willed movement complements single neuron studies and also indicates that electrical activity all over the brain precedes the activity of the motor area. The electrical signals recorded are so small that the records from many hundreds of identical movements must be averaged to distinguish the signals from other ongoing brain activity. An example is the complex potential shown in Fig. 1.14(b) which both preceded and followed a finger movement in a human subject (Deeke *et al.,* 1969). This record, of the type expected from electrode 1 in Fig. 1.14(a), shows a slowly increasing negativity of the brain just a little less than a second before the movement is recorded (Fig. 1.14b time 0). It was called by its discoverers the "readiness potential." This potential would be recorded from all the other electrodes shown in Fig. 1.14(b). About 50 msec before the movement, the record shows a sudden increase in negativity known as the "motor potential." Electrode 1, as indicated in Fig. 1.14(a), would be expected to show the largest motor potential, since motor potentials are generated by activity of the cells of the motor area and electrode 1 lies over the finger area. The finger movement begins (Fig. 1.14 time 0) when the nerve impulses generated in the finger area reach the finger muscles.

Motor function and willed movement. Despite the complex nature of the control exerted by the motor area, it is obvious that this area is only a servant of the rest of the brain. Conscious men who have had their motor areas or their pyramidal tract stimulated report that they did not *will* the movement produced by stimulation (see Question 1.6); they were aware of it but knew it was not under their control. The complex potentials recorded from the cerebral cortices before a move-

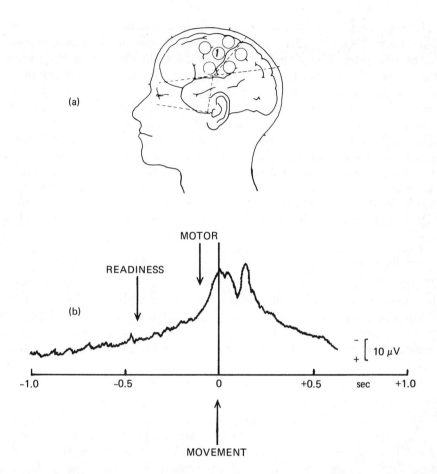

(a)

(b)

READINESS

MOTOR

10 μV

−1.0   −0.5   0   +0.5   sec   +1.0

MOVEMENT

Fig. 1.14 Brain potentials associated with finger movement. (a) shows the electrode placing and (b) a typical record obtained from electrode 1 in (a) following a finger movement. Further description in text. (With permission from Deecke, *et al.,* Distribution of readiness potential, pre-motion positivity, and motor potential of the human cerebral cortex preceding voluntary finger movements. *Exp. Br. Res. 7*, 158–168, 1969.)

ment have been suggested as the neural correlates of decision-making processes. This seems unlikely because similar potentials are recorded before reflex movement, that is, a movement not involving mental activity.

The completely automatic nature of the movements set in train by signals from the motor area is emphasized by the goals of a new laboratory recently set up at the National Institutes of Health. This is the Laboratory of Neural Control, where scientists are charged with developing devices to take information in and out of the nervous system, bypassing injured sense organs, nerves, or muscles.

It is possible to use action potentials in motor paths to control external devices such as artificial limbs directly. Action potentials may be recorded from cortico-spinal tract axons, cerebellar neurons, brainstem nuclei, motoneurons, peripheral nerves, or muscles, depending on the level of the lesion. One approach to the problem (Moss Rehabilitation Hospital, 1968) has been to use ten pair of electrodes to record from the surface, the activity of neck, shoulder, and chest muscles secondarily related to the prime movements of the lower arm. An analysis of these secondary components in a normal individual, recorded together with action potentials from his normal forearm, enables time-potential records to be made. From this type of record it is possible to decide from the movement of neck, shoulder, or chest what forearm movements are called for. A simple electronic device has been built that executes these decisions and controls the movements of an artificial arm. Newly fitted amputees operate such arms immediately, no learning being required, as the action potentials in their upper arms are driving the artificial lower arm.

2. The autonomic system

While the somatic system is concerned with detection of events in and reactions to the environment, the autonomic system is concerned with the regulation of body function in response to internal and external needs. As Fig. 1.15 indicates, this system consists of groups of neurons in the spinal cord and brainstem (reticular formation and cranial nuclei), together with neurons of the diencephalon (hypothalamus) and cortex.

As in the somatic system, there are specific receptor and effector paths.

(a) *Receptors.* The receptors of the autonomic system are found both peripherally and in the brain itself. The peripheral receptors are all internal and in many cases are involved in reflex arcs concerned with maintenance of circulation and respiration. Those receptors, such as the stretch receptors of bladder or rectum, whose signals reach consciousness, have a three-neuron path to the cortex as has been similarly described for somatic receptors (Fig. 1.12).

The brain receptors are hypothalamic neurons sensitive to changes in the temperature, osmotic pressure, and glucose level of body fluids. Sensations of thirst, hunger, and behavioral responses to these sensations and to unpleasant temperatures are believed to be mediated by these neurons.

(b) *Effectors.* Autonomic neurons are to be found, like the somatic effectors, in the spinal cord and brainstem. There is, however, a two-neuron chain rather than one neuron connecting the neurons with their target organs. From the spinal cord and brainstem the axons of autonomic neurons (preganglionic) pass out to synapse with neurons in peripheral ganglia which are the final effectors. Their axons (postganglionic) make contact with muscles and glands. It is known that the transmitter at the ganglion synapse is acetylcholine as at the neuromuscular junction.

Three components comprise the organization of the peripheral effectors. As Fig. 1.15 shows, there is a component carried by certain of the cranial nerves (III,

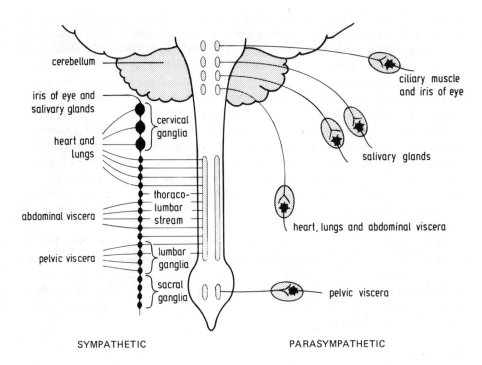

SYMPATHETIC   PARASYMPATHETIC

Fig. 1.15 A schematic drawing of the peripheral distribution of the autonomic nervous system. Note that the sympathetic supply to blood vessels and sweat glands which travels with somatic motor nerves is not shown.

VII, IX, and X) to ganglia, which are situated close to the organs they innervate. A second component has its preganglionic neurons in the sacral cord, and the ganglia are again close to the innervated viscera. These sacral and cranial components, known as the *parasympathetic* system, also use the same transmitter, acetylcholine, to influence the target organs.

The third and largest component of the autonomic effector system is the *sympathetic*, in which the cell bodies of the preganglionic neurons lie in the thoracolumbar spinal cord while the postganglionic neurons are in the sympathetic ganglia which lie on each side of the vertebral column. The postganglionic neurons of the sympathetic system in many, but not all cases, use the transmitter 1-norepinephrine to influence their target organs.

3. *Functions of the autonomic system*

The functions of the autonomic system may be broadly characterized as homeostasis, expression of the emotions, and regulation of hormonal function (see Question 1.7).

(a) *Homeostasis.* This word was introduced by Cannon, a famous American investigator of the autonomic system, to describe the processes by which the conditions surrounding tissue cells were kept in a steady state. Both divisions of the autonomic system participate in this role. The sympathetic system is, for instance, involved in temperature regulation. The normal vasoconstrictor output to the skin blood vessels is increased in cold weather and diminishes in hot weather. Similarly, the rate of sweating is controlled by sympathetic activity.

The cranial component of the parasympathetic is also involved in a variety of protective actions (Fig. 1.15). The heart is normally under control of inhibitory fibres of the vagus, while the activity of the third cranial nerve produces pupillary constriction. The 7th and 9th cranial nerves control the rate of secretion of saliva. The vagus (10th) is concerned in the secretion of the gastric and pancreatic juices and in the promotion of the tone and movement of the esophagus, stomach, and small intestine.

The sacral division of the parasympathetic (Fig. 1.15) was described by Cannon (1929) as the "emptying division" because stimulation of these nerves caused contraction of the rectum, distal colon, and the bladder. These contractions will occur as an automatic consequence of stretch produced by filling of the appropriate organ, unless prevented due to inhibition of the sacral division by connections from cortical levels.

(b) *Expression of the emotions.* The sympathetic system is active together with the somatic system in emotional behavior and in stressful conditions. Stimulation of sympathetic effectors results in pupil dilatation, a dry mouth (because of an inhibition of salivary secretion), stoppage of gut contraction, an increased heart rate and blood pressure, cold hands (from contractions of skin blood vessels), and erection of hairs. This constellation of effects is well known as the accompaniment of fear and rage. Only portions of the system may be activated, as in blushing.

A concomitant and reinforcing factor in sympathetic action is neural stimulation of the medulla of the adrenal glands, small comma-shaped structures sitting above the kidneys. The result of nerve stimulation is the release by the adrenal medulla of two hormones into the blood (epinephrine and norepinephrine). These hormones reinforce the effects of sympathetic stimulation. Injection of epinephrine will cause palpitations of the heart, nervous tremors, flushing, and accelerated breathing. The mouth is dry and the skin cold. The basis of these signs is a rise in blood pressure, heart rate, and breathing rate together with a rise in brain and muscle blood flow. Salivary secretions stop and the blood supply to the skin is reduced. Blood sugar increases and the blood is found to clot more quickly than normal. Activity of the sympathetic division and the effects of the hormones of the adrenal medulla are thus synergic. The advantage of having two systems is probably that the nervous system responds quickly, whereas the hormone action takes ten to fifteen minutes for completion but has a prolonged effect.

It will be noted that, where an organ is innervated from both the sympathetic and parasympathetic division, it will be excited by one and inhibited by the other. For instance, while our hearts are normally under a degree of vagal slowing, when we are excited, the vagal depression is removed and a sympathetic acceleration takes place.

(c) *Hormonal control.* Just below the hypothalamic nuclei at the base of the brain (Fig. 1.16) lies an important organ known as the pituitary gland or hypophysis. The pituitary has an anterior and a posterior lobe, each of unique embryological origin and histological appearance. Each lobe is a storehouse of hormones, which are released into the bloodstream in minute but enormously potent amounts to be carried in the blood to their target.

As Fig. 1.16 indicates, the anterior lobe, also known as the adenohypophysis, contains and releases the steroid hormones. These are growth hormone (GH), thyroid stimulating hormone (TSH), the adrenocorticotrophic hormone (ACTH), and the hormones controlling the menstrual cycle, the sex glands, and the mammary glands. These include the luteinizing hormone (LH), follicle-stimulating hormone (FSH), and prolactin (PRL). From the posterior lobe (neurohypophysis), the two peptide hormones—vasopressin, which controls the reabsorption of water from the blood in the kidney, and oxytocin, which stimulates the release of milk during lactation and the contraction of the uterus during childbirth—are released.

The hormones of the neurohypophysis are manufactured by neurons of the paraventricular and supraoptic nuclei of the hypothalamus (Fig. 1.17) and packaged into vesicles of twice the diameter of synaptic vesicles. The vesicles travel inside their axons, which form part of the pituitary stalk of the neurohypophysis. At axon terminals the boutons, which are enormously expanded, make contact with blood vessels (Fig. 1.18c). Release of the hormones into the blood is initiated, just as at synapses, by action potentials. As Fig. 1.18(a), (b), and (c) indicates, the whole process is analogous to synaptic transmission, except that the hormone is released into blood vessels rather than being released into the synaptic cleft.

The hormones of the adenohypophysis are both manufactured and stored there. Release into the bloodstream is triggered, as in the neurohypophysis, by action potentials in hypothalamic neurons (as shown in Fig. 1.18d). These hypothalamic neurons manufacture tripeptides known as hypothalamic releasing or regulating factors. Nine types are postulated, of which two have been isolated. Most of these releasing factors induce gland cells to release their specific hormones. In three cases, however, one factor promotes release of a specific hormone and a different one slows release of the same hormone (reviewed by Schally *et al.,* 1973).

As in the neurohypophysis, these substances are packaged in vesicles and released from axon terminals into blood vessels. The small capillary vessels unite to form the hypophyseal portal vein (Fig. 1.17) which passes down the pituitary stalk and breaks up into a fresh capillary bed in the adenohypophysis. The release factors are then able to induce the gland cells to secrete their hormone (Fig. 1.18d).

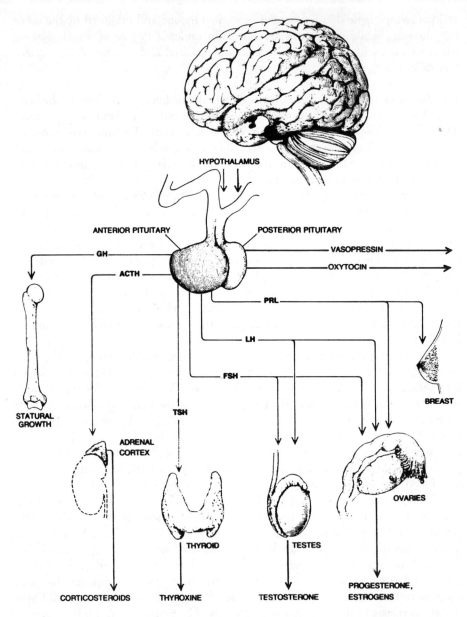

Fig. 1.16 The situation and function of the pituitary gland. The posterior lobe of the pituitary stores and passes on to the general circulation two hormones manufactured in the hypothalamus: vasopressin and oxytocin. The anterior lobe secretes a number of other hormones: growth hormone (GH), which promotes statural growth; adreno-corticotrophic hormone (ACTH), which stimulates the cortex of the adrenal gland to secrete corticosteroids; thyroid-stimulating hormone (TSH) which stimulates secretions

Most of the hormones of the adenohypophysis are normally under negative feedback control from their target organ hormones. The level of activity in such systems is set by hypothalamic activity. For instance, TSH stimulates release of the thyroid hormone, thyroxine. This hormone reaches both its target organs (where it stimulates metabolism) and the anterior pituitary via the bloodstream. In the anterior pituitary it inhibits TSH release. Through the synaptic action of different parts of the brain on hypothalamic neurons this system can be set at appropriate levels. For instance, in a cold environment part of the body's response is an increased metabolic rate. This response follows secretion of thyrotrophic releasing factor (TRF) by hypothalamic neurons as a result of synaptic input from other hypothalamic neurons involved in temperature-sensing functions. TRF in turn stimulates TSH secretion, which in turn stimulates thyroxin secretion. The final result is that thyroxin acts on its target organs and brings about an increased metabolic rate.

The hormones which are not under feedback control, such as growth hormone, are served by releasing and release-preventing hypothalamic factors.

(d) *Hormonal control and behavior.* The subtle interaction between hormone levels and behavior is shown by studies of testosterone levels in male rhesus monkeys. Testosterone is the masculinizing hormone secreted by the testis under the stimulation of the hypothalamus and pituitary. In an initial study (Rose *et al.,* 1972), individual rhesus monkeys were allowed for two weeks into a yard with a group of adult female rhesus monkeys. The males enjoyed themselves greatly, rapidly assuming a position of dominance, receiving frequent expressions of esteem from the females, and indulging in copulation to the limit of their powers. Under this regime their blood testosterone level rose twofold. Within a week after removal from this environment their testosterone level was back to normal. In the next phase of the study, the same monkeys were individually placed for two hours only in a yard with a well-established group of thirty adult male rhesus monkeys, hitherto strangers. Rhesus monkeys are intolerant of strangers. The test monkey was immediately beaten up by them and eventually assumed a very submissive pose when in contact with other members of the group. After this brief experience of defeat, blood testosterone levels fell drastically, the mean fall being 80 per cent (four monkeys). Upon introduction to females again, their blood testosterone level rose.

---

by the thyroid gland, and follicle-stimulating hormone (FSH), luteinizing hormone (LH), and prolactin (PRL), which in various combinations regulate lactation and the functioning of the gonads. Several of these anterior pituitary hormones are known to be controlled by releasing factors from the hypothalamus, two of which have now been synthesized. (From "The Hormones of the Hypothalamus" by Roger Guillemin and Roger Burgus. Copyright © 1972 by *Scientific American,* Inc. All rights reserved.)

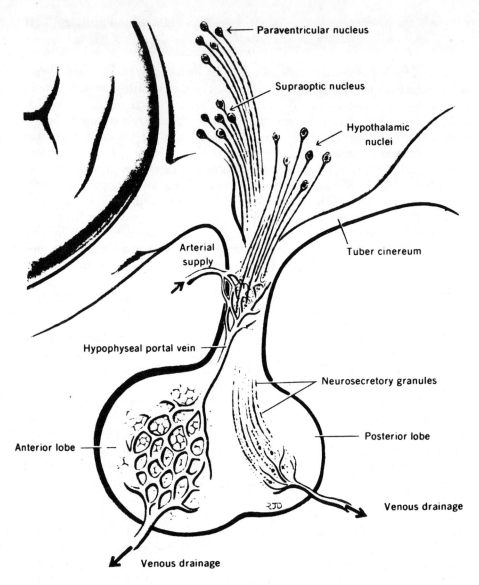

Fig. 1.17 An idealized picture of the hypothalamic control of pituitary secretions. Note that the anterior lobe actually enfolds the posterior lobe and that the pituitary stalk connects the posterior lobe with the hypothalamus. There is no stalk connecting the anterior lobe with the hypothalamus. Neurosecretions are transported via nerve fibres of the hypothalamic-hypophyseal tract from the supraoptic and paraventricular nuclei to the posterior lobe of the hypophysis; they are conveyed from this lobe via the bloodstream. Other neurosecretions, elaborated in other hypothalamic nuclei, are conveyed via the hypophyseal portal vein to the anterior lobe of the hypophysis. (From *The Human Nervous System: Basic Elements of Structure and Function* by C. R. Noback and R. J. Demarest. Copyright 1967, McGraw-Hill, Inc. Used with permission of McGraw-Hill Book Company.)

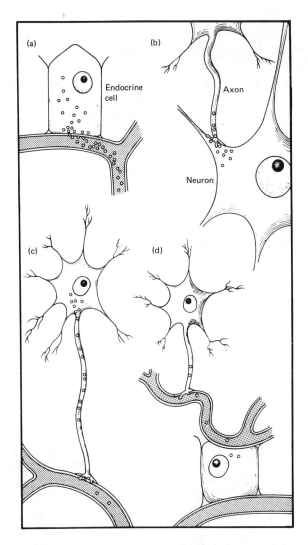

Fig. 1.18 Comparison of synaptic, endocrine, and neurohumoral secretions involved in hypothalamic-pituitary interactions. A classical endocrine cell (such as those in the anterior pituitary, or the adrenal cortex, for example) secretes its hormonal product directly into the bloodstream (a). At the classical synapse, the axon, or fibre, from one nerve cell releases locally a transmitter substance that activates the next cell (b). In neurosecretion of oxytocin or vasopressin, the hormones are secreted by nerve cells and pass through their axons to be stored in axon terminals and eventually secreted into the bloodstream (c). Hypothalamic (releasing factor) hormones go from the neurons that secrete them into local capillaries, which carry them through portal veins to endocrine cells in the anterior lobe, whose secretions they in turn stimulate (d). (Drawn with some alterations from "The Hormones of the Hypothalamus" by Roger Guillemin and Roger Burgus. Copyright © 1972 *Scientific American*, Inc. All rights reserved.)

While strictly comparable studies have not been done on men, there is some evidence that human hormone levels are adjusted in a similar way (see Question 1.8).

It will be noted that the control function of the hypothalamus is analogous to the similar function of the motor cortex. Motor cortex and hypothalamus are both servants of the rest of the brain. The commands which put these neuron assemblies into action come from elsewhere.

REFERENCES

Cannon, B. W. (1929) *Bodily Changes in Pain, Hunger, Fear and Rage* (2nd edition), Harper & Row, New York, Evanston, and London.

Cobb, S. (1958) *Foundations of Neuropsychiatry* (6th edition), The Williams & Wilkins Co., Baltimore.

Curtis, B. A., S. Jacobson, and E. M. Marcus (1972) *An Introduction to the Neurosciences.* W. B. Saunders Co., Philadelphia.

Delgado, J. M. R. and D. Mir (1969) Fragmental organization of emotional behavior in the monkey brain. *N. Y. Acad. Sci. 159*, 731–751.

Deecke, L., R. P. Scheid, and H. H. Kornhuber (1969) Distribution of readiness potential, pre-motion positivity, and motor potential of the human cerebral cortex preceding voluntary finger movements. *Exp. Brain Res. 7*, 158–168.

Eccles, J. C. (1965) The Synapse, *Sci. American,* January, p. 56.

Evarts, E. V. (1972) Activity of motor cortex neurons in association with learned movement. *Intern. J. Neuroscience 3*, 113–124.

Gloor, P. (1969) ed. Hans Berger (1873–1941). *On the Electroencephalogram of Man: The Fourteen Original Reports on the Human Electroencephalogram.* Translated from the original German and edited by P. Gloor. Elsevier, Amsterdam.

Grant, J. C. B. (1972) *An Atlas of Anatomy* (6th ed.) The Williams & Wilkins Co., Baltimore.

Guillemin, R. and R. Burgus (1972) The hormones of the hypothalamus. *Sci. American 227* (5), 24–33.

Hodgkin, A. L. and P. Horowicz (1959) Movements of Na and K in single muscle fibres. *J. Physiol. 145*, 405–432.

Hodgkin, A. L. and B. Katz (1949) The effect of sodium ions on the electrical activity of the giant axon of the squid. *J. Physiol. 108*, 37–77.

Hodgkin, A. L. and R. D. Keynes (1955) Active transport of cations in giant axons from Sepia and Loligo. *J. Physiol. 128*, 28–60.

Hubbard, J. I. (1971) Handedness not a function of birth order. *Nature* (London) *232*, 276–277.

Jouvet, M. (1969) Coma and other disorders of consciousness, in *Handbook of Clinical Neurology,* Vol. 3, pp. 62–79, P. J. Vinken and G. W. Bruyn, Eds. Amsterdam, North Holland.

Katz, B. (1966) *Nerve, Muscle and Synapse.* McGraw-Hill, New York.

Kuhlenbeck, H. (1959) Further remarks on the brain and consciousness. The brain-paradox and the meanings of consciousness. *Confin. neurol.* (Basel) *19,* 462–484.

Loewenstein, W. R. (1960) Biological transducers. *Sci. American 203* (2), 98–108.

Loewenstein, W. R., C. A. Terzuolo, and Y. Washizu (1963) Separation of transducer and impulse-generating processes in sensory receptors. *Science, 142,* 1180–1181.

Moss Rehabilitation Hospital (1968) *Quarterly Progress Report,* May, June, July. Social and Rehabilitation Service, Knisen Center for Research and Engineering, Philadelphia.

Noback, C. R. and R. J. Demarest (1967) *The Human Nervous System: Basic Elements of Structure and Function.* McGraw-Hill, New York.

Purves, M. J. (1972) *The Physiology of the Cerebral Circulation.* Cambridge University Press, Cambridge.

Roberts, L. (1955) Handedness and cerebral dominance. *Trans. Amer. Neurol. Assn. 80,* 143–148.

Rose, R. M., T. P. Gordon and I. S. Bernstein (1972) Plasma testosterone levels in the male rhesus: influences of sexual and social stimuli. *Science, 178,* 643–645.

Schally, A. V., A. Arimura and A. J. Kastin (1973) Hypothalamic regulatory hormones. *Science, 179,* 341–350.

Woodbury, J. W. (1965) Action potential: properties of excitable mechanisms, pp. 26–72, in *Neurophysiology,* T. C. Ruch, H. D. Patton, J. W. Woodbury and A. L. Towe, Eds. W. B. Saunders Co., Philadelphia.

SUGGESTED FURTHER READING

Scientific American Reprints

Baker, P. F. *The nerve axon.* March, 1966, p. 74 (offprint 1038).

Dicara, L. V. *Learning in the autonomic nervous system.* January, 1970, p. 30 (offprint 525).

Eccles, J. C. *The synapse.* January, 1965, p. 56 (offprint 1001).

Fisher, A. E. *Chemical stimulation of the brain.* June, 1964, p. 60 (offprint 485).

Heimer, L. *Pathways in the brain.* July, 1971, p. 48 (offprint 1227).

Katz, B. *The nerve impulse.* November, 1952, p. 55 (offprint 20) and *How cells communicate.* September, 1961, p. 209 (offprint 98).

Keynes, R. *The nerve impulse and the squid.* December, 1958, p. 83 (offprint 58).

Loewenstein, W. R. *Biological transducers.* August, 1960, p. 98 (offprint 70).

Luria, A. R. *The functional organisation of the brain*. March, 1970, p. 66 (offprint 526).

Miller, W. H., F. Ratliff, and H. K. Hartline. *How cells receive stimuli*. September, 1961, p. 222 (offprint 99).

Books

Hodgkin, A. L. (1964) *The Conduction of the Nervous Impulse*. Liverpool University Press, Liverpool.

Katz, B. (1966) *Nerve, Muscle and Synapse*. McGraw-Hill, New York.

Lowenstein, O. (1966) *The Senses*. Pelican Books A835. Harmondworth, England.

Parr, G. and D. Hill, Eds. (1963) *Electroencephalography*. (2nd Edition), MacDonald, London.

QUESTIONS

More advanced students may like to try answering the following questions using the references as a starting point.

1.1 *What is the function of glia?*

Burnham, R., O. Raiborn, and S. Varon (1972) Replacement of nerve-growth factor by ganglionic non-neuronal cells for the survival *in vitro* of dissociated ganglionic neurons. *Proc. U.S. Nat. Acad. Sci. 69*, 3556–3560. See also, "Requirements for neuron culture," *Nature New Biol. 242*, 65 (News).

Hydén, H. and R. Egházi (1963) Glial RNA: changes during a learning experiment in rats. *Proc. U.S. Nat. Acad. Sci. 49*, 618–624.

Kuffler, S. W. and J. G. Nicholls (1966) The physiology of neuroglial cells. *Ergebnisse der Physiologie 57*, 1–90.

1.2 *How are action potentials generated?*

Armstrong, C. M. and F. Bezanilla (1973) Currents related to movements of the gating particles of the sodium channels. *Nature* (London) *242*, 459–461.

Baker, P. F., A. L. Hodgkin, and T. I. Shaw (1962b) The effect of changes in internal ionic concentrations on the electrical properties of perfused giant axons. *J. Physiol. 164*, 355–374.

Hodgkin, A. L. and B. Katz (1949) The effect of sodium ions on the electrical activity of the giant axon of the squid. *J. Physiol. 108*, 37–77.

Hodgkin, A. L., A. F. Huxley, and B. Katz (1952) Measurement of current-voltage relations in the membrane of the giant axon of *Loligo*. *J. Physiol. 116*, 424–448.

Hodgkin, A. L. and A. F. Huxley (1952a) Currents carried by sodium and potassium ions through the membrane of the giant axon of *Loligo*. *J. Physiol. 116*, 449–472.

Hodgkin, A. L. and A. F. Huxley (1952b) The components of membrane conductance in the giant axon of *Loligo*. *J. Physiol. 116*, 473–496.

Hodgkin, A. L. and A. F. Huxley (1952c) The dual effect of membrane potential on sodium conductance in the giant axon of *Loligo*. *J. Physiol. 116*, 497–506.

Hodgkin, A. L. and A. F. Huxley (1952d) A quantitative description of membrane current and its application to conduction and excitation in nerve. *J. Physiol. 117*, 500–544.

Hodgkin, A. L. and A. F. Huxley (1953) Movement of radioactive potassium and membrane current in a giant axon. *J. Physiol. 121*, 403–414.

Hodgkin, A. L. and R. D. Keynes (1955) Active transport of cations in giant axons from *Sepia* and *Loligo*. *J. Physiol. 128*, 28–60.

Moore, J. M., M. P. Blaustein, N. C. Anderson, and T. Narahashi (1967) Basis of tetrodotoxin's selectivity in blockage of squid axons. *J. Gen. Physiol. 50*, 1401–1411.

1.3 *Does electrical transmission exist at a mammalian synapse?*

Auerbach, A. A. and M. V. L. Bennett (1969) A rectifying electrotonic synapse in the central nervous system of a vertebrate. *J. Gen. Physiol. 53*, 211–237.

Baker, R. and R. Llinas (1971) Electrotonic coupling between neurons in the rat mesencephalic nucleus. *J. Physiol. 212*, 45–63.

Bennett, M. V. L. (1966) Physiology of electrotonic junctions. *Ann. N.Y. Acad. Sci. 137*, 509–539.

Furshpan, E. J. (1964) "Electrical transmission" at an excitatory synapse in a vertebrate brain. *Science, 144*, 878–880.

Pappas, G. D. and M. V. L. Bennett (1966) Specialized junctions involved in electrical transmission between neurons. *Ann. N.Y. Acad. Sci. 137*, 495–508.

1.4 *Outline the mechanism of neuromuscular transmission.*

Clark, A. W., W. P. Hurlbut, and A. Mauro (1972) Changes in the fine structure of the neuromuscular junction of the frog caused by black widow spider venom. *J. Cell. Biol. 52*, 1–14.

Del Castillo, J. and B. Katz (1954a) Quantal components of the end-plate potential. *J. Physiol. 124*, 560–573.

Fatt, P. and B. Katz (1951) An analysis of the end-plate potential recorded with an intra-cellular electrode. *J. Physiol. 115*, 320–370.

Fatt, P. and B. Katz (1952) Spontaneous subthreshold activity at motor nerve endings. *J. Physiol. 117*, 109–128.

Heuser, J. E. and T. S. Reese (1973) Evidence for recycling of synaptic vesicle membrane during transmitter release at frog neuromuscular junctions. *J. Cell. Biol. 57*, 315–344.

Katz, B. and R. Miledi (1967a) The release of acetylcholine from nerve endings by graded electric pulses. *Proc. Roy. Soc. B. 167*, 23–38.

Katz, B. and R. Miledi (1967b) The timing of calcium action during neuromuscular transmission. *J. Physiol. 189*, 535–544.

Takeuchi, A. and N. Takeuchi (1960) On the permeability of end-plate membrane during the action of transmitter. *J. Physiol. 154*, 52–67.

1.5 *Outline the mechanisms which are brought into play when an approximate stimulus excites a receptor and an action potential is generated in the receptor axon. Mention the steps in general and give a specific example.*

Pacinian corpuscle:

Alvarez-Buylla, R. and J. R. de Arellano (1953) Local response in Pacinian corpuscles. *Amer. J. Physiol. 172*, 237–244.

Diamond, J., J. A. B. Gray, and D. R. Inman (1958) The relation between receptor potentials and the concentration of sodium ions. *J. Physiol. 142*, 382–394.

Gray, J. A. B. and M. Sato (1953) Properties of the receptor potential in Pacinian corpuscles. *J. Physiol. 122*, 610–636.

Hubbard, S. J. (1958) A study of rapid mechanical events in a mechanoreceptor. *J. Physiol. 141*, 198–218.

Hunt, C. C. (1961) On the nature of vibration receptor in the hind limb of the cat. *J. Physiol. 155*, 175–186.

Loewenstein, W. R. (1959) The generation of electrical activity in a nerve ending. *Ann. N.Y. Acad. Sci. 81*, 367–387.

Ozeki, M. and M. Sato (1964) Initiation of impulses at the non-myelinated nerve terminal in Pacinian corpuscles. *J. Physiol. 170*, 167–185.

Schiff, J. and W. R. Loewenstein (1972) Development of a receptor on a foreign nerve fiber in a Pacinian corpuscle. *Science, 177*, 712–715.

Crayfish stretch receptor:

Eyzaguirre, C. and S. W. Kuffler (1955a) Processes of excitation in the dendrites and in the soma of single isolated sensory nerve cells of the lobster and crayfish. *J. Gen. Physiol. 39*, 87–119.

Eyzaguirre, C. and S. W. Kuffler (1955b) Further study of soma, dendrite, and axon excitation in single neurons. *J. Gen. Physiol. 39*, 121–153.

Obara, S. (1968) Effects of some organic cations on generator potential of crayfish stretch receptor. *J. Gen. Physiol. 52*, 363–386.

1.6 *How close are brain physiologists to finding the seat of the will?*

Deecke, L., P. Scheid, and H. H. Kornhuber (1969) Distribution of readiness potential, pre-motion positivity, and motor potential of the human cerebral cortex preceding voluntary finger movements. *Exp. Brain Res. 7*, 158–168.

Evarts, E. V. (1966) Activity of pyramidal tract neurons during postural fixation. *J. Neurophysiol. 32*, 375–385.

Evarts, E. V. (1972) Studies on the cerebral mechanisms of motor control. *Intern. J. Neuroscience 4*, 89–92.

Evarts, E. V. (1973) Motor cortex reflexes associated with learned movement. *Science, 179*, 501–503.

Järvilehto, T. and H. Fruhstorfer (1970) Differentiation between slow cortical potentials associated with motor and mental acts in man. *Exp. Brain Res. 11*, 309–317.

1.7 *Has an Indian Yogi any special powers? If so what are they and could you develop them?*

Anand, B. K., G. S. Chhina, and B. Singh (1961) Studies on Shri Ramanand Yogi during his stay in an air tight box. *Ind. J. Med. Res. 49*, 82–89.

Dicara, L. V. (1970) Learning in the autonomic nervous system. *Sci. American 222*, January 32–39 (offprint 525).

Wallace, R. K. and H. Benson (1972) The physiology of meditation. *Sci. American 226*, February, 84–90 (offprint 1242).

Wallace, R. K., H. Benson, and A. F. Nelson (1971) A wakeful hypometabolic physiologic state. *Am. J. Physiol. 221*, 795–799.

1.8 *Why does a sailor's beard grow faster the day before he gets shore leave?*

Anonymous (1970) Effects of sexual activity on beard growth in men. *Nature* (London) *226*, 869–870.

Ismail, A. A. A. and R. A. Harkness (1967) Urinary testosterone excretion in men in normal and pathological conditions. *Acta Endocrinol. 56*, 469–480.

Rose, R. M., T. P. Gordon and I. S. Bernstein (1972) Plasma testosterone levels in the male rhesus: influence of sexual and social stimuli. *Science, 178*, 643–645.

Rose, R. M., J. W. Holaday, and I. S. Bernstein (1971) Plasma testosterone dominance rank and aggressive behaviour in male rhesus monkeys. *Nature* (London), *231*, 366–368.

PSYCHONEURAL PARALLELISM EXPLORED

2

The aim of this chapter is not only to explore the generally accepted idea that mental activity is paralleled by brain activity (psychoneural parallelism) but also to explore how far the content of consciousness is influenced by brain activity.

I. SENSATION

A. Evoked potentials and sensation

The arrival of action potentials in the primary receiving areas of the cerebral hemispheres is an easily detected event. After a brief stimulus, such as a flashing light or a clicking sound, a bi- or triphasic wave can be recorded followed by slower individual waves (Fig. 2.1b-d) which have to be extracted from other on-going brain activity with an averaging computer. These potential changes are known as "evoked potentials" (see Question 2.1). Evoked potentials can be recorded from the surface of the brain and even, with delicate equipment, from the scalp itself. As Fig. 2.1(a) indicates, evoked potentials are the sum of the EPSPs and IPSPs generated in a 1–6 mm^2 area.

The form of a visual (Fig. 2.1d) or an auditory "evoked potential" (Fig. 2.1b) is very constant in a given subject but there is much variance if different subjects are compared using the same stimuli, or as Fig. 2.1(b)-(d) indicates, if the stimulus type is changed, in the same subjects. The response to a single, brief stimulus typically lasts for a period up to a second. The early components represent the arrival of action potentials in the cortex. The late components appear to be due to interaction between neurons in the primary cortical receiving areas and thalamic neurons.

Evoked potentials were once thought to signal the onset of sensation because in early experiments the threshold for detection of evoked potentials (with scalp elec-

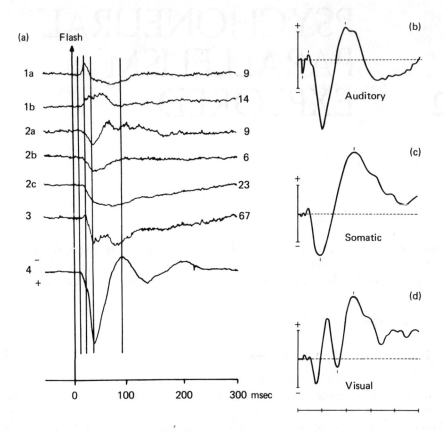

Fig. 2.1 Evoked potentials and their relationship to brain neural activity. (a) Averaged neuron membrane potential changes (1–3) and evoked potential (4) of the visual cortex after a strong stroboscopic flash (at time zero). No background illumination. Cells of the same response type were selected and the respective membrane potential changes (intracellular recording) were averaged. The numbers at the right indicate the number of neurons from which the averaged responses were calculated. Upward deflection represents depolarization. 1a, b: Neurons with primary excitation 2a, b, c: Neurons with primary inhibition. 3. Averaged response of total population. 4. Cortical evoked potential; downward deflection indicates positivity. (With permission from O. D. Creutzfeld, *et al., J. Neurophysiol.,* 1969. *32,* 127–139). (b), (c), (d). Averaged evoked potential responses obtained from eight adult subjects to the indicated stimulus type. Each tracing is the computed average of 4,800 individual responses. Calibration 10 μV, 100 msec per division. (With permission from H. G. Vaughan, Jr., "The Relationship of Brain Activity to Scalp Recordings at Event-Related Potentials," in E. Donchin and I. B. Lindsley, Eds., *Average Evoked Potentials: Methods, Results, and Evaluations,* NASA/SP-191, 1969, pp. 45–75, NASA, Washington, D.C.

trodes) coincided with the subject's conscious detection of the stimulus. Later experiments have shown these ideas were mistaken, presumably because small evoked potentials could not be detected through the scalp and skull.

If evoked potentials are recorded directly from the surface of the brain in conscious subjects (undergoing operation for intractable epilepsy), there is no correlation between perception of a skin stimulus (a touch) and the arrival of or size of the evoked potential. The stimuli have to be repeated or made stronger until there are late components to the primary evoked potential (Libet *et al.*, 1967). *Conscious sensation is associated with the appearance of these later components.* Conversely, these components disappear in conditions such as anaesthesia or sleep (Jasper, 1966).

What is the nature of these late components? As Fig. 2.2(a) shows, a typical evoked potential has a number of waves classified as negative (N1, N2, N3) or positive (P1, P2, P3). Interesting variations in the magnitude of the wave known as P3, as it is the third positive going component (P3), were investigated by Sutton and his colleagues in 1965. A typical situation for displaying this component is to record average evoked potentials in human subjects in response to clicks or light flashes. The stimuli, click or flash, are paired, but while the first always occurs, the second may not, and the subject has to guess whether or not it will come. The evoked potential in response to the second stimulus now differs from normal in having a large positive wave (Fig. 2.2a, dotted outline, P3), with a maximum latency about 300 msec after the stimulus. The size of this wave varies with the attention and alertness of the subject and the meaningfulness of the stimulus for him (see Question 2.2).

Even more interesting is the potential change recorded from the scalp or cortex which precedes a stimulus requiring *some action* by a subject. This potential charge, known as the contingent negative variation (CNV), was discovered by Grey-Walter and his colleagues in 1964, and is the first electrophysiological correlate of a mental state. Typically, it is recorded in a stimulus situation in which the first stimulus—a click, for example, tells the subject that a second click will follow, and then the subject must do something, like turning on a switch. The CVN is a large negative going potential change which occurs, as Fig. 2.2(b) shows, *between* the two clicks. It is so large, compared with an evoked potential that it hides the evoked response to the second stimulus (Fig. 2.2b, arrow). There is considerable evidence that this potential is related to selective attention by the subject and it may well be that the CNV and the P3 are aspects of the same phenomenon. It has been found, for instance, that a loud noise or other distracting stimuli when the subject is expecting a stimulus leading to action reduces both his reaction time and his CNV.

B. Brain stimulation and sensation

It is thought that conscious sensation follows the spread of signals from primary receiving areas to the nearby areas of cortex, which were given the name "associa-

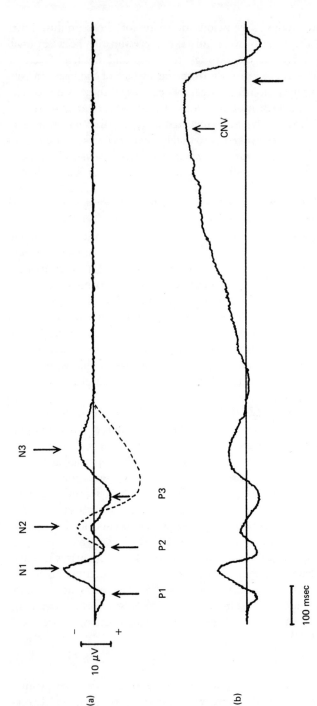

Fig. 2.2 Evoked potentials (a) and the contingent negative variation (CNV)(b). In (a) the various waves of an idealized evoked potential (Fig. 2.2a) are labelled according to whether they are positive (P) or negative (N) to the baseline [straight line in (a)] and according to their order from time 0 (N, 1–3, P, 1–3). The dotted line in (a) shows variation in the evoked potential known as P–3 which occurs when the evoked potential is associated with increased attention of the subject. (Based on the account of Sutton, Braren and Zubin, 1965, *Science 150*, 1187–1188).

In (b), the contingent negative variation (CNV) is shown following the same evoked potential as in (a). It terminates [arrow in (b)] when the second signal arrives and the subject makes the expected reaction. (Note the 10 μV scale.) Special precautions are needed to record such tiny signals. They cannot be recorded by the usual hospital EEG machine. (Based on the account of Grey-Walter, *et al.*, 1964, *Nature* (London), *203*, 308–384).

tion areas" to denote the "elaboration" of the crude sensation. Strong support for such ideas comes from experiments of the Canadian neurosurgeon Penfield and his colleagues upon epileptic patients (Penfield, 1958). In these operations the skull was opened under local anesthetic, so that the patients were conscious while a surgeon stimulated various cortical areas with electrical pulses. The purpose of the operation was to find the places where the epilepsy was being generated and destroy the responsible neurons. The surgeon knows he has found such a place when the patient reports that an aura has been generated after stimulation.

When primary sensory areas are stimulated, patients report crude sensations, unlike anything previously experienced. For the auditory area for instance, patients report clicks, buzzing, clanging, knocking, or rushing sounds. Activity in primary sensory areas is evidently not accompanied by normal perception.

When a stimulating electrode is applied to surrounding brain areas, patients report more organized sensations. For instance, Penfield recorded that when he stimulated the primary auditory area in one patient she heard a buzzing sound. When the electrode was applied to the associated area, she said, "someone is calling." Other patients similarly stimulated reported that they heard music and could even hum what they were hearing. Several heard orchestras playing. Similar reports came from the visual area.

In experiments of this type made by the American investigator, Libet and his colleagues (Libet et al., 1964, Libet, 1966) it was found that to be perceived and reported by conscious subjects, stimulation had to continue for at least 0.5–1 sec. The finding that sensation is associated with prolonged cortical stimulation and the late components of evoked potentials raises a number of interesting problems. One problem which has been investigated is how the long time (0.5–1 sec.) required for perception can be reconciled with the much shorter reaction time of men and animals. It seems probable that the action may be brought about by processes not initiating mental activity, signalled by the earlier parts of the evoked potential. A further corollary could be that learning may involve shifting a learned task to a subconscious level which would allow more rapid initiation of and automatic progression of the steps of the task. Direct evidence that this may be the case has come from experiments with monkeys which were trained to almost 100 per cent reliability in choosing between a square and a triangle flashed briefly on a screen (Fehmi et al., 1969). It was found that a blank flash of light, following closely upon the test flash could prevent the discrimination. Under these conditions the evoked potential from the test flash could not be recorded in the visual receiving area of the cortex. Other experiments suggested that there was interference between the test and the blank flashes at the level of the retina, and the evoked potential which would normally arise from the test flash was suppressed. It was possible to separate the test and masking (blank) flashes by increasingly longer intervals. As the interval lengthened, an increasing proportion of the signals from the retina generating an evoked potential to the test flash escaped interference, and more and more of the evoked potential could be recorded from the cortex.

The monkey began to make correct discriminations again when only the *initial* part of the evoked potential, the primary evoked part, was present. Thus the information necessary to perform an already learned task was present very early in the course of the evoked response and was not dependent upon later or secondary components.

C. Receptor function and sensation

It is obvious that while we may imagine different worlds we can only sense the world about which our receptors send information to the brain. Those readers who own a dog will be aware that their pets live in a rather different and much more smelly world than they do. However, we see our world in color when the dog does not. Our receptors then define the world we can immediately sense. Of course we may extend the range of our receptors by machines such as spectacles, microscopes, telescopes, and hearing aids.

It does not follow that we must be conscious of receptor activity to take action. There is no doubt that much information from our eyes and ears, and presumably from our other receptors too, is translated to the brain without any attention on our part (see Question 2.3). This information may enter memory and even influence quite complex actions such as car driving. An experiment which demonstrates this involved measuring the movements and particularly the fixation of a subject's eyes (Thomas, 1968). Near the center of the human retina (at the fovea) the anatomical and functional organization is most favorable for detailed vision. Our eyes therefore are in constant motion, pausing briefly to fix part of the scene on the foveas of the two eyes. Helmets can be constructed with attached equipment for measuring these eye movements while a subject does things such as driving a car, watching a film, etc. Such experiments indicate that enormous amounts of information are sent to the brain from the retina without being perceived, that is, without being given conscious attention. Hundreds of fixations of the eye, e.g., while driving a car, can be seen and, with ancillary equipment such as a television monitor, even what was being looked at can be determined. Complex motor acts are performed based on information received during the apparently unconscious situation. Apparently only "important" information is attended to, that is, becomes the subject of conscious thought. Experimentally it was found that "importance" was determined by the subject's previous experience, for eye fixation and motor action were determined not only by obvious hazards such as dangers to life and limb, but also by more subtle points such as emotional reactions to the object of fixation. It was found, for instance, that people avoided accepting and remembering visual information associated with strong emotions. They might even deny looking at a distasteful object even though their eye movements showed that they had been looking. Indeed, as the investigator of eye movements, Dr. Llewellyn Thomas (1968) has said:

Part of the brain appears to function rather like a secretary who handles routine matters without consulting her employer and apprises him of important points in incoming letters—but who sometimes makes mistakes.

1. *Modality*

It is again obvious that the type of sensory gate opened will determine the type of sensation. Eyes are specialized to respond to light, and a punch on the eye, even though not the usual stimulus, still evokes a flash of light. For skin receptors we have direct evidence that the type of receptor which is activated determines the type of sensation (see Question 2.4). This evidence comes from experiments on German students in which, under local anesthetic, a superficial branch of the radial nerve, supplying the skin over the back of the little and ring fingers and half the middle finger, was sectioned (Hansel and Boman, 1960). Individual nerve fibres, each the axon of a receptor neuron, were teased out of the peripheral end and placed on recording electrodes. When finger skin was stimulated it was found that individual fibres were connected to receptors sensitive to either mechanical or thermal stimuli. (After the experiment the nerve fibres were sewn together and complete recovery of function occurred in two or three months.)

Other types of experiments indicate that the quality of sensation depends not only on the receptor but also on its central connections. It is known, for instance, that if the pathway from a receptor to the cortex is artificially stimulated anywhere along the pathway, sensation appropriate to the receptor may be perceived, localized to the peripheral receptor field (see Question 2.5).

2. *Intensity*

A more subtle aspect of receptor activity arises from the relationship between the intensity of receptor stimulation and the intensity of the resulting (conscious) sensation.

In all cases so far investigated, the threshold for sensation has corresponded with the receptor threshold—that is, the weakest stimulus that can be perceived is the weakest stimulus that will generate an action potential. It seems probable too that under laboratory conditions the intensity of suprathreshold sensation is a function of the intensity of receptor activation.

The most direct approach to this problem has come from the studies of patients having middle-ear operations in a Swedish hospital (Borg et al., 1967). During the course of the operation a nerve, the chorda tympani, is exposed which carries action potentials from taste receptors in the tongue. Before the operation the patients tasted various sweet or sour solutions and were asked to grade the intensity of their sensations on a seven-point scale as a function of the concentration of citric acid, salt (NaCl), or sucrose applied. Many investigators have done this sort of thing and it is quite easy to teach people to do. The relationship between the strength of the various solutions and the intensity of sensation in one patient is shown in Fig. 2.3 (Psychophysical), which indicates that the logarithm of the intensity of sensation is linearly related to the logarithm of the stimulus intensity (molarity of citric acid). A similar relationship between the logarithm of the stimulus strength and sensation has been reported also for auditory and visual sensation by other investigators. For some sensations, however, for instance touch on a non-hairy skin, intensity is a simple linear function of stimulus strength (Mount-castle, 1967).

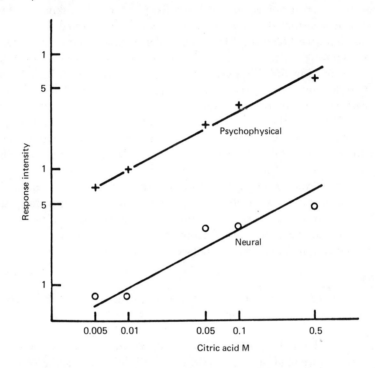

Fig. 2.3   The relationship between intensity of sensation and the intensity of receptor activation. Graphs from one patient showing subjective intensity (psychophysical) and frequency of action potentials recorded from the chorda tympani nerve (neural) plotted against molarity of citric acid on a log-log scale. (With permission from Borg, Diamant, Strom & Zotterman, *J. Physiol., 192*, 13–20, 1967.)

During the operation it was possible to record action potentials from the chorda tympani. The frequency of action potentials in response to the same range of concentration of the same solutions was measured. Exactly the same relationship (Fig. 2.3 Neural) between citric acid concentration and action potential frequency (response intensity) was found as had been found for the relationship between sensation and concentration.

Similar experiments, demonstrating "psychoneural parallelism" have been reported by workers comparing the sensation of touch and of cold in themselves (as sensation) and in monkeys (as frequency of action potentials). From experiments of this type (see Question 2.4 and Darian Smith *et al.*, 1973; Johnson *et al.*, 1973) it has been concluded that the *intensity of stimulation is signalled to the brain by the frequency of action potentials.* Furthermore, in all cases so far investigated, it appears that the intensity relationship was determined by receptor properties and faithfully preserved as it was transferred to higher levels of the brain. This finding implies that synaptic transmission does not alter the frequency characteristics of the signal (see Question 2.6).

It should be noted that the perceived intensity of a stimulus under other than strict laboratory conditions may very well not be a function of the intensity of receptor stimulation. Previous experiences, present attention, and future expectations can all play a part in determining the perceived "intensity" of a stimulus.

3. *Place*

More subtle aspects of receptor functions are involved in the perception of the spatial position of a particular stimulus. It is instructive to consider this aspect of sensation in the context of the skin and touch sensation. A human subject can, without looking and with only 1–2 mm error, reproduce the position of a light touch to the tip of the finger. In the same area, two points, such as the blunted points of a compass, can be appreciated as two points when only 2 or 3 mm apart. Table 2.1, based on the work of the great nineteenth-century German physiologist Ernst Weber (1846), shows that two-point discrimination is greatest for the fingertips and lips and is much reduced elsewhere.

Underlying the difference in two-point discrimination in different skin areas is undoubtedly a difference in the density of touch-receptor distribution. Apart from the lips and finger tips, distribution is spot-like. When such spots have been marked, cut out, and sectioned for histology, examination of the sections shows that each spot contains terminal branches of several receptor neurons; that is, a particular neuron innervates several such spots. Nevertheless, only one type of sensory experience can be derived from such a spot (e.g., touch, or cold, or warm, or pain), so long as the appropriate stimulus is confined to the specific area.

When in the course of a two-point test the points of a compass are placed together on the skin, and gradually separated, the subject will report, in turn, that he or she feels a line, a double-paddle shape, a dumbbell shape, and, finally, two points. Only the two points faithfully represent physical reality; the other perceptions must be classed as illusions. Illusions are commonplace to students of all modalities of sensation. Their detection does not necessarily contradict psychoneural parallelism. Indeed, it can be shown that in many cases the illusion arises because of the way the nervous system is constructed.

A good example of an illusion with a probable neural basis comes from recent studies not of two-point but of three-point discrimination (Gardner and Spencer, 1972a, b). In these studies, three brass rods (each 2.5 mm in diameter and with

3.5 g mass) were allowed to fall freely on the skin of the middorsal forearm of human subjects. Brief backward and forward (shearing) movements of the probes were the stimulus.

When a single probe moved, subjects reported a brief tap-like sensation located superficially in the skin and within ±10 mm of the actual site. When the three probes moved simultaneously, the subjects reported only a single sensation. When asked to locate the site of sensation (which they could not see), they pointed in about 60 per cent of trials to the *middle* probe site. Indeed, even if the subjects were allowed to watch the three probes in operation, they still reported the tap-like sensation was felt only under the middle probe with no sensation located under the lateral probes. Similar results were obtained when the probes were 10, 15, or 20 mm apart. At probe distances of greater than 40 mm, the subjects sometimes reported distinct sensations. This is a similar distance to that needed for two-point discrimination (Table 2.1) on the back of the forearm.

TABLE 2.1
Two-point discrimination after Weber (1846).

Location	Distance apart at which two points are felt distinctly (mm).
Anterior thigh	67.5
Dorsal forearm	40.5
Back of hand	31.4
Forehead	22.5
Lips	4.5
Finger tips	2.3

A further feature of the simple sensation elicited by the three-probe movement was that, while the subjects could accurately rate the intensity of the stimulus for movements from 25 μ to 600 μ, the sensation produced by three probes felt stronger than the sensation produced by a single probe driven the same distance. Some subjects also felt that the three-probe sensation felt slightly broader in extent than did the single-probe sensation, although this "broader" sensation was still narrower than the span of the probes.

It might be thought that the illusions resulted because the subjects' receptors were not capable of resolving the three probes. This could occur, for instance, if one receptor neuron had branches innervating touch receptors in contact with all three probes. Alternatively, the stimulus might travel as a wave through the skin to stimulate receptors under all the probes. Such explanations could not explain the intensity difference.

Experiments in which the same stimuli were applied to the forearm of cats suggest that such explanations do not hold. The peripheral receptors could accurately signal to the nervous system of the cat the position and intensity of the stimulation applied to all three probes. Such an investigation is very difficult. It is not possible to record directly from the peripheral receptors. Instead, nerves supplying the forearm skin were cut, single fibres (axons) dissected out, and the peripheral ends of these fibres placed on recording electrodes. Stimuli were then systematically applied to the skin area of interest with a fine probe. When the probe was stimulating the receptors innervated by the appropriate axons, action potentials could be recorded with a frequency proportional to the intensity and site of stimulation. Over 200 separate axons were dissected out and their receptors localized in this way. Several types of receptors were involved. Figure 2.4 shows the responses of one type (touch corpuscles). This type of receptor forms a dome-like elevation in the skin about 150 μ to 400 μ in diameter and is innervated by a single nerve fibre. As Fig. 2.4 (a–e) indicates, a strong response occurs only when a probe touches a corpuscle and the presence of other probes does not influence its activity.

Study of a population of such receptors suggests that three simultaneous stimuli activated three groups of receptors just as would single probes at the three points. Touch receptors directly contacted would give the highest frequency of impulses, receptors grazed by a probe would be less excited, and nontouched receptors would not respond.

These studies showed that the predominant spatial and intensity features of the three-pronged stimuli were transmitted to the central nervous system of the cat.

The experiments were then repeated, stimulating the skin of the forepaw as before, but recording from neurons in the somatosensory area of the cortex (Fig. 2.5) rather than isolated nerve fibres. Glass microelectrodes were used to record the impulses generated by probe stimuli of the skin receptors. As before, the relationship of the probes to skin receptors was determined until a profile could be built up showing the magnitude of neural responses.

As Fig. 2.5 indicates, the profile was slightly different from that obtained for peripheral nerve fibres (Fig. 2.4). Stimulation by the skin probes now produced a broad excitatory focus of activity in the cortex with most intense response from those cortical neurons connected to receptors which were maximally stimulated by the middle probe. The results suggest that movements of the three-probe array are recorded by the nervous system as if only a single probe lying in the site of the middle probe had moved. The profile of the cortical responses was similar to that expected from the description of the human sensation. The greater intensity of the sensation when three probes moved, compared with one, could also be explained. The profile of response to three pulses was spatially similar to that produced by a single probe, but the frequency of firing of cortical neurons was greater over the range. Both the spatial and intensity properties of the illusion then were paralleled by similar changes in the response of cortical cells to the peripheral input.

Separate issues of interest are the meaning of the blurring of the receptor input

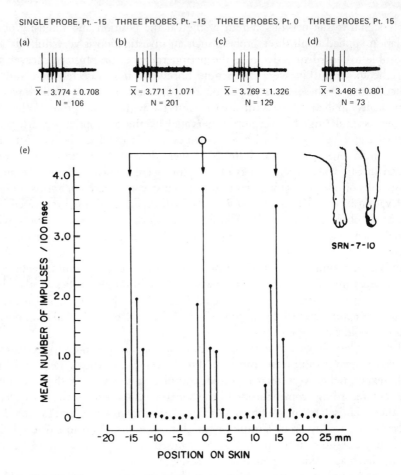

Fig. 2.4 Profile of responses of a type 1 touch corpuscle to three probes presented simultaneously. The touch corpuscle was located on a cat's peraxial dorsal foreleg slightly proximal to the wrist. Three probes, 15 mm apart, were placed horizontally on the foreleg, and the skin was stimulated in the manner described in the text. Mapping was begun with all three probes proximal to the touch corpuscle, and the array was moved distally in 1.25-mm steps. The abscissa plots the distance of the middle probe from the touch corpuscle; the ordinate the mean number of spikes recorded at each stimulus site. To facilitate the reading of this figure, the three-probe array has been drawn above the bar graph in (e) so that each point of the abscissa corresponds spatially to the experimental orientation of the three probes with respect to the touch corpuscle. The three-probe array produces three distinct peaks of activity; a strong response occurs only when one of the probes contacts the touch corpuscle, while no response occurs when two adjacent probes straddle the corpuscle. See text for further details. The upper part of the figure shows typical oscilloscope traces of the first 100 msec of the response to shearing stimuli at selected points in the

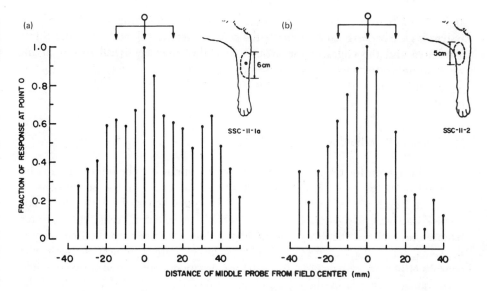

Fig. 2.5 Profiles of responses of typical cortical hair units to shearing stimuli from an array of three probes, 15 mm apart. Receptive field boundaries and field centers are indicated on the inset drawings. The abscissa denotes the distance of the middle probe of the three-probe array from the field center. Positive distances refer to probe orientation with the middle probe distal to the field center, while negative distances refer to proximal positions of the middle probe. Graphs plot the mean unit response to shearing stimuli at each probe orientation as a fraction of the unit response to three-probe stimuli when the middle probe was on the field center. Evoked activity was recorded as long as one of the probes was contained within the receptive field. Maximum activity occurred when the middle probe was placed on the field center; other responses were graded as a function of the distance of the middle probe from the field center. The unit activity when the proximal probe was on the field center (point +15) or when the distal probe was on the field center (point −15) was only 60 per cent as intense as the maximum response. There were no consistent peaks in profiles at these points. Unit SSC-11-1a. Response at point 0 = 0.88 spikes/response. Probe excursion, 190μ. (With permission from Gardner and Spencer, *J. Neurophysiol. 35*, 954–977, 1972b).

---

field. The type 1 touch corpuscle is the large spike in the records; the smaller spike visible in some traces was produced by a type 11 touch receptor (unit SRN–7–11) which has a slightly more proximal receptive field. (a): point −15, single (proximal) probe. (b): point −15, three probes, proximal probe on field center. (c): point 0, three probes, middle probe on field center. (d): point +15, three probes, distal probe on field center. The response amplitude is independent of which of the three probes contacts the touch corpuscle and the total number of probes on the skin. Unit SRN–7–10. Probe excursion, 400μ. (With permission from Gardner and Spencer, *J. Neurophysiol. 35*, 925–953).

and the mechanisms involved in blurring. Insofar as meaning is concerned, the system is clearly designed to improve the contrast between the center of the stimulated area and the edges of the area. This ability may be useful in amplifying weak stimuli which would otherwise not be perceived. For instance, the human threshold for the three-probe stimulus was lower than the threshold for a single probe.

D. "Surround" inhibition

The major reason for the blurring of the receptor input is to be found in a mechanism operative at each of the three relays which exist on the somatosensory, visual, and auditory pathways. As Fig. 2.4 shows, when each of the three skin probes is active, each generates action potentials in receptor axons without interference one between the other. Let us now follow the system to the first relay in the spinal cord, where each receptor axon makes excitatory connections with relay neurons (Fig. 2.6a, spinal cord). Consider the situation wherein one of two receptors is activated, as shown by the record of action potentials recorded in the first relay cell in the spinal cord in response to the maintained stimulus (Fig. 2.6b). When the adjoining receptor is activated, it will be seen that this neuron falls silent (Fig. 2.6b, stimulus to inhibitory surround). The mechanism involved, known as "surround" inhibition, involves interactions between the terminals of the receptor axons, as shown in Fig. 2.6(a) at the first relay. Terminals of a receptor neuron end not only on the appropriate relay cell but also on interneurons whose axons end, in turn, on the terminals of other receptor axons. When active, these axoaxonal synapses reduce the effectiveness of the nearby relay synapse.

This synaptic mechanism is known as presynaptic inhibition. Basically, this mechanism arises because the amplitude of an action potential in a neuron is a function of the magnitude of the resting potential of that neuron. When an axoaxonic synapse operates, it releases an excitatory transmitter (Fig. 2.6a, spinal

---

Fig. 2.6 Surround (afferent) inhibition. Illustration of interaction of excitatory and inhibitory effects upon neuron of postcentral gyrus which was produced by stimuli delivered to its peripheral receptive field on the contralateral forearm. Cell was excited by stimuli delivered to the field on preaxial side of arm and inhibited by stimuli delivered anywhere within a large surrounding area (Fig. 2.6a). Graph in (b) plots impulse frequency versus time during excitatory inhibitory interactions. Application of excitatory stimulus evoked high-frequency onset transient discharge that declined toward a steady plateau until interrupted by application of inhibitory stimulus. Upon removal of the latter, sequence was repeated in response to continuing excitatory stimulus. In (a), some of the connections thought to be responsible for the effects of inhibitory stimulation are shown diagrammatically. (Area b. with permission from V. B. Mountcastle and T. P. R. Powell, Central neural mechanisms subserving cutaneous sensibility, with special reference to the role of afferent inhibition in sensory perception and discrimination. *Bull. Johns Hopkins Hosp. 105*, 201–232, 1959.)

cord, +) which causes a depolarization of the receptor axon terminal. This depolarization does not itself generate action potentials. Its existence does, however, affect the amplitude of action potentials propagating up to the depolarized terminals after receptor activity. An action potential set up in the depolarized terminal is reduced in amplitude. Normally an action potential is of an unvarying amplitude (see Chapter 1) and therefore releases about the same amount of transmitter substance from axon terminals each time. Experimentally, however, it can be shown that if one varies the action potential amplitude, either upward by hyperpolarization of the terminals or downward by depolarizing the terminals, there is

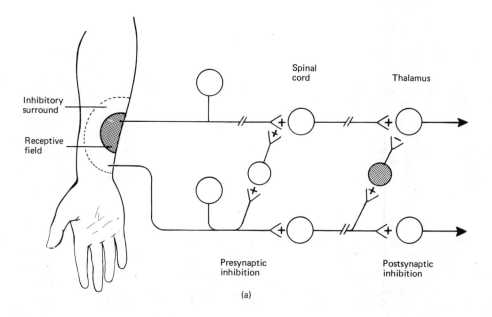

(a)

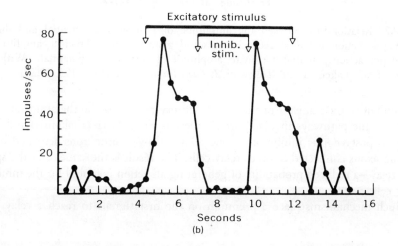

(b)

a corresponding change in the amount of transmitter released. As Fig. 2.7 indicates, the relationship is very steep. A small decrease in action potential amplitude will bring about a large fall in transmitter release and thus a smaller EPSP. A smaller EPSP, in turn, means a reduced probability of setting up an action potential; an inhibition is thus generated presynaptically.

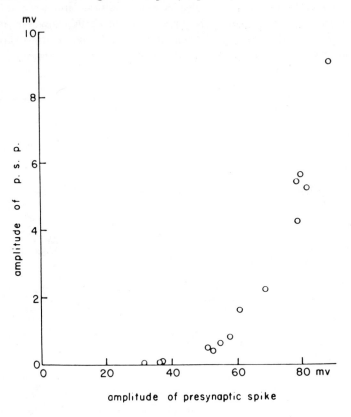

Fig. 2.7 Relationship between the amplitude of postsynaptic potential and that of presynaptic action potential recorded at squid giant synapse. Abscissa, amplitude of presynaptic action potential. Ordinate, amplitude of postsynaptic potential. (With permission from Takeuchi and Takeuchi, *J. Gen. Physiol.* 45, 1181–1193, 1962.)

Inhibitory mechanisms operate at all sensory relays. At the thalamic and cortical relays the pathways involved are simpler, as Fig. 2.6(a) (thalamus) indicates. There is postsynaptic inhibition of one relay cell by interneurons activated by incoming axons connected to other relay cells. The result is the same as at the spinal cord relay—a reduced probability of generating an action potential for the inhibited relay cell.

Such mechanisms place a premium on the first signals to reach a relay. The first signal will not only be transmitted onward but will cause inhibition of other relay cells, thus diminishing the probability that these cells will generate action potentials. The receptor field of each receptor neuron is then surrounded by a field of potential competitors. In the case of two- and three-point discrimination, the two or three points are appreciated as one because the one (felt) point activates receptors and receptor axons which presynaptically inhibit the action potentials, which would otherwise be produced by stimulation of adjoining areas by the other (not felt) points. In skin sensation this is a useful mechanism for improving localization and threshold. In the visual system similar mechanisms operate to produce contrast (edge detection). A great generalization which emerges from such studies is that receptor activation does not guarantee perception.

II. ATTENTION AND AROUSAL

While receptor activation does not guarantee perception, perception is guaranteed if *attention* is paid to the source of stimulation. As Adrian (1954) remarked, "the signals from the sense organs must be treated differently when we attend to them than when we do not." Abundant evidence is now at hand to confirm the truth of this statement and the underlying mechanisms have been explored in some depth. It appears that there are both general and particular mechanisms underlying attention. The general mechanism underlies what is commonly termed "arousal," while the particular mechanism underlies the paying of attention to something specific.

A. Arousal

When a drowsy cat or man is suddenly startled by a noise, a number of changes in behavior can be catalogued. In addition to the obvious change in posture which takes place as the man or cat sits up and looks for the source of stimulation, there are objective signs shown by an EEG tracing. As Fig. 2.8 (CTX) indicates, the EEG in the drowsy state consists of large amplitude slow (4–6 sec) waves. At the onset of the stimulus (arrow in Fig. 2.8), and at the time behavioral arousal occurs, the tracing changes to a low-amplitude, irregular trace with no particular frequency of the voltage changes (desynchronized). The mechanism involved in this EEG change is complex. Neurons in both thalamus and cortex take part.

We have previously considered receptor activation in the somatic system (Chapter 1) as causing nerve impulses to travel over defined paths through the spinal cord and brainstem to the thalamus and receiving areas of cortex. The pathways from receptors, however, also include another route to the cerebral hemisphere which in the brainstem diverges from that previously considered. Largely owing to the work of Magoun and Lindsley (e.g., Magoun, 1952, and Lindsley, 1960), we now know that the axons passing to the thalamic sensory nuclei send branches in the brainstem to cells of reticular nuclei. The reticular nuclei con-

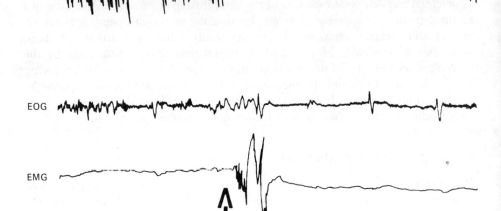

Fig. 2.8 Arousal (arrow) as shown by EEG, EOG (eye movement) and EMG (electromyogram). Records were obtained from a cat in slow-wave sleep upon presentation of an auditory stimulus (arrow). (With permission from Vern and Hubbard, *Electroenceph. Clin. Neurophysiol. 31*, 573–580, 1971.)

cerned are found throughout the medulla, pons, and midbrain, particularly in the midline. The reticular neurons, in turn, send their axons up to certain thalamic nuclei and to cortical neurons as well as down to the spinal cord (reticulospinal tracts).

Two fundamental types of nucleus are found in the thalamus. The type previously considered (specific sensory) receives input from receptors (eye-lateral geniculate nucleus, ear-medial geniculate nucleus, somatosensory-ventrolateral nucleus) and sends axons to appropriate cortical neurons (visual, visual area; auditory, auditory area; somatosensory, post central gyrus). The type presently considered receives input from the reticular formation, which is not modality specific. The projection to the cortex is, in turn, widespread and diffuse.

While activation of the specific thalamic system results in the appearance of evoked potentials in cortical receiving areas (Fig. 2.1), activation of the generalized system results in the desynchronized EEG shown in Fig. 2.8. Microelectrode studies of the synaptic linkages involved (Purpura, 1970) show that the thalamic neurons of the generalized system send excitatory input to cortical neurons and, via thalamic interneurons, inhibit the neurons of the specific sensory thalamic nuclei. As a result, as Fig. 2.9 (2) indicates, during the drowsy state, signals reaching cortex and thalamus are attenuated by this inhibitory feedback. Upon arousal, however, which involves more rapid firing of the generalized thalamic system, the

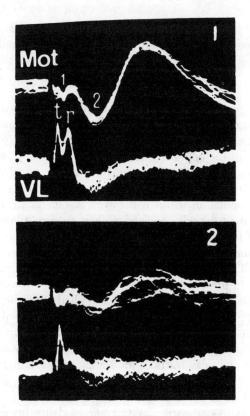

Fig. 2.9 Modifications produced in the response to stimulation of red nucleus neurons recorded in the ventrolateral nucleus of the thalamus (below) and motor cortex (above) during (1) wakefulness; (2) drowsiness. (With permission from Steriade *et al.*, 1969. *J. Neurophysiol. 32*, 251–265.)

inhibitory input is attenuated. Apparently the inhibitory interneurons are unable to transmit at high rates. The inhibition is thus lifted and, as Fig. 2.9 (1) indicates, a much bigger cortical signal is generated.

Midbrain reticular formation activity is particularly important in the generation of arousal. Thalamic neurons are unable to generate a desynchronized EEG in the presence of lesions in the reticular formation. There are differences, however, in the arousal generated by thalamic and midbrain stimulation. The thalamic arousal is shortlived whereas the midbrain arousal is prolonged and intense, as is its cortical facilitory effect. The differences presumably reflect the fact that midbrain reticular neurons are connected to cortical neurons not only by thalamic relays but also by other relays, such as those through hypothalamic nuclei. It is of some interest, too, that the midbrain neurons are excited by norepinephrine. It appears that the "arousal" produced by this substance is also exerted by a dual action—firstly and rapidly by exciting the reticular neurons and secondly and more slowly by a blood-born action on cortical neurons (Bonvallet *et al.,* 1954).

B. Attention

In addition to the general mechanism of arousal, another system controlling the flow of information to the brain is in operation. The mechanism involved in this system may underlie attention or the lack of attention.

Tracts running in the opposite direction from the sensory tracts, that is from cortex to thalamus and cortex to relay junctions in the spinal cord, comprise the anatomical substrate of this system. The axons of these tracts terminate on the same interneuron population which is involved in "surround inhibition." Experimentally, stimulation of the cells involved or their axons has been shown to inhibit the forward flow of information in sensory tracts. The inhibitory effects are exerted by postsynaptic inhibition in thalamus and cortex and by presynaptic inhibition in the spinal cord. There is reason to believe this system is always active (Livingston, 1959). Earlier in this chapter, evoked potentials were considered as indicators that action potentials set up by receptor activation had, after the appropriate relays, excited cells in the cortical receiving areas. It has been observed that these evoked potentials are much larger in anesthetized animals than in an active, awake animal. Furthermore, if the potentials set up by receptor activation are studied at lower levels, e.g., in the relay tracts of the spinal cord, it is found that these cord potentials increase in amplitude if the cord is sectioned in the cervical region, thus cutting off the descending inhibitory systems.

To pay attention to one particular receptor modality involves a choice from several simultaneously ongoing receptor inflows. The result is choice of one and neglect of the others. Both processes—choice and rejection—have been studied and appear to have a neural basis. An effect of attention upon evoked potential amplitudes has been well documented, but the interpretation of this finding is controversial. For instance, one of the most often-quoted experiments dealing with the effects of nonattention is the story of the cat and the sardine (e.g. Hernandez Peon, 1969). In this experiment, evoked potentials were recorded from the occipital cortex of an awake, unrestrained cat in response to flashes of light. When the cat's attention was attracted by the odor of sardines, blown through its cage, the evoked potential produced in response to the flash was markedly reduced. This result was taken by the experimenters to indicate that attention to the sardine *odor* led to the inhibition of the visual input. It was pointed out by Horn (1960), however, that cats attended to the sardine odor by sniffing and *looking* toward its source. Horn raised the possibility that the depression of evoked responses actually occurred in the modality being used. Later he was able to provide evidence for his hypothesis. In these experiments, evoked responses to a flash, recorded from the visual cortex of active unrestrained cats with implanted electrodes, were reduced when a series of tones was delivered *only if there was some visual searching* involved in the cat's response to the acoustic stimuli. The searching has, as a con-comitant, inhibition of the signals generated by the flash. This reduction in evoked potential presumably was brought about by a large number of neurons no longer working together but processing more information in a state of desynchrony.

The enhancing effects of attention on neural activity are better documented. For instance, there are neurons in the auditory cortex of awake unrestrained cats which generate an action potential in response to an auditory stimulus only when the animal is attending to the stimulus (Hubel *et al.*, 1959). Neurons have also been detected in monkey visual systems which give an enhanced response to a spot of light if an animal is attending to the spot (Goldberg & Wurtz, 1972). In the experiments the monkeys were trained to make eye movements toward a bright spot in their visual field. Neuron responses (number of action potentials) could be compared when the appropriate stimulus was the object of eye movement and when it was not. In the attended condition, the response was more regular, vigor-ous, and prolonged than in the nonattended condition. It has also been shown that attention will enhance synaptic transmission in man. For instance, Jouvet & Lapras (1959) recorded evoked potentials from thalamic neurons in a man before an operation which was to involve the destruction of this area. The potentials gen-erated by light taps to the face were markedly enhanced when the subject counted them.

III. PERCEPTION

In traditional neurology a distinction was drawn between sensation and percep-tion. Sensation was thought to be the result of experiencing the "raw" stimulus—explicable in terms of receptors, relays, and cortical function, probably to the level of a primary receiving area. Perception was thought to involve the total experience of apprehending and comprehending an object in space and time with appropri-ate emotions and associated memories. The neurological basis of perception was conceived of as activity in neurons of the association cortex. Today it is difficult to make such a clear distinction, and perception is often used in a more restricted way to mean the process by which certain features or patterns in a receptor field are thought to be recognized. It is in this limited sense that perception is discussed here.

A. Neural basis of perception

Neurons in a primary receiving area are arranged in such a way that they repre-sent the whole receptor field to which they are connected. In the somatosensory area, for instance, the whole body surface is represented in proportion to receptor density. On such a map then, lips and fingers are represented by larger areas than arms and legs.

Recent studies indicate that within the primary receiving area further order exists. At any particular spot, say the leg portion of the somatosensory area, the neurons of the six layers of neocortex lie in columns. Two forms of order occur within a column. The stimulus dimension is represented vertically. All the neurons in a column (Fig. 2.10) are connected to receptors of the same modality with the same, or very similar, receptor fields. Horizontally, cells are in layers with a hierarchical order. The entering axons from the thalamic neurons synapse on cells in layer IV—the simple cells. Higher order neurons (with more rigorous stimulation parameters) are in upper and lower layers.

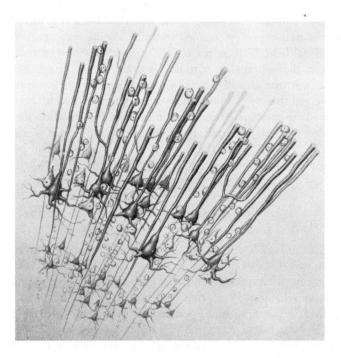

Fig. 2.10 Perspective schematic drawings of the cerebral cortex based upon a stereoscopic observation of Nissl counter-stained Golgi sections. Columnlike units, formed by elongated aggregates of cells and their processes, are shown. The figure also illustrates how the spread of the basal dendrites of pyramidal cells in one column invades a number of neighboring columns and how the branching of their apical dendrites may contribute to the function of one or more adjacent cell columns in layers above the level of their division. (With permission from G. von Bonin and W. R. Mehler, On columnar arrangement of nerve cells in cerebral cortex, *Brain Research 26*, 1–9, Figure 2, 1971.)

Still more recent studies indicate that a single neuron in the primary sensory area may have, in its dendritic tree, a representation of its receptor field. In the somatosensory area, for instance, it appears possible that synapses are made on dendrite trees in a way that reproduces the spatial position of receptors on the skin surface (Whitsel *et al.*, 1972).

The detailed map—area, column, dendritic tree—is the basis of perception. How is it used? The most advanced studies have been made in cat and monkey primary and secondary visual areas (Hubel and Wiesel, 1962, 1965, 1968). In the primary visual cortex, some neurons (simple cells) are most effectively stimulated by a long, narrow rectangle of light (slit) arranged at a particular orientation to the vertical and located in a particular part of the visual field, thus stimulating a particular part of the retina. Cells in the same column share similar orientation and position preferences. Presumably this is because each of the simple cells is connected to a particular, linearly arranged group of retinal receptors (Fig. 2.11). In adjacent areas of visual cortex, however, the stimulus requirements needed before a neuron is excited are more complicated. Some columns of neurons (complex cells) respond to a slit of a particular orientation *anywhere* in the receptor field. In still other areas columns of neurons (hypercomplex cells) are found for which the adequate stimulus is a slit of light of a particular *length* anywhere in the receptor field. Too long or too short a slit is not an optimal stimulus. Neurons have even been found requiring an intersection of slits at a particular angle for their excitation. Results of this type are currently explained by connection of cell columns (Fig. 2.11). Appropriate connections of hierarchies of neuron columns can be imagined so that a visual neuron would be excited only if a triangle or a square were the stimulus (see Question 2.7).

Our preference for Euclidean geometry, with its postulate that parallel lines never meet, may perhaps be explained by the preference of our visual cortex neurons for straight-line stimuli. It seems probable that we have an arrangement of cell columns with receptor fields like those of cat and monkey. First, it is known that bars or spots of light appear in the visual fields of men and women when their primary visual area is stimulated. One study reports that an attempt was made to rectify the blindness of one woman by putting many small stimulating units on her primary visual area (Brindley and Lewin, 1968). Some sixty units were installed which were to be activated by radio pulses, and which, if activated in sequence, would hopefully produce lines or patterns. The lady reported "seeing" flashes of light, apparently in front of her eyes, but because only a few of the stimulators worked, the experiment was not fully successful. Second, a common visual hallucination, associated with migraine headaches, is manifest as a fortification pattern (Fig. 2.12), which consists of bars of light arranged rather like a barricade. This is just the appearance expected if columns of cells in a primary visual area are being activated, with the activation spreading out from column to column (Richards, 1971). There are certainly enough cells in our visual cortices to account for pattern-detecting abilities. Anatomists report 540 million cells in each human primary area and 760 million in the surrounding secondary area.

Feature-detecting cells are known in other parts of the cortex. In the monkey somatosensory area, for instance, neurons have been detected which are connected

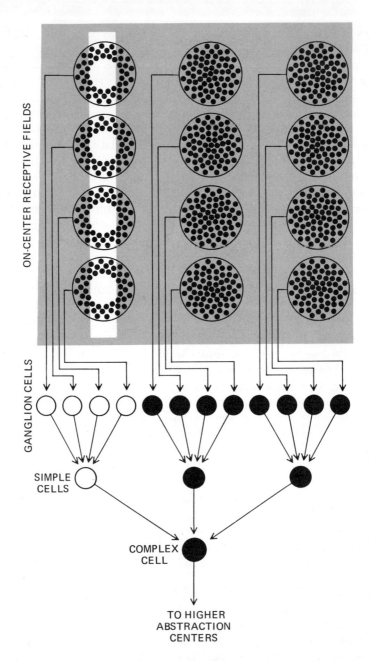

Fig. 2.11 Neuronal circuitry involved in perception, thought to exist within a cat's visual cortex, is illustrated schematically. "It begins with a rectangular array of receptive fields. The array is comprised of three parallel vertical rows and each row contains four receptive fields. The axons from the retinal ganglion cells that correspond to each

Fig. 2.12 Fortification pattern seen by sufferers from some types of migraine preceding an attack. The prototype of this figure was drawn by a student of mine subject to such attacks. The successive rows are thought to be generated by the activation of successive columns of simple neurons in the visual area of the brain. The activation is thought to spread like the waves from a stone tossed in a pond.

with hairs and are only excited when the hair moves in a certain direction. Investigations of this sort have revealed that feature detectors are not active all the time. Their activity then signals the detection of the feature (Whitsel *et al.*, 1972).

More complex feature detectors include cells in the cat parietal association areas which respond only to a fixed number of stimuli—two or three or six or

---

row converge on one of three simple cortical cells; the axons from the simple cells then converge on one complex cortical cell. A bar of light (left) falling on a row of receptive fields excites the four ganglion cells corresponding to that row and also the simple cortical cell connected to them." (With permission from "Cellular Communication" by Gunther S. Stent. Copyright © 1972 by *Scientific American*, Inc. All rights reserved.)

seven—and the stimuli may be sounds, light flashes, or touches (Thompson *et al.*, 1970). The detection of such cells, which may be termed "gnostic" (knowing), certainly indicates that feature or pattern detection plays an important role in neural basis of perception. The effects of the parietal lobe lesions considered in the next section indicates, however, that a further large number of very complex operations are necessary for normal perception.

B. Parietal lobe lesions and disorders of perception

Clinical evidence based on examination of patients with injuries or disease of brain areas adjacent to primary receiving areas has shown the essential correctness of the view that perception involves identification of many individual units (aspects of a stimulus), the integration of these aspects into groups, and finally the selection of meaningful groups. Patients with injuries to the parietal lobe have been particularly helpful in the formulation of this view.

The parietal lobe contains in the postcentral gyrus the somatosensory area. It borders on the occipital lobe containing the visual area and the temporal lobe including the auditory area. Neurons in the broad region between the three receiving areas may receive inputs from all three sources and the vestibular (balance) system as well. Lesions in this region are fortunately rare, but, because of their great interest, have been much studied. Patients with such lesions commonly are found to have, for instance, normal visual acuity but gross defects in perception (visual agnosia). The account of such lesions that follows is based on the fascinating account given by the Russian neurologist A. R. Luria in his book *Higher Cortical Functions in Man* (1966, Chapter 3).

1. *Lesions of visual cortex and visual agnosia*

Lesions of the primary visual area (Fig. 1.8) do not lead to disturbance of complex visual perception, but to central blindness. Patients with bilateral lesions outside this area, especially if such lesions extend out into the parietal lobe, may have normal visual acuity but cannot recognize what they see. There appear to be several possible reasons for such defects.

The basic defect in some patients, according to Luria, is a disturbance of the ability to synthesize isolated visual elements into an integral whole. Characteristically, such patients pick out one aspect of a picture; for instance, one of Luria's patients called a pair of spectacles a bicycle because, the patient said, since there was a circle and another circle and some sort of crossbar, it must be a bicycle. It should be noted that such patients have no speech defect and try and use speech associations to identify the object. Figure 2.13 indicates the nature of the evidence on which Luria's opinion is based. A patient attempted to copy a drawing of an elephant (Fig. 2.13, specimen) but could only draw isolated elements—legs, trunks (Fig. 2.13, copy)—and could not synthesize them into a complete picture.

Grosser forms of this defect are known in which the ability to synthesize visual elements is so restricted that the patient can only perceive one object at a time

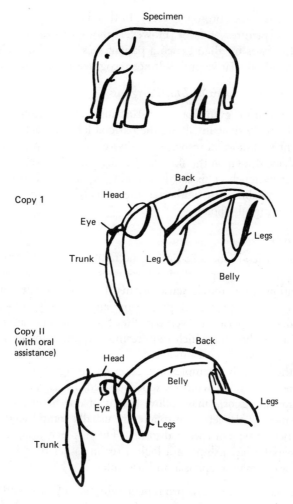

Fig. 2.13 Visual agnosia. Drawings by a patient with agnosia following a bilateral wound of the occipital region of the brain. The patient made two attempts to copy a drawing of an elephant (specimen). Copy 1 was his effort to complete a drawing that had been started. Copy 2 is a drawing made with the aid of spoken instructions. (With permission from *Higher Cortical Functions in Man* by A. R. Luria, authorized translation from the Russian by Basil Haigh, © 1966 Consultant Bureau Enterprises, Inc. and Basic Books, Inc.

regardless of its size. Some patients with bilateral occipito-parietal lesions for instance, when looking at a fork and spoon, see only one of them; if they look at the spoon the fork disappears.

This brain defect in other patients is apparently not in perceiving objects or pictures but in recognizing their nature. A common form of this disorder is an inability to recognize faces (prosopagnosia). In this disorder, patients have no trouble seeing faces or pictures of faces. However, they fail to realize the particular significance of the faces for them; such a patient sees a face but fails to recognize it as that of a friend or relative and will not recognize himself in a photograph.

2. *Lesions of the parietal cortex and tactile agnosia*

Lesions of the postcentral gyrus lead to disturbances of sensation on the contralateral half of the body. Lesions involving the parietal lobe just outside this area may result in a patient with normal responses to discrete touch or pain, but an inability to recognize a shape drawn on the skin, or the direction of travel of a moving stimulus, or an object by touch. This tactile agnosia, like visual agnosia, can be attributed mainly to an inability to synthesize the units of primary sensory data into coherent and meaningful wholes.

3. *Spatial disorientation*

That part of the parietal lobe adjacent to the temporal lobe (interoparietal area) contains neurons receiving input of visual, somatosensory, and vestibular origin, as well as information from muscle sense organs. Patients with lesions in this area commonly have defects in spatial perception and spatially organized activity. Signs of such defects appear in everyday life. Such patients cannot dress themselves or make a bed, both of which require more appreciation of spatial relationships than they possess. They cannot tell the time either, for the estimation of the position of the hands is a complex operation requiring appreciation of the symmetry of the clock face upon which is superimposed the asymmetry of the hands.

Unilateral spatial agnosia may follow lesions of one hemisphere (usually the right). Disturbances of the left hemisphere are usually complicated by an association with a particular type of speech disorder. These speech disorders demonstrate a disorder of spatial relationships in a logical realm rather than in external space. Two examples are semantic aphasia and acalculia.

(a) *Semantic aphasia.* The most prominent symptom of this syndrome is an inability to remember the name of an object. If given the first sound of the word, patients do remember, suggesting that the defect resides in an inability to fit the basic sound details together into a whole. Patients with this defect cannot understand instructions involving spatial relationships. For example, when one of Luria's patients was asked to draw a triangle below a circle, the patient drew a triangle and a circle in that order, but expressed an inability to relate them.

(b) *Acalculia.* Operations involving numbers appear to be learned in a way that involves spatial relationships. A child first develops number concepts by manipulating the elements in an external spatial field, e.g., playing with blocks. Later these operations are replaced by visual images and more complex abstractions. Apparently, however, the spatial character of the mathematical element is retained. Patients with acalculia appreciate the magnitude of individual numbers but can neither write nor read compound numbers, i.e., they cannot point to the units of 10s or 100s in a three-figure number accurately. Given such a number, they may take account only of the individual numbers within the whole, i.e., the number 387 may appear larger than 401. Such patients may remember their multiplication tables but cannot carry out division or manipulate fractions.

IV. EMOTION

Any emotion has three facets—first, an origin in an external or internal stimulus; second, a central process, which results (third) in an appropriate response to the stimulus in terms of past experiences and future expectations.

A distinction can be usefully made between emotion (affect), i.e., whether one is happy, sad, frightened, angry, despairing, etc., which is essentially private, and the emotional behavior which signals these states to an observer. In animal experiments, behavior is studied and emotions, if considered at all, can only be inferred. In fact, the distinction has an anatomical basis, for brain stimulation experiments in man have shown that emotional states and emotional behavior can be elicited by stimuli of different brain areas. Of course in any real situation an emotion will be accompanied by the appropriate behavior. It is convenient to consider the neuronal basis of emotional behavior before the neuronal basis of emotion, as theories of emotion have historically been dependent on the current state of animal research.

A. The neural basis of emotional behavior

In Chapter 1 the expression of emotions was dealt with as one of the functions of the sympathetic division of the autonomic system, which included release of epinephrine from the adrenal gland. The muscles of the somatic system are of course also involved in an emotional response, as in the instances of the growling, barking, jaw opening, snarling, and lowering of the head of a dog about to attack. Clearly, an emotional response involves coordination of the sympathetic and somatic systems. The reticular neurons of the midbrain arousal system are also concerned, for emotional states are commonly accompanied by a desynchronized EEG (Lindsley, 1951).

The integration of somatic, autonomic, and arousal systems is achieved by hypothalamic neurons. Animals with an intact hypothalamus (even if they lack all the brain above the hypothalamus) display a vigorous pattern of rage in response to a light touch or a pattern of fear in response to a high-pitched sound. The responses in all cases outlast the stimulus. Electrical stimulation of particular hypothalamic areas will elicit complete patterns of behavior characteristic of rage, terror, or fear. It may be noted that effects of hypothalamic stimulation have their counterpart in human cases of disease and injury involving this area. There is no doubt that emotional behavior is organized by hypothalamic neurons in men and monkeys as well as cats and dogs (review in Gellhorn and Loofbourrow, 1963; Bard, 1968).

Gellhorn and his colleagues (e.g., Gellhorn and Loofbourrow, 1963) have pointed out that the autonomic activity of the hypothalamus is expressed through both sympathetic and parasympathetic channels, the balance depending on the particular emotion and its intensity. In general, unpleasant emotions of mild intensity are associated with sympathetic discharges, while pleasant emotions of mild intensity are predominately associated with parasympathetic discharges. As the intensity of an emotion increases, both divisions become involved. For instance, increased motor activity of bladder and rectum (parasympathetic signs) may accompany fear and anxiety.

The gray matter of the hypothalamus is continuous with that of the midbrain and some midbrain neurons also have integrating functions in emotional responses. When cats and dogs with no neural tissue above the midbrain are handled, they display brief reactions characteristic of rage, fear, or terror which do not outlast the stimulus (Brady, 1960). These reactions occur because midbrain reticular neurons play a central role in effecting emotional responses. Excited by hypothalamic neurons, these neurons in turn send their axons in the reticulospinal tracts to autonomic and somatic motoneurons, thus influencing movement, heart rate, vessel diameter, salivary and sweat secretions, and epinephrine secretion. The role of midbrain reticular neurons in mediating arousal has already been mentioned (Section III).

Several groups of investigators, impressed by the abnormal ease with which the "rage" reaction of hypothalamic cats is evoked, considered the possibility that cortical neurons normally exerted an inhibiting influence upon hypothalamic neurons. Figure 2.14 shows some of the connections of hypothalamic neurons which have proved to be important. Most of the gray matter of the hypothalamus is situated close to the midline in specific nuclear masses. More laterally on each side lies a mass of axons—the median forebrain bundle—formed in part by axons passing to and from the hypothalamus.

The outflow of hypothalamic neurons passes in several directions. Already considered is the projection to the midbrain reticular neurons which form part of the median forebrain bundle. Another projection, shown in Fig. 2.14, passes from the mammillary nuclei (one of the medial hypothalamic groups) to the anterior thalamic nuclei. These project, in turn, to the cingulate gyrus. Finally, some hypothalamic nuclei project to the pituitary gland controlling endocrine function.

Hypothalamic neurons receive connections from the cerebral cortex, the hippocampus, and the amygdaloid nucleus. The hippocampus plays a key role in projections to the hypothalamus. As Fig. 2.14 indicates, hippocampal axons form the fornix and are distributed to the corresponding mammillary body and septal region (a small area of cortex beneath the rostrum of the corpus callosum). Axons of cells in the septal region synapse with cingulate gyrus neurons which project back to the hippocampal neurons. Collaterals of the septal axons pass via the median forebrain bundle to synapse with hypothalamic neurons.

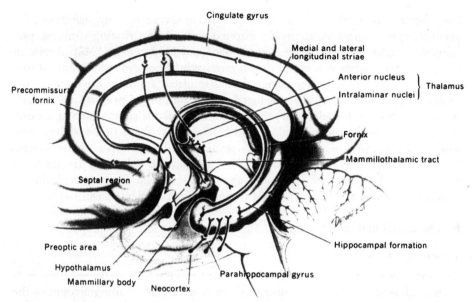

Cingulate gyrus

Medial and lateral
longitudinal striae

Anterior nucleus

Intralaminar nuclei } Thalamus

Precommissur
fornix

Fornix

Mammillothalamic tract

Septal region

Preoptic area

Hippocampal formation

Hypothalamus

Mammillary body

Parahippocampal gyrus

Neocortex

Fig. 2.14 Schema of some connections of the limbic system. The "Papez circuit" includes tracts from hippocampal to mammillary body via the fornix; from mammillary
body to anterior nucleus of thalamus via mammillothalamic tract; from anterior nucleus to cingulate gyrus; and from cingulate gyrus via several neurons back to the
hippocampus. (With permission from *The Human Nervous System* by C. R. Noback
and R. J. Demarest. Copyright 1967, McGraw-Hill, Inc. Used with permission of Mc-
Graw-Hill Book Company.)

The amygdaloid nuclei, masses of gray matter in the anterior end of the roof of
the inferior horn of each lateral ventricle, also project to the hypothalamic nuclei.
These structures are not shown in Fig. 2.14 but are related to the corresponding
hippocampus, which forms the floor of the inferior horn of each lateral ventricle. In
each hemisphere, amygdaloid neurons, like hippocampal neurons, are connected
with the cingulate gyrus.

It is convenient to apply the term *limbic lobe* (*limbic* meaning "ring" or "border") to the cortex on the medial side of each hemisphere (limbic cortex) together
with associated structures (septal area, hippocampus, and amygdaloid nucleus).

The brain structures controlling emotional behavior can best be regarded as a
series of overlapping control circuits. In cats (Bard and Mountcastle, 1947), the
hypothalamic rage reaction is normally held in check by amygdaloid and cingulate
gyrus neurons; the destruction of these areas results in the rage reaction appearing
in an otherwise intact cat. In contrast, the destruction of neocortex, leaving the
limbic lobe, makes cats extraordinarily tame and placid. Apparently then, neocortex provides excitatory drive to the hypothalamic integrating neurons, thus modify-
ing the inhibitory effects of the limbic system. It should be noted that neocortex

has other effects on the rage reaction. Cats made savage by amygdalectomy, for instance, show aggression accurately directed toward the irritating stimulus, presumably because they possess neocortex (Bard and Mountcastle, 1947). Again, in normal animal studies it is found that aggressive behavior evoked by brain stimulation is expressed to a greater degree if the stimulated animal is *dominant* in the group. Presumably, cortically mediated social inhibition prevents electrically induced hostility (Delgado, 1969)! Unfortunately for this simple story it appears that in man (and Macaque monkeys and Norway rats) the neurons of the limbic lobe excite aggressive behavior and are restrained by the neurons of the neocortex. In man, bilateral amygdalectomy results in an apathetic individual (reviewed in Bard, 1968); Delgado (1969) reports aggressive behavior by a patient during stimulation of one of her amygdaloid nuclei through implanted electrodes.

B. The neural basis of emotion

1. *Response theories*

The three facets of emotion—stimulus, central process, and response—have each been considered primary determinants of emotion. An entertaining account of the work of the pioneers in this field can be found in Cannon's book (Cannon, 1929). It was, according to James and Lange (Cannon, 1929, Chapter 18), the afferent nerve impulses from the disturbed organs which by their effect on the brain neurons produced the substratum of emotion. This theory lost support when Sherrington (1900), who transected the spinal cord and cut the vagal nerves of dogs, and Cannon and his coworkers, who removed the entire sympathetic division of the autonomic nervous system from cats (Cannon, 1929, p. 348), found that even after surgery these animals displayed unchanged emotional behavior, except for the disappearance of elements whose connections with the brain had been cut. Cannon (1929, p. 356) also pointed out that norepinephrine injection, which induces the bodily changes typical of emotion, does not include the correspondingly appropriate psychic states.

Consider, for instance, the experiments of Schacter and Singer (1962). In these experiments students were given epinephrine injections to mimic sympathetic activity. The bodily reactions that occur are of course identical. The students often reported no emotional response, or occasionally said they felt as if they were afraid. Fear is of course one of the emotional states in which sympathetic activity occurs, but in this case the students obviously doubted whether the feelings were genuine. Schacter and Singer's experiment involved giving the students an opportunity to interpret their state as an emotion-arousing event. They did this by separating the two components, epinephrine injection and the event. Students were told they were to take part in trials of a new drug. In fact, half of them were injected with epinephrine, half with a weak salt solution. One group of the subjects received an explanation of the expected bodily changes which might follow the injection. Another group got no information or incorrect information. These were the groups that, it was hoped, would label their epinephrine-aroused states in correspondence with whatever emotion they were exposed to at the time. The interpretation component involved placing the students with persons who were ostensibly other subjects, but were actually trained experimenters who had been instructed to generate excitement or anger in various ways. For instance, to generate excitement, a subject was alone in a room with a stooge who followed a standard routine consisting of such things as flying paper airplanes and hula hooping, all the while keeping up a standard patter and occasionally trying to get the subject to join in. Anger was provoked by asking subjects to fill in a long personal questionnaire with numbers of infuriating questions. A stooge filled in the questionnaire at the same time and got obviously more and more annoyed, finally ripping up the questionnaire in a rage and stomping out of the room.

Schacter and colleagues watched the resultant activity through a one-way mirror and later asked the students about their mood and activity. The results were just as predicted. Students who had no accurate knowledge of what to expect from epinephrine injection became either excited or angry, depending on the experience they had had. Students who knew what to expect or who were injected with salt solution did not become very excited or very angry and indeed found the behavior of their aroused but ignorant fellow students somewhat strange.

Presumably in everyday life, cortical connections with hypothalamic, midbrain, and spinal autonomic neurons trigger sympathetic activity, and the nature of the initiating stimulus determines the nature of the emotional label. For example, when threatening objects initiate emotional behavior, we label our experience as "fear."

2. Central process theories

The neuronal systems which facilitate or inhibit emotional behavior (Section IV-A) have all been considered at one time or another as "the seat" of the emotions. Cannon (1929), for instance, suggested that the hypothalamus, which by then had been shown to be essential for emotional behavior, was the seat of the emotions. As the preceding section makes clear however, the hypothalamic neurons, while capable of organizing integrated emotional responses, are themselves controlled by the limbic lobe and neocortex. Modern theories of emotion take account of more recent neurophysiological findings, together with the results of brain stimulation in man and animals. The Papez-McLean theory, for instance, states that the neural structures found on the medial aspect of the cerebral hemispheres (Fig. 2.14)—the hippocampus, fornix, mammillary body, mammillothalamic tract, anterior nucleus of thalamus, and cingulate cortex are involved also in the control of emotions. Papez (1937) postulated that emotions were elaborated in the hippocampus and the results shunted via the mammillothalamic tract to the anterior thalamus and thence to the cingulate gyrus (Fig. 2.14). The Papez theory was apparently supported by the famous studies of Kluver and Bucy (1939), who demonstrated that bilateral temporal lobectomy in monkeys—removing the lower half of the Papez circuit—indeed resulted in changes in emotional behavior. The monkeys became tame and docile and repeatedly exposed themselves to painful or harmful situations. For instance, one such animal tried again and again to lick a lighted match. It is now clear, however, as the preceding section indicates, that this result was due to a removal of the amygdala, *not* the hippocampus, as the Papez theory would indicate.

McLean (e.g. 1960) has amended the Papez theory by stressing the importance of the amygdaloid nuclei and their connections with the septal area and with the hypothalamus and brainstem (median forebrain bundle). This region of the brain is also important in memory and learning (Chapter 3), which may be significant in understanding how emotional responses are modified by past experience.

Striking support for the dependence of emotion on structures of the Papez circuit has come from attempts to treat psychiatric patients by surgical destruction of parts of the circuit (psychosurgery) and from brain stimulation experiments in man.

(a) *Psychosurgery.* Surgeons attempting to treat psychiatric disorders in this manner today use stereotactic techniques to make very localized brain lesions (Hitchcock *et al.*, 1972). Undercutting the cingulate gyrus (cingulotractotomy), for instance, appears to be a very successful treatment for severe chronic depression which does not respond to any other form of treatment. For instance, of fifty treated patients in an Australian study, forty-four were able to return to work, thirty-three without any further treatment or supervision. Patients with such good results included a dentist and three high school teachers (Bailey *et al.*, 1971). Enthusiasm for such operations should be tempered by the possibility that the improvement may not be permanent. Mingrino & Schergna (1972), for instance, found that half of their patients initially improved by cingulotomy had relapsed within fifteen to thirty-two months of the operation. Such patients are left with permanent brain damage (see Question 2.8).

(b) *Brain stimulation studies.* Olds and Milner (1954) found that rats with stimulating electrodes implanted in the brain could be trained to press a lever which turned on stimulating current. Regions of brain could be classified by the percentage of time the animals spent lever pressing. Brain areas with high scores were the septal area; less dramatic but still noteworthy was stimulation in the cingulate cortex and the mammillothalamic tract (Fig. 2.14). The hippocampus was less often stimulated by rats but still at rates above control levels. Olds and Milner suggested that brain stimulation rewarded bar-pressing behavior. The most notorious area in this regard is the median forebrain bundle, which, among other functions, connects the hypothalamic nuclei with the septal nucleus (Fig. 2.14). It was found that if a rat had a stimulating electrode implanted here, it continually pressed the bar which turned on stimulation. Indeed, given a choice between feeding and pressing, a rat would rather stimulate its median forebrain bundle than eat. Some brain areas were nonrewarding, i.e., animals *avoided* stimulating such areas. A number of questions are raised by these studies; notably, what the meaning of "reward" is in this context.

Fortunately the studies are not species specific. Studies with similar results have been carried out in cats, dogs, monkeys, and man. Studies on men are few but have particular value, for only in men can affect and behavior be separated. The reports of Heath and his coworkers (1955, 1964, 1972) indicate that "rewarding" brain stimulation is pleasurable. One of Professor Heath's patients, for instance, was provided with a small stimulator connected to several electrodes implanted in his brain. A counter connected to the stimulator counted the number of times he stimulated the various electrodes. The highest score was recorded from one point in the septal region (Fig. 2.15) which the patient declared made him feel "good"—he felt as if he was building up to a sexual orgasm although he was not able to reach the endpoint; he also often felt impatient and anxious. Other patients also enjoyed septal self-stimulation and reported similar feelings.

Unpleasant emotions can likewise be evoked by brain stimulation in man; for instance, fear can be induced by stimulation of parts of the temporal lobe in the region of the amygdala (Van Buren, 1961). In these cases there was no overt cause for the induced emotion and "fear" was limited to the duration of stimulation. In-

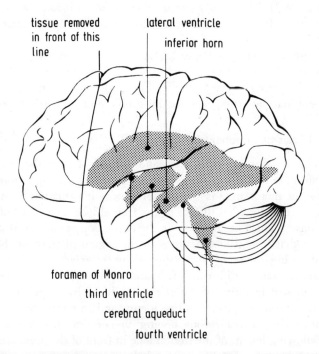

Fig. 2.15 Frontal lobotomy. The figure shows the extent of the brain removal or undercutting in the most extensive type of lobotomy. (Based on Rylander, 1939.)

dividual variation of the results of stimulation was marked, however. One patient laughed whenever he was stimulated in the same area. Extremely unpleasant emotions are also reported during the pathological electrical stimulation of temporal lobe neurons produced by epilepsy, and the emotion can be unpleasant enough to induce sufferers to commit suicide.

A further problem with these Olds and Milner studies (1954) is the nature of the stimulated structures, and recent studies (see Question 2.9) may have resolved this problem. It seems probable that the structures, stimulation of which is found "rewarding" in rats, are axons of certain neurons found in the midbrain and medulla. These neurons contain, and presumably release at synapses, either dopamine (midbrain) or norepinephrine (medulla). Their axons of both groups run forward in the median forebrain bundle, thus accounting for the uniquely satisfying nature of stimulation here. The norepinephrine-containing neurons are concerned also in arousal and attention (Section II this chapter) and in sleep and wakefulness (Chapter 4).

3. Stimulus theories

A recent theory of emotion, which places primacy on the role of the initiating stimulus as the genesis of emotion, is known as the activation theory (Lindsley, 1951; Zanchetti, 1967). This theory stresses the role of an incoming stimulus and/ or internal stimulus from cortical mechanisms in setting up reticular and hypothalamic activity and thus excitation of limbic and neocortical areas. Theories of this type are congruent with the Papez-McLean theory in that the activation theory explains how the Papez-McLean circuit is excited. Arousal, signalled by a desynchronized EEG would provide the background stimulation which facilitated the specific neuronal patterns generated by limbic and neocortical neurons.

C. The neural basis of personality

The frontal lobe contains the motor areas and in front of them the premotor areas so that the neurons of this lobe play a role in the processes leading to motor activity. Converging on the motor areas is a wealth of sensory information from all sensory areas. Furthermore, the medial surface of the frontal lobe forms part of the limbic lobe, the neurons of which are involved in the regulation of emotional states. Luria (1966) suggests that frontal lobe neurons in the region in front of the premotor area are the site of integration of information about the external world and information about internal states. With this information, presumably, behavior of an animal can be regulated in terms of the effects produced by its actions. This brain area may be destroyed by tumors and accidents, and in recent years has been selectively removed by neurosurgeons hoping to cure mental disorders (frontal lobotomy). Following lesions of the frontal lobe in front of the premotor area (Fig. 2.15) it is found that specialized functions such as speech, movement, vision, hearing, and intellectual operations, appear normal. Behavior is abnormal, however, in subtle ways. Significantly, epilepsy generated by lesions in this region is without a motor or sensory aura but is accompanied by a general loss of consciousness.

Rylander (1939) carefully studied the personality of thirty-two patients with frontal lobe tumors before and for several years after operation (Fig. 2.15). Furthermore, the patients were compared with control subjects without tumors, of the same sex, and similar age and occupation. Dr. Rylander's conclusion was that after operation, regardless of age, sex, or occupation, the patients suffered a change in their character or identity, that is, a change of personality. Perhaps the most obvious changes were in mood. In her series, twenty patients became euphoric. These patients in whom the trait was most prominent were spontaneously happy and contented no matter what their circumstances, laughing and joking upon the slightest provocation. In other cases, particularly when patients were very shy before operation, they became calmer, found it easier to meet with other people, and were less embarrassed. A few patients who were very depressed for years before surgery did not become euphoric but became even more despondent. It was noticeable too that after surgery patients showed a lack of tact, which was a considerable embarrassment to their relatives and friends. For instance, one patient, a clergyman, after his operation was quick to notice whether anything was lacking on the table and at once told his hostess of any deficiency in a careless and awkward way.

Intellectual changes after frontal lobotomy are difficult to detect in ordinary psychological tests. It was found, however, that patients who had undergone surgery had difficulty in remembering for more than two to three hours. For instance, they had much greater difficulty in learning and remembering nonsense syllables than did control subjects. Reading and writing were not affected but more complicated intellectual functions were weakened, which was demonstrated in Rylander's cases by the less satisfactory result of operation in patients with more complex jobs. A manual laborer did not appear much changed to himself or associates. An office manager, however, worked more slowly and found it difficult to undertake new work though he did his old routine work well. A clergyman two years after surgery no longer studied religious literature and when asked to preach could not write a new sermon but adapted an old one.

Dr. Rylander later studied an additional thirty-two patients who suffered frontal lobotomy because of mental disorders (Rylander, 1947). Like the tumor patients after operation these patients became tactless, emotionally labile, and in many cases euphoric. Their close relatives were convinced that there had been a personality change as a result of this operation. One wife said, "Doctor, you have given me a new husband, he isn't the same man." Other relatives of patients reported the loss of daughters, sons, and friends who had been replaced by unpleasant strangers. The patients themselves appeared superficially satisfactory after operation, but upon detailed questioning revealed they could not feel deep happiness or deep sorrow, that they forgot things, and that they had lost most of their interests.

It has long been known that animals with the anterior part of both frontal lobes removed show no sensory deficit and no gross disturbance of movement, but again abnormal behavior. Dogs, for instance, no longer recognize their masters and no longer search for food but take and chew any object. Russian workers have done much work in this field. Pavlov, for instance, favored the hypothesis that the essential deficit in frontal lobe destruction is the disintegration of goal-directed behavior. Later Russian workers have refined these concepts (e.g., Luria, 1966, Chapter 5). They have suggested that frontal lobe damage leads to a disturbance of the preliminary synthesis of individual signals which precede movement. An illustration of such an effect is the fact that dogs deprived of their frontal lobes, shown two feeding bowls, one of which contains food, run aimlessly from one to the other instead of going to the food filled bowl, as would a normal dog.

American experimenters (e.g. Pribram, 1959) suggest that in addition to the disturbance of the preliminary synthesis underlying regulation of complex motor operations, laboratory animals display a loss of the normal evaluation of the effects of their own actions which is essential for goal-directed behavior. It appears that patients with frontal lobe lesions can recognize the errors made by themselves and others but do not utilize this knowledge to control their own behavior (Konow and Pribram, 1970).

REFERENCES

Adrian, E. D. (1954) The physiological basis of perception, in J. F. Delafresnaye, ed., *Brain Mechanisms and Consciousness*, pp. 237–248. Oxford, Blackwell Scientific Publications.

Bailey, H. R., J. L. Dowling, C. H. Swanson, and E. Davies (1971) Cingulotractotomy in the treatment of severe affective illness. *Med. J. Aust. 1*, 8–12.

Bard, P. (1968) The hypothalamus. In *Medical Physiology*, Ch. 80, 12th edition, V. B. Mountcastle, Ed., C. N. Mosby Co., St. Louis.

Bard, P. and V. B. Mountcastle (1947) Some forebrain mechanisms involved in the expression of rage with special reference to suppression of angry behavior. *Proc. Ass. Res. Nerve. ment. Dis. 27*, 362–404.

Bonin, G. von and W. R. Mehler (1971) On columnar arrangement of nerve cells in cerebral cortex. *Brain Res. 27*, 1–9.

Bonvallet, M., P. Dell, and G. Hiebel (1954) Tonus sympathique et activité électrique corticale. *Electroenceph. clin. Neurophysiol. 6*, 119–144.

Borg, G., H. Diamant, L. Strom, and Y. Zotterman (1967) The relation between neural and perceptual intensity: a comparative study on the neural and psycho-physical response to taste stimuli. *J. Physiol. 192*, 13–20.

Brady, J. P. (1960) Emotional behavior, in *Handbook of Physiology*, Vol. III, pp. 1529–

1552, H. W. Magoun, Ed., Neurophysiology section. The Williams & Wilkins Co., Baltimore.

Brindley, G. S. and W. S. Lewin (1968) The sensations produced by electrical stimulation of the visual cortex. *J. Physiol. 196*, 479–493.

Cannon, B. W. (1929) *Bodily Changes in Pain, Hunger, Fear and Rage*. Harper & Row, New York, Evanston and London.

Creutzfeld, O., A. Rosina, M. Ito, and W. Probst (1969) Visual evoked responses of single cells and of the EEG in primary visual area of the cat. *J. Neurophysiol. 32*, 127–139.

Darian-Smith, I., K. O. Johnson, and R. Dykes (1973) "Cold" fibre population innervating palmar and digital skin of the monkey: response to cooling pulses. *J. Neurophysiol. 36*, 325–346.

Delgado, J. M. R. (1969) *Physical Control of the Mind*. Harper & Row, New York.

Fehmi, L. G., Adkin, J. W. and Lindsley, D. B. (1969) Electrophysiological correlates of visual perceptual masking in monkeys. *Exp. Brain Res. 7*, 299–316.

Gardner, E. P. and W. A. Spencer (1972a) Sensory funneling. I: Psychophysical observation of human subjects and responses of cutaneous mechanoreceptive afferents in the cat to patterned skin stimuli. *J. Neurophysiol. 35*, 925–953.

Gardner, E. P. and W. A. Spencer (1972b) Sensory funneling: II. Cortical neuronal representation of patterned cutaneous stimuli. *J. Neurophysiol. 35*, 954–977.

Gellhorn, E. and G. N. Loofbourrow (1963) *Emotions and Emotional Disorders*, Harper & Row, New York and Evanston.

Goldberg, M. E., and R. H. Wurtz (1972) Activity of superior colliculus in behaving monkey: II. Effect of attention on neuronal responses. *J. Neurophysiol. 35*, 560–574.

Grey-Walter, W., R. Cooper, V. J. Aldridge, W. C. McCallum, and A. L. Winter (1964) Contingent negative variation: an electric sign of sensorimotor association and expectancy in the human brain. *Nature (London), 203*, 380–384.

Heath, R. G. (1963) Electrical self-stimulation of the brain in man. *Am. J. Psychiat. 120*, 571–577.

Heath, R. G. (1972) Pleasure and brain activity in man: deep and surface encephalograms during orgasm. *J. nerv. ment. Dis. 54*, 3–18.

Heath, R. G., R. R. Monroe, and W. A. Mickle (1955) Stimulation of the amygdaloid nucleus in a schizophrenic patient. *Am. J. Psychiat. 111*, 862–863.

Hensel, H. and K. K. A. Boman (1960) Afferent impulses in cutaneous sensory nerves in human subject. *J. Neurophysiol. 23*, 564–578.

Hernández-Peón, R. (1969) Neurophysiologic aspects of attention, in *Handbook of Clinical Neurology*, Vol. 3, pp. 155–186, P. J. Vinken and G. W. Bruyn, Eds., Amsterdam, North Holland.

Hitchcock, E., L. Laitinen, and K. Vaernet, Eds. (1972) *Second International Conference on Psychosurgery* (Proceedings). Charles Thomas, Springfield, Ill.

Horn, G. (1960) Electrical activity of the cerebral cortex of the unanesthetized cat during attentive behaviour. *Brain, 83,* 57–76.

Hubel, D. H. and T. N. Wiesel (1962) Receptive fields, binocular interaction, and functional architecture in the cat's visual cortex. *J. Physiol. 160,* 106–154.

Hubel, D. H. and T. N. Wiesel (1965) Receptive fields and functional architecture in two non-striate visual areas (18 and 19) of the cat. *J. Neurophysiol. 28,* 229–289.

Hubel, D. H. and T. N. Wiesel (1968) Receptive fields and functional architecture of monkey striate cortex. *J. Physiol. 195,* 215–243.

Hubel, D. H., G. O. Henson, A. Rupert, and R. Galambox (1959) "Attention" units in the auditory cortex. *Science, 129,* 1279–1280.

Jasper, H. H. (1966) Pathophysiological studies of brain mechanisms in different states of consciousness, pp. 256–282 in *Brain Mechanisms and Consciousness,* J. C. Eccles, Ed., Springer-Verlag, Berlin.

Johnson, K. O., I. Darian-Smith and C. LaMotte (1973) Determinants of temperature discrimination in man: a correlative study of responses to cooling skin. *J. Neurophysiol. 36,* 347–370.

Jouvet, M. and C. Lapras (1959) *Variation des réponses électriques somesthésiques au niveau du thalamus chez l'homme au cours de l'attention. C. R. Soc. Biol. (Paris) 153,* 98–101.

Kluver, H. and P. C. Bucy (1939) Preliminary analysis of functions of the temporal lobes in monkeys. *Arch. Neurol. Psychiat. 42,* 979–1000.

Konow, A. and K. H. Pribram (1970) Error recognition and utilization produced by injury to the frontal cortex in man. *Neuropsychologia 8,* 489–491.

Libet, B. (1966) Brain stimulation and the threshold of conscious experience, pp. 165–176 in *Brain and Conscious Experience,* J. C. Eccles, Ed., Springer-Verlag, Berlin.

Libet, B., W. W. Alberts, E. W. Wright, L. D. Delattre, G. Levin, and B. Feinstein (1964) Production of threshold levels of conscious sensation by electrical stimulation of human somatosensory cortex. *J. Neurophysiol. 27,* 546–578.

Libet, B., W. W. Alberts, E. W. Wright, and B. Feinstein (1967) Responses of human somatosensory cortex to stimuli below threshold for conscious sensation. *Science, 158,* 1597–1600.

Lindsley, D. B. (1951) Emotion, pp. 473–516, in *Handbook of Experimental Psychology,* S. S. Stevens, Ed., John Wiley & Sons, New York.

Lindsley, D. B. (1960) Attention, consciousness, sleep and wakefulness, pp. 1553–1593, in *Handbook of Physiology,* Vol. III, H. W. Magoun, Ed., Neurophysiology section. The Williams & Wilkins Co., Baltimore.

Livingston, R. L. (1959) Central control of receptors and sensory transmission systems, pp. 741–760, *Handbook of Physiology,* Vol. I, H. W. Magoun, Ed., Neurophysiology section. The Williams & Wilkins Co., Baltimore.

Luria, A. R. (1966) *Higher Cortical Functions in Man.* Translated from the Russian by B. Haigh. Tavistock Publications, London.

McLean, P. D. (1960) Psychosomatics, in *Handbook of Physiology*, Vol. III, pp. 1723–1744, H. W. Magoun, Ed., Neurophysiology section. The Williams & Wilkins Co., Baltimore.

Magoun, H. W. (1953) An ascending reticular activating system in the brain stem. *Harvey Lect. 47,* 53–71.

Mingrino, S. and E. Schergna (1972) Stereotaxic anterior cingulotomy in the treatment of severe behavior disorders. Ch. 26 in *Psychosurgery*, ed. E. Hitchcock, L. Laitinen, and K. Vaernet, Eds., Charles Thomas, Springfield, Illinois.

Mountcastle, V. B. (1967) The problem of sensing and the neural coding of sensory events, pp. 393–408 in *The Neurosciences: A Study Program*, Eds. G. C. Quarton, T. Melnechuk, and F. O. Schmitt, Rockefeller University Press, New York.

Mountcastle, V. B. and T. P. S. Powell (1959) Neural mechanisms subserving cutaneous sensibility with special reference to the role of afferent inhibition in sensory perception and discrimination. *Bull. Johns Hopkins Hosp. 105,* 201–232.

Noback, C. R. and R. J. Demarest (1967) *The Human Nervous System: Basic Elements of Structure and Function*, McGraw-Hill, New York.

Olds, J. and P. Milner (1954) Positive reinforcement produced by electrical stimulation of septal area and other regions of rat brain. *J. comp. Physiol. Psychol. 47,* 419–427.

Papez, J. W. (1937) A proposed mechanism of emotion. *Arch. Neurol. Psychiat. 38,* 725–743.

Penfield, W. (1958) *The Excitable Cortex in Conscious Man.* Liverpool University Press, Liverpool.

Pribram, K. H. (1959) The intrinsic systems of the forebrain, in *Handbook of Physiology*, Vol. II, pp. 1323–1344, H. W. Magoun, Ed., Neurophysiology section. The Williams & Wilkins Co., Baltimore.

Purpura, D. P. (1970) Operations and processes in thalamic and synaptically related neural subsystems, pp. 458–470 in *The Neurosciences: A Second Study Program*. F. O. Schmitt, Ed. Rockefeller University Press, New York.

Richards, W. (1971) The fortification illusions of migraine. *Sci. American 224* (5), 89–96.

Rylander, G. (1939) *Personality Changes after Operation on the Frontal Lobes.* Humphrey Milford, Ed. Oxford University Press, London.

Rylander, G. (1947) Personality analysis before and after frontal lobotomy. *Res. Proc. Ass. nerv. ment. Dis. 27,* 691–705.

Schachter, S. and J. Singer (1962) Cognitive, social, and physiological determinants of emotional state. *Psychol. Rev. 69*, 379–399.

Sherrington, C. S. (1900) Experiments on the value of vascular and visceral factors for the genesis of emotion. *Proc. Roy. Soc. London 66*, 390–403.

Stent, G. S. (1972) Cellular communication. *Sci. American 227* (3), 42–51.

Steriade, M., G. Iosif and V. Apostol (1969) Responsiveness of thalamic and cortical motor relays during arousal and various stages of sleep. *J. Neurophysiol. 32*, 251–265.

Sutton, S., M. Braren, and J. Zubin (1965) Evoked potential correlates of stimulus uncertainty. *Science, 150*, 1187–1188.

Takeuchi, A. and N. Takeuchi (1962) Electrical changes in pre- and post-synaptic axons of the giant synapse of Loligo. *J. gen. Physiol. 45*, 1181–1193.

Thomas, J. E. (1968) Movements of the eye. *Sci. American 219* (2), 88–95.

Thompson, R. F., K. S. Mayers, R. T. Robertson and C. J. Patterson (1970) Number coding in association cortex of the cat. *Science, 168*, 271–273.

Vaughan, H. G., Jr. (1969) The relationship of brain activity to scalp recordings, in *Averaged Evoked Potentials: Methods, Results, Evaluations.* E. Donchin, and D. B. Lindsley, Eds., NASA, Washington, D.C.

Van Buren, J. M. (1961) Sensory, motor and autonomic effects of mesial temporal stimulation in man. *J. Neurosurg. 18*, 273–288.

Vern, B. and J. I. Hubbard (1971) Reinvestigation of the effects of gammahydroxybutyrate on the sleep cycle of the unrestrained intact cat. *Electroenceph. clin. Neurophysiol. 31*, 573–580.

Weber, E. H. (1846) Der Tastsinn und das Gemeingefühl. In *Handworterbuch der Physiologie 3* (2), R. Wagner, Ed., reported in Boring, E. G. (1942) *Sensation and Perception in the History of Experimental Psychology,* Appleton Century Crofts, Inc., New York.

Whitsel, B. L., J. R. Roppolo, and G. Werner (1972) Cortical information processing of stimulus motion on primate skin. *J. Neurophysiol. 35*, 691–717.

Zanchetti, A. (1967) Subcortical and cortical mechanisms in arousal and emotional behavior, pp. 602–614, in *The Neurosciences,* G. C. Quarton, T. Melnechuk, and F. O. Schmitt, Eds., Rockefeller University Press, New York.

SUGGESTED FURTHER READING

Scientific American Reprints

Sensation and perception:

Crombie, A. C. *Early concepts of the senses and the mind.* May, 1964, p. 108 (offprint 184).

Hubel, D. H. *The visual cortex of the brain.* November, 1963, p. 54 (offprint 168).

Julesz, B. *Perception, texture and visual.* February, 1965, p. 38 (offprint 318).

Kennedy, D. *Inhibition in visual systems.* July, 1963, p. 122 (offprint 162).

Pettigrew, T. D. *The neurophysiology of binocular vision.* August, 1972, p. 84 (offprint 1255).

Ratliff, F. *Contours and contrast.* June, 1972, p. 90 (offprint 73).

Wald, G. *Eye and camera.* August, 1950, p. 32 (offprint 46).

Wilson, V. J. *Inhibition in the central nervous system.* May, 1966, 102 (no offprint available).

Emotion:

Berlyne, D. E. *Conflict and arousal.* August, 1966, p. 82 (offprint 500).

Funkenstein, D. H. *The physiology of fear and anger.* May, 1955, p. 74 (offprint 428).

Brain stimulation:

Fisher, A. E. *Chemical stimulation of the brain.* June, 1964, p. 60 (offprint 485).

Olds, J. *Pleasure centers in the brain.* October 1956, p. 105 (offprint 30).

Books

Cannon, B. W. (1929) *Bodily Changes in Pain, Hunger, Fear and Rage.* Harper & Row, New York, Evanston and London.

Delgado, J. M. R. (1969) *Physical Control of the Mind.* Harper & Row, New York, Evanston, and London. (This is the best modern account of brain stimulation in monkey and man. It is designed for popular reading.)

Glass, D. C., Ed. (1967) *Neurophysiology and Emotion.* Rockefeller University Press, New York.

QUESTIONS

More advanced students may want to try answering the following questions using the references as a starting point.

2.1 *How can the electrical activity of the brain be recorded in a conscious man? What are the electrical correlates of perception?*

Bostock, H. and M. J. Jarvis (1970) Changes in the form of the cerebral evoked response related to the speed of simple reaction times. *Electroenceph. Clin. Neurophysiol.* 29, 137–145.

Libet, B. (1966) Brain stimulation and conscious experience, in *Brain and Conscious Experience,* J. C. Eccles, Ed., pp. 165–176, Springer-Verlag, Berlin.

Libet, B., W. W. Alberts, L. D. Delattre, G. Levin, and B. Feinstein (1964) Production of threshold levels of conscious sensation by electrical stimulation of human somatosensory cortex. *J. Neurophysiol.* 27, 546–589.

Libet, B., W. W. Alberts, E. W. Wright, and B. Feinstein (1972) Cortical and thalamic activation in conscious sensory experience, pp. 157–168, in *Neurophysiology Studied in Man*, G. G. Somjen, Ed., Excerpta Medica, Amsterdam.

2.2 *Are there any electrical correlates of mental activity?*

Grey-Walter, W., R. Cooper, V. J. Aldridge, W. C. McCallum and A. L. Winter (1964) Contingent negative variation: an electric sign of sensorimotor association and expectancy in the human brain. *Nature* (London), 203, 380–384.

Sutton, S., M. Braren, and J. Zubin (1965) Evoked potential correlates of stimulus uncertainty. *Science, 150,* 1187–1188.

Tecce, J. J. and N. M. Scheff, (1969) Attention reduction and suppressed direct current potential in the human brain. *Science, 164,* 331–333.

Weinberg, H., W. Grey-Walter, and H. J. Crow (1970) Intracerebral events in humans related to real and imaginary stimuli. *Electroenceph. Clin. Neurophysiol. 29,* 1–9.

2.3 *Speculate on the biological basis of "sex appeal" in the light of the following references.*

Brownlee, R. G., R. M. Silverstein, D. Muller Schwartz, and A. G. Singer (1969) Isolation, identification and function of the chief component of the male tarsal scent in black-tailed deer. *Nature* (London), 221, 284–285.

Comfort, A. (1971) Likelihood of human pheromones. *Nature* (London), 230, 432–433.

Gleason, K. K. and Reynierse, J. H. (1969) The behavioral significance of pheromones in vertebrates. *Psych. Bull. 71,* 58–73.

Mann, T. (1969) The science of reproduction. *Nature* (London), 224, 649–654.

Michael, R. P. and E. B. Keverne (1968) Pheromones in the communication of sexual status in primates. *Nature* (London) 218, 746–749.

Wilson, E. O. (1972) Animal communication. *Sci. American, 227* (3) 52–60 (offprint 1258).

2.4 *What determines the relation of a mammal to its environment so far as the sense of touch is concerned?*

Franzén, O. and K. Offenloch (1969) Evoked response correlates of psychophysical magnitude estimates for tactile stimulation in man. *Exp. Brain Res. 8,* 1–18.

Hagbarth, K. E., A. Honwell, R. G. Hallin, and H. E. Torebjork (1970) Afferent impulses in median nerve fascicles evoked by the tactile stimuli of the human hand. *Brain Res. 24,* 423–442.

Harrington, T. and M. M. Merzenich (1970) Neural coding in the sense of touch: human sensations of skin indentation compared with the responses of slowly adapting mechanoreceptive afferents innervating the hairy skin of monkeys. *Exp. Brain Res.* *10*, 251–264.

Hensel, H. and K. K. A. Boman (1960) Afferent impulses in cutaneous sensory nerves in human subjects. *J. Neurophysiol. 23*, 564–578.

2.5 *How can a receptor deficit be overcome by artificial means?*

Bach-y-Rita, P. (1972) *Brain Mechanisms in Sensory Substitution.* Academic Press, New York and London.

Bach-y-Rita, P., C. C. Collins, F. A. Saunders, B. White and L. Scadden (1969) Vision substitution by tactile image projections. *Nature* (London), *221*, 963–964.

Brindley, G. S. and W. S. Lewin (1968) The sensations produced by electrical stimulation of the visual cortex. *J. Physiol. 196*, 479–493.

2.6 *What is the neural code and has it been broken?*

Borg, G., H. Diamant, L. Strom, and Y. Zotterman (1967) The relation between neural and perceptual intensity: a comparative study on the neural and psychophysical response to taste stimuli. *J. Physiol. 192,* 13–20.

Mountcastle, V. B. (1967) The problem of sensing and the neural coding of sensory events, in *The Neurosciences: A Study Program.* G. C. Quarton, T. Melnechuk, and F. O. Schmitt, Eds. Rockefeller University Press, New York, pp. 393–409.

Osterhammel, P., A. Terkildsen, and K. P. Zilstorff (1969) Electro-olfactograms in man. *J. Laryngol. Otol. 83*, 731–733.

Stevens, S. S. (1970) Neural events and the psychophysical law. *Science 170*, 1043–1050.

2.7 *Can perception be explained by hierarchies of neurons? Are there alternative models? Is there a hierarchy?*

Hubel, D. H. and T. N. Wiesel (1962) Receptive fields, binocular interaction and functional architecture in the cat's visual cortex. *J. Physiol. 160*, 106–154.

Hubel, D. H. and T. N. Wiesel (1965) Receptive fields and functional architecture in two non-striate visual areas (18 and 19) of the cat. *J. Neurophysiol. 28*, 229–289.

Hoffman, K. P. and J. Stone (1971) Conduction velocity of afferents to cat visual cortex: a correlation with cortical receptive field properties. *Brain Res. 32*, 460–466.

Stone, J. and B. Dreher (1973) Projection of X- and Y-cells of the cat's lateral geniculate nucleus to Area 17 and 18 of visual cortex. *J. Neurophysiol. 36*, 551–567.

Alternative models:

Pribram, K. H. (1969) The neurophysiology of remembering. *Sci. American 220* (1) 73–86 (offprint 520).

Pollen, D. A., J. R. Lee, and J. H. Taylor (1971) How does the striate cortex begin the reconstruction of the visual world? *Science, 173,* 74–77.

2.8 *Is psychosurgery ever justified?*

Pro:

Andy, O. J. (1966) Neurosurgical treatment of abnormal behavior. *Amer. J. Med. Sci. 252,* 232–238.

Delgado, J. M. R. (1969) *Physical control of the mind.* Harper & Row, New York.

Editorial, Brain surgery for sexual disorders. (1969) *Brit. Med. J.* (4) 250–251.

Mark, V. H., W. H. Sweet, and F. R. Ervin (1967) Role of brain diseases in riots and urban violence, *J.A.M.A. 201,* 895. See also *J.A.M.A. 202,* 663 and *J.A.M.A. 203,* 368.

Con:

Breggin, P. (1972a) The return of lobotomy and psychosurgery. *U.S. Congressional Record, 118,* No. 26. Feb. 24, 1972.

Breggin, P. (1972b) New information in the debate over psychosurgery. *U.S. Congressional Record,* 118, E3380.

Holden, C. (1973) Psychosurgery: legitimate therapy or laundered lobotomy? *Science, 179,* 1109–1112.

2.9 *Is there any neuroanatomical basis for the concept of "reinforcement"?*

Crow, T. J. (1971) A map of the cat mesencephalon for electrical self-stimulation. *Brain Res. 36,* 265–273.

Crow, T. J. and G. W. Arbuthnott (1972) Function of catecholamine-containing neurons in mammalian central nervous system. *Nature New Biology 238,* 245–246.

Crow, T. J., P. J. Spear, and G. W. Arbuthnott (1972) Intracranial self-stimulation with electrodes in the region of the locus coeruleus. *Brain Res. 36,* 275–287.

Olds, J. and P. Milner (1954) Positive reinforcement produced by electrical stimulation of septal area and other regions of rat brain. *J. Comp. Physiol. Psychol. 47,* 419–427.

Olds, M. E. and J. Olds (1963) Approach-avoidance analysis of rat diencephalon. *J. Comp. Neurol. 120,* 259–295.

Stinus, L., A. M. Thierry, G. Blanc, J. Glowinski, and B. Cardo (1973) Self stimulation and catecholamines: III. Effect of imposed or self stimulation in the area ventralis tegimenti on catecholamine utilization in the rat brain. *Brain Res. 64,* 199–210.

Ungerstedt, U. (1971) Sterotaxic mapping of the monamine pathways in the cat brain. *Acta Physiol. Scand. Suppl. 367,* 1–48.

3 MEMORY AND LEARNING

Man is a learning animal. It has been mentioned that the brain is that part of the nervous system essential for learning (Chapter 1). Furthermore, to learn one must be awake (Chapter 4), and attentive (Chapter 2). If these parameters are assumed, the learning process can be further circumscribed by its beginning and end points. Everything that can be learned must be initially represented in the nervous system as nerve impulses. In Chapter 1 it was mentioned that certain aspects of the environment are detected by receptors and represented by trains of nerve impulses. Chapter 2 took this idea a little further by suggesting that as nerve impulses were generated afresh at each synaptic relay, there was further processing which, as exemplified in the visual system, leads to representation of external events by the activity of certain cortical cells. Thus the words you are now reading are encoded in cell activity representing areas of dark and light. At higher stages of the visual system the encoding is in lines, and at a still higher stage, angles. The concept (as yet unproved) that letters and groups of letters or words may be similarly encoded follows logically. Furthermore, this abstracting process is quite automatic, as it is wired into the structure of the nervous system and is not under conscious control.

In the same way, everything once learned which is recalled or recognized will be presented as activity of neurons. This activity may take the form of a pattern of action potentials in motor nerves as some motor skill is displayed, or be detectable as in an evoked potential if the remembered item is an unexpressed thought. The evidence for this latter statement comes from experiments in which recordings were made from brains of patients being treated for psychiatric disorders (Weinberg *et al.,* 1970). The patients had to guess, in separate experiments, whether they would be given a shock to a finger, hear a click, or see a light flash. In each case they moved a lever to the right if they expected a stimulus and to the left if not. They were rewarded for three correct guesses. The switch started an on-line computer analyzing the evoked potentials. The striking finding is that when the subject expected, but did not receive, a stimulus, an evoked potential was recorded, similar in form to that evoked by the appropriate stimulus. Its latency was less than the event produced by a real stimulus, suggesting a rise in cortical excitability with expectancy. This striking finding suggests that the remembering process is being observed. Indeed, experiments of this type have given rise to the hypothesis that recognition of a particular stimulating event depends on comparison of the pattern of nerve impulses from the appropriate receptor with a pattern stored in the nervous system.

This chapter is devoted to the processes which lie beyond the abstracting process in which the abstracted material becomes the content of consciousness for a short time (short-term memory) and may then be stored (long-term memory) and remembered at will (recall) or failed to be remembered (forgotten).

Some children and a very few adults have a "photographic," memory which is called by psychologists "eidetic" imagery. Such people can recall at will an image of what they have seen, apparently localized in space in front of their eyes. Detailed investigation suggests this visual image is an alternative means of storing information distinct from, but not more effective than, ordinary memory (Haber, 1969). Nothing at present is known of the physiological basis of this ability (see Question 3.1).

I. SHORT- AND LONG-TERM MEMORY

We are all aware that we remember some things only for a short time. For instance, telephone numbers are remembered just long enough to make the call. Other things we remember all our lives. An as yet unresolved question is whether short-lived memories are of the same nature as long-term memories—that is, are they at opposite ends of a continuum or are they different phenomena (see, e.g., Weiskrantz, 1970)?

A. Evidence for two processes

1. *Capacity*

The number of items that can be recalled after a short exposure (visual or oral) is small; for instance, a popular experimental method of examining short-term memory capacity is the tachistoscopic technique in which photographs, printed letters and records, diagrams, and drawings can be flashed on a screen for very short, precisely-controlled intervals of time—for instance, one-twentieth of a second. Surprisingly, subjects can only recall four or five of a row of letters, although the row may be made up of many more (Miller *et al.,* 1954). This contrasts with the storage capacity of long-term memory which is presumably very large, though no quantitative estimates are available. There are, however, accounts of men with phenomenal memories, perhaps the most sensational being *The Mind of a Mne-*

monist (Luria, 1968), which deals with a man observed by Luria, a Russian neurologist, for a thirty-year period. This man had no distinct limits to the capacity of his memory, for the Russian professor was never able to give the man a list of words so long that his subject could not remember it perfectly.

2. *Duration*

In the tachistoscopic type of experiment, short-term memory decays in a few seconds. It appears that long-term memory may be permanent in that at least some information is retained for the life of the subject. For instance, Luria's subject appeared to have no limit on the length of time he retained material. The most striking example of this was that the man could reproduce any lengthy series of words even if, as was several times the case, the test was fifteen or sixteen years after the man originally learned the words. His memory was such that he could recall the place where the test was first presented to him, how Luria was dressed, where Luria sat, etc.

The strongest evidence for long-term memory comes from the work of neurologists who have occasion to stimulate the brain of conscious patients during surgery. The Canadian neurosurgeon Penfield, for instance, found that when he stimulated particular points in his patients' brains, they reported fragments of past experiences (Penfield, 1958). These experiences were hallucinations in which the patients saw, heard, and felt everything which occurred long ago, taking place at the same rate as it did originally. There appeared to be nothing in these hallucinations not previously experienced, that is, things not in the focus of the patient's attention at the time of the original experience were not present in the hallucination. Many of the patients studied by Penfield suffered from epilepsy. Their attacks were preceded by "flashbacks" consisting of the recall of experiences from their past. These "flashbacks" could also be evoked by brain stimulation. It is important to note that patients reported that the material elicited by stimulation or coming into consciousness before an epileptic attack was much more distinct than anything they could normally recall. Penfield was convinced that his patients had records of their experiences in their brain which were normally not completely available to them.

3. *Methods of recall*

The material in the short-term store is rehearsed acoustically (Conrad, 1964). This was first picked up when it was found that volunteers in tachistoscopic experiments were rehearsing the material they had learned by mumbling, either overtly or covertly. This, in turn, led to the discovery that in remembering letters, mistakes were made between letters which sounded alike and thus could be confused when spoken—that is, letters that sound alike were confused even though the subjects were only shown them visually. The same mistakes were made, in fact, whether the subjects were shown the material or it was spoken. If experiments of this type are done with long-term memory, confusion has a semantic basis rather than an acoustic basis; that is, words which have a similar meaning are confused rather than words with a similar sound (Baddeley, 1966).

4. *Separation of the two processes*

Recently a man has been found with a normal long-term memory but a defective short-term memory. He could put new information into his long-term memory, suggesting that material need not be in short-term memory before going into long-term memory (Shallice and Warrington, 1970).

The converse situation—a normal short-term memory but an apparent inability to get information into long-term memory—is well known (the amnesic syndrome) and has been much investigated. Bilateral damage to any part of the Papez circuit—hippocampus, fornix, mammillary body, medial hypothalamus, and the parts of the thalamus connected with the mammillary bodies—has the same effect, a remarkably severe and persistent memory disorder (Ojemann, 1966). The most dramatic examples are men with bilateral injuries to their hippocampal cortices. Occasionally bilateral surgical resection of the hippocampal cortices is necessary to prevent intractable epilepsy. Milner (1959), for instance, reports one such patient, a twenty-nine year old high school graduate. After surgery, this man was unable to live a normal life for he could recall nothing of day-to-day events, could not remember where objects of continual use were kept; would do the same puzzle or read the same magazine repeatedly without showing any evidence of learning; thirty minutes after lunch he could not remember eating; could not learn a new home address or find his way to a new house. He had short-term memory, for if not disturbed, he could retain a three-figure number or a pair of unrelated words for several minutes; but as soon as his attention was diverted, there was no recollection of the figure or words. For example, he was able to retain the number 584 for at least fifteen minutes in the following way: "It's easy. You just remember 8. You see, 5, 8 and 4 add to 17. You remember 8, subtract it from 17, and it leaves 9. Divide 9 in half and you get 5 and 4, and there you are. Easy." Psychological tests revealed good motivation, and no deficits in perception, abstract thinking, or, reasoning. This man could not recall any portion of the period of hospitalization prior to operation; could not recognize the hospital staff; did not remember the death of a favorite uncle three years before; but could recall some minor events that had occurred just prior to his admission. There was no impairment of distant memory and no change of personality and emotion. A similar clinical picture, defective learning and defective memory of ongoing events, may be found in Korsakoff's psychosis, which occurs in some chronic alcoholics and is associated with damage to the mammillary bodies and adjoining parts of the medial hypothalamus (Baddeley and Warrington, 1970).

Analysis of many case histories confirms that patients with damage to the hippocampal system show no loss of preoperatively acquired skills and that intelligence, as measured by formal tests, is unimpaired. But with the possible exception of acquiring motor skills, they seem largely incapable of adding new information to their long-term store. Nevertheless, the immediate registration of new input appears to take place normally, and material which can be rehearsed verbally is held for many minutes. Interruption of the rehearsal, however, produced immediate forgetting of what went before. Material in long-term store is unaffected by the lesion. Apparently then, the long-term store remains with the patient but the lesions have produced a breakdown either in the ability to put new information into the long-term store or to retrieve new information from it.

B. The relationship between short- and long-term memory

Despite these differences, there must be some interaction between the short- and long-term stores, for it has been known for over two thousand years that it is possible, using coding procedures, to increase the material retained in a short-term store. This coding relies on associations with previously learned material (Paivio, 1969), which is presumably in the long-term store. Coding systems are known as *mnemonics* and are of great antiquity. A famous and very effective mnemonic system, known to the ancient Greeks, for instance, consists in imagining a house or some other building with many rooms. In each room is placed an object representing a key word in the material one wishes to remember. As one talks, one travels about the house in a previously determined order. Each object, as one enters the room, provides a fresh series of associations with the material to be remembered. Medical students today use mnemonics to aid them in remembering such things as the names of the cranial nerves. One such, kindly supplied by a reviewer of this book, runs "On Old Olympus's Towering Tops, A Finn And German Viewed Some Hops." More formal experimental tests have shown that the short-term memory span can be increased by coding procedures (see, e.g., Dale and McGlaughlin, 1970) from 5 to 7 to over 50 items. In these tests each bit of the code represented up to 10 items.

C. Multiple representation of memories?

It is common knowledge that motor skills such as riding a bicycle are remembered far better than other more verbal types of memory. In preceding sections it was mentioned too that hippocampal damage did not prevent learning of motor skills, although other types of material could not be retained. It is easiest to explain such findings by postulating several different types of memory perhaps represented in different parts of the brain. Experiments on animals subjected to brain lesions are in accord with the hypothesis. Lashley (1950) for instance, showed that once a rat had learned to run a maze for a reward, it would continue to do so after being blinded (using as subsequent lesions showed, olfactory clues); or after having its hind legs paralyzed (by dragging itself along with its front paws) and after loss of olfactory and visual clues (apparently by remembering the turning sequence). Lashley explained his results by postulating that almost all parts of the cortex were equivalent so far as memory was concerned. Nowadays it is fruitful to consider a different interpretation (see Question 3.2). The animals could be considered to have made several different types of learning; visual, olfactory, motor, conceptual, all taking place in different parts of the brain and all available for direction of behavior. This position is supported by modern neurophysiological research (see Section III and Question 3.4).

II. REMEMBERING AND FORGETTING

Psychologists working on recall of verbal material by men and of motor responses by animals have concluded that forgetting is analogous not to a loss of a book from a library but to an unsuccessful hunt for the book. The hunt is unsuccessful because of a phenomenon known as "interference." The nature of interference can be gathered from the story told of the professor of ichthyology (study of fishes) who complained that whenever he learned the name of a new student he forgot the name of a fish! The idea is that forgetting results from interference or confusion between the associations a man carries in his memory storage system. The items for which the search is made are not lost, they merely cannot be brought to mind!

There is ample evidence that interference with brain function which has been thought to cause permanent memory loss actually prevented recall. One example is the effect of electroconvulsive shock, often used as a treatment for suicidal depression. After treatment, some patients forget their anxieties and are able to function normally again. When interviewed later however, under the influence of the sedative barbiturate drug sodium amytal, they can recall their troubles, showing that these were not permanently forgotten but simply not recalled in the normal waking state (Bogoch, 1954). Another example comes from studies of patients with head injuries. Their memory of events before injury is often lost (retrograde amnesia). These events of course are often very dramatic and must have been registered by the nervous system. Yet quite often the subject has no memory of the events for up to an hour before injury. During recovery, the length of the period of retrograde amnesia shrinks markedly and interestingly; association of ideas may aid this process. W. R. Russell (1959) for instance, quotes the case of a soldier whose last memory was of setting out on a journey, driving a truck in the dark. This was more than an hour before his accident. Some months later, he was at a movie and saw a plane crash, with the usual noisy sound track. This noise suddenly brought back to the soldier the noise his truck made as he crashed.

III. NEUROPHYSIOLOGICAL STUDIES OF LEARNING

For many years investigators have tried to track down the processes involved in learning by observing what goes on in learning brains. One difficulty is that recording must, at least initially, be made from many areas in an awake, alert animal carrying out its learning task. Encouraging progress has been made with this approach (Olds *et al.*, 1973) in rats learning to associate presentation of food pellets with one of two *tones* (CS+ and CS−). The food was available for 7 sec only after the presentation of the selected tone (CS+) and was then automatically withdrawn. The rat therefore had to move quickly in order to be fed; they were only 70 per cent of normal weight and presumably hungry.

Before the tests the animals were equipped with ten nichrome recording electrodes placed by stereotactic procedures in sites in the auditory pathways, the hippocampus, various parts of the cortex and thalamus, and in the reticular system. An eleventh electrode was a length of bare hearing-aid wire which was not connected to the brain (open circuit) and served as an indicator of animal movement. After the experiment the animals were sacrificed and the position of the brain electrodes was checked by histological methods. The electrodes were connected to a holder cemented to an animal's skull. As is usual in such operations, the rats were housed in cages which had a central connector cable, fixed to the animal's holder and arranged so that the animal had maximum freedom of movement. Extracellular action potentials recorded from the electrodes were amplified and counted for later analysis. In control experiments the action potentials were recorded in response to either of the two tones used in the experiment. Neither tone was consistently associated with the food reward but the recording established a base-line level of action potential frequency at the selected points.

The food reward was now associated with only one of the tones (CS+) and the animal's learning was judged by the number of times it retrieved a food pellet, its movements being recorded. Recordings from the ten brain electrodes were monitored and particular notice was taken of new responses, appearing at short intervals after CS+ which were not detected in the base period.

The earliest of these responses occurred in the sensorimotor and frontal cortex (Fig. 3.1e, f, g, 10 msec), confirming the long-held belief that these areas are important in learning. By 20 msec new responses were detected in a number of areas. As Fig. 3.1 shows, such responses were found along the auditory pathways (Fig. 3.1b, h) but also in part of the hippocampus (Fig. 3.1g) and certain thalamic nuclei (Fig. 3.1a, b) and in the reticular formation of the brainstem (Fig. 3.1d). Some of the areas explored did not show marked new activities (Fig. 3.1i, j).

At later times responses were detected from widely scattered areas of the brain. In the first 80 msec after the tone, four patterns of new responses were detected. The first group of structures to show new activity included the hypothalamus and amygdala and other areas associated with the median forebrain bundle (see Chapter 2, Emotion). The second set included cortex near the motor cortex, central midbrain, and thalamic nuclei—possibly indicating involvement of motor systems. Third in time was activity in the basal ganglia and posterior nuclei of the thalamus which have to do with purposive motor behavior. Finally, sensory cortex, the thalamic nuclei of the auditory system (medial geniculate), and hippocampus came into action.

These results clearly suggest that there are specific learning areas and that learning goes on simultaneously in various parts of the brain. The pattern of ac-

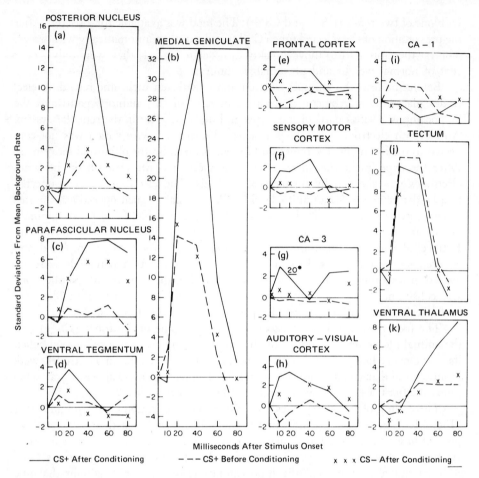

Fig. 3.1 Neural activity in different brain areas associated with learning. In these post-stimulus histograms, the number of responses for 100 msec before the stimulus was used to establish a mean response rate. Then the 80 msec after stimulus onset was taken in 20-msec periods, and the average number of responses in each 20-msec period was stated as a number of standard deviations from the mean background rate. Also, the first poststimulus 10 msec was considered separately as a number of standard deviations from the mean background rate. Thus, the 10-msec point was based on only half as many data as the other four points, and its data were also included in those of the 20-msec point. (With permission from Olds *et al., J. Neurophysiol. 35,* 202–219, 1973.)

tivity further suggests that this multiple representation is not redundant but has to do with specific aspects of the learning situation.

Another type of experiment has shown that the areas found by Olds, *et al.,* 1973, to display new responses during learning may be important for memory. In the first of these experiments (Thompson, 1969), rats were trained to distinguish between pairs of cards (one pair differed in whiteness, one pair in direction of stripes, and one pair in shape). Eighty-four animals were trained and then subjected to small brain lesions. These were made in all parts of the brain, but only twelve animals showed defects in retention of their learning. These animals had lesions in either visual cortex (occipital cortex), posterior thalamus, or ventral midbrain. The distribution of areas was then (allowing for the visual rather than auditory task) very similar to the areas (Fig. 3.1a and d) in which new responses occurred in experiments of Olds *et al.,* 1973. In a later series of experiments with monkeys (Thompson and Myers, 1971), similar training in visual discrimination was given (blue vs. yellow, triangle vs. disc, black vs. black and white stripe). Bilateral lesions were made in cortex, diencephalon, and midbrain. Only lesions in infratemporal cortex (where visual discrimination tasks are represented), posterior thalamus (Fig. 3.1a) and associated midbrain areas (Fig. 3.1d) affected learning. While there were several differences between the critical areas in rat and monkey, the measurement of agreement was startling.

IV. THE ROLE OF THE HIPPOCAMPUS AND ITS CONNECTIONS IN MEMORY

It has been mentioned (this chapter, IA-4) that bilateral injuries to the hippocampus and its connections interfere with the laying down of long-term memories in men and animals. The cortical connections of the hippocampal neurons are most important in memory functions. For instance, bilateral injuries to the cingulate gyri may cause a temporary memory deficit (Whitty and Lewin, 1960). The effects of a temporal lobe injury or removal are much more severe. It was this part of the brain that Penfield stimulated when he evoked fragments of past experiences from his patients. If the medial parts of the temporal lobes of each cortex are removed, the patient no longer has a memory of past experience. There are reports of surgical cases who suffered from epileptic seizures apparently originating in the temporal lobes. To try to cure the epilepsy the medial part of each temporal lobe was cut away. After surgery, one particular patient did not know where he was, could not read or write, had increased sexual activity, and very odd dietary and emotional behavior (Terzian and Ore, 1955). The memory difficulty was indeed serious. After performing a similar operation Scoville, an American neurosurgeon and Brenda Milner, who did the testing, report that their patient did not remember anything at all of what had recently happened, nor could he remember anything of his past. When asked about his house, his family, or the city he lived in, the patient did not even seem to understand these questions, as if their objective was entirely unknown to him. Dr. Milner could not fully analyze her patient's memory function under these circumstances but posited that the patient felt completely isolated with neither a past nor a future (Scoville and Milner, 1957). Four years after the operation, a grave memory defect persisted, although there was some improvement of the patient's ability to pay attention (Milner, 1965). As Nathan, a British neurologist, remarks, "When certain parts of the temporal lobes are cut out, the record of a life is cut out with them. It is as if one's memory is in a filing cabinet and someone has taken it away" (Nathan, 1969, p. 351).

These striking results might suggest that the temporal lobes and the hippocampus are the sites at which long-term memories are stored. In the case of the hippocampus this cannot be true, for patients with bilateral hippocampal damage still have a short-term memory and can acquire motor skills and also verbal long-term memories by special techniques in which they are given part of the information and have to supply the rest. In both types of learning they are as effective as normal subjects (Warrington and Weiskrantz, 1970). Animal studies suggest that hippocampal lesions prevent the suppression of old information which is apparently needed for the storage of new information. This result arises from studies of rats and monkeys in which the hippocampus has been removed on both sides; such animals react to new stimuli much more sluggishly than normal animals. Furthermore, they are very slow to reverse responses in the type of study in which the subject has to respond alternatively to one of two situations, e.g., the right or the left. These animals also continue giving a response for much longer in the absence of a reward than do normal animals (Douglas & Pribram, 1966; Kimble, 1969).

The role of the temporal lobe is more difficult to discern. Recently acquired memories are very easily affected by interference with temporal lobe function. Bickford, et al. (1958), for instance, placed electrodes in the temporal lobe of three patients in the region which Penfield stimulated. Electrical stimulation caused temporary amnesia. Five-second stimulation caused forgetting of the day's events for several hours, while ten-second stimulation caused an amnesia for the events of several days past. Experiments with rats similarly indicate transient amnesia during bilateral KCl injections which stopped electrical activity in the hippocampus and surrounding regions (Hughes, 1969). It seems unlikely in view of the evidence for multiple storage of memories that the temporal lobes are the "filing cabinets" suggested by Nathan (1969). Speculatively it seems more probable that they represent a directory which enables one to track down material in the cabinets, i.e., the temporal lobe neurons represent a higher order set in a hierarchy of "learning" neurons.

V. THE PHYSIOLOGICAL BASIS OF SHORT-TERM MEMORY

All that is known about short-term memory is explicable in terms of nerve impulses circulating in defined paths. In particular, the need for acoustic reinforcement and the short-lasting nature of this form of memory make it seem likely that there is no other form of store. The short but persistent retrograde amnesia found after head injury and electroconvulsive therapy (Russell, 1959) can be presumably explained by the temporary cessation of normal brain activity at the time of injury.

Well-known synaptic mechanisms may account for the prolonging of short-term memory by rehearsal. Synaptic transmission may become more effective during, and for a period after, repetitive activation (post-tetanic potentiation); (see Question 3.3). Not all synapses show such behavior, but in the brain, synapses on hippocampal neurons are found to demonstrate both processes to an unusual degree. It is found for instance that during stimulation at 10/sec, synaptic transmission is much improved in that the likelihood of each stimulus evoking an action potential is much increased. After several brief bursts of stimulation (20/sec for 15 sec), synaptic transmission was more effective for several hours (Bliss and Lømo, 1973). There seems no doubt that such repeated stimulation must happen in normal brains, particularly if the stimulating impulses are travelling in a circular path, returning to the same synapses at intervals. This explanation for the reinforcement of short-term memory is supported by experiments with chickens (Mark and Watts, 1971; Watts and Mark, 1971), in which the animals were trained to peck at a wet target and then presented with another target dipped in an aversant drug instead of water. After one peck, chickens would not peck at the target during the next 30 sec. Drugs which inhibit the development of post-tetanic potentiation (Gage and Hubbard, 1966) were then injected into the forebrain of the chickens. Chickens injected with saline showed no memory loss (as measured by absence of pecking at the aversive target) over the 90 minutes following drug injections. Drug-injected chicks showed a progressive increase in pecking with time so that by 90 minutes after injection all chickens pecked again at the aversive target; presumably indicating complete memory loss.

VI. THE PHYSIOLOGICAL BASIS OF LONG-TERM MEMORY

Long-term memory is not preserved as ongoing, continuous electrical activity of the brain in the way that short-term memory is thought to be preserved, for when the electrical activity of the brain is stopped, long-term memory is not lost. There are several ways of stopping brain activity—for example, deep anesthesia and electroconvulsive shock (passing electric currents between electrodes on the head so that the currents pass through the brain), cooling, and convulsive drugs. Accidents involving head injuries are another test, nature's own. The result in all cases is clear—existing memories are preserved (see, e.g., Jarvik, 1970); they are not in the form of nerve impulses.

This clearcut result suggests that the permanent trace must be structural and further suggests the question: "How do nerve impulses initiate the formation of this trace and how are they recovered when we recall the memory?" Two broad alternatives have been suggested. One may be termed the chemical or molecular theory. Synaptic activity is thought to result in *alteration of a chemical code in the cell,* thus preserving a record of the activity. The second alternative, which may be termed synaptic, is that synaptic transmission results in *a change in the active synapse,* making it more effective. The two theories of course can be combined in the suggestion that the activation of the coding mechanism results in the presumed synaptic change. Unfortunately, the present results of much activity in the molecular memory field are both exciting and confusing.

A. A chemical code?

The genetic material desoxyribonucleic acid (DNA), ribonucleic acid (RNA), and proteins have all been considered as the coding elements. Figure 3.2 shows

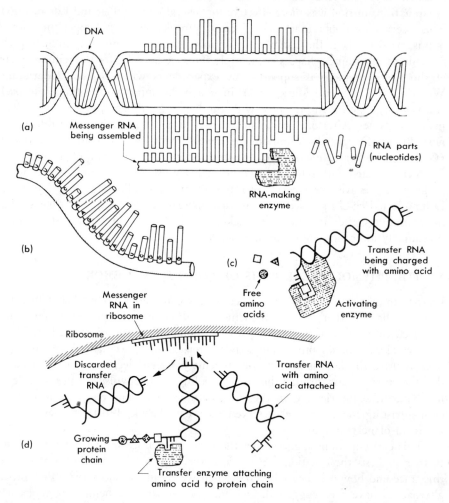

Fig. 3.2 A highly diagrammatic representation of protein synthesis by nucleic acids. (a) The DNA chains unwind temporarily, exposing the sequence of nitrogenous bases. The separation allowing this unwinding occurs at the union of the paired bases. The messenger RNA is built on the template from the DNA subunits, located in the nucleoplasm of the cell. The sequence of bases on the completed messenger RNA will bear a

diagrammatically the role of these chemicals in protein formation and should be studied by those unfamiliar with this triumph of molecular biology. The sequence of events can be represented as DNA, RNA, and proteins. DNA is stable, of the right size to code memories, and already has an information function in the cell. It has been found, however, that it is too stable. Indeed, unless one postulates that the DNA of nerve cells has some special property, for which there is no evidence, DNA could not have any direct function in memory.

1. RNA

Many investigators have found that the cytoplasmic RNA in neurons is increased following increased brain activity and is decreased when brain activity is reduced. More specifically, changes in the composition of nuclear RNA have been found (RNA contains four bases—adenine, cytosine, guanine, and uracil). For example, Table 3.1 shows the changes found in rat brain neuron nuclear RNA when spontaneously right-pawed rats were forced to reach for food with their left paws (Table 3.1—number of successful reaches). The control neurons were the cortical neurons in layers 5 and 6 on the left side, while the test neurons were the comparable right-sided neurons, presumably active during the forced reaching. As Table 3.1 indicates, there were increases in total RNA which became larger as the experiment continued. A fall in cytosine and a rise in adenine were also found (Table 3.1, RNA composition of control and test neurons). In a similar experiment

---

definite relationship to the DNA sequence. The relationship is like that of an automobile fender to the mold in which it was shaped. At this stage, it is theoretically possible to determine the DNA sequence by examining the RNA, just as the design of the fender tells a great deal about the shape of the mold. After the completion of this step, the role of the DNA in protein synthesis is essentially finished. (b) The completed messenger RNA molecule leaves the DNA template. The RNA passes out of the cell nucleus and moves to the ribosomes. These are located along the endoplasmic reticulum of the cell, where they have ready access to entering raw materials. The enlarged view here shows the substitution of the base uracil for thymine. (c) Meanwhile, transfer RNA molecules become bonded to free amino acids within the cell cytoplasm. These amino acids may have been derived from proteins which had previously been digested and absorbed. The type and sequence of the unpaired triplet of bases at the end of each transfer RNA molecule determines the kind of amino acid to which it attaches. (d) Molecules of transfer RNA, with their amino acid attached, enter the ribosomes. The type and arrangement of the unpaired bases in the triplet now determine where each molecule of transfer RNA fits onto the messenger RNA. The attachment of transfer RNAs side by side on the messenger RNA automatically brings the amino acids which they carry into close contact. Here, the transfer enzyme can unite them to form protein chains. Thus the genetic code of the DNA molecule establishes the sequence of amino acids along the protein, which, in turn, determines the protein's characteristics. (With permission from: *Matter, Energy and Life,* by J. J. W. Baker and G. E. Allen. Copyright © 1968 by Addison-Wesley Publishing Co.)

TABLE 3.1
RNA composition of neurons related to performance (from Hyden, 1967)

Animal	Training periods 2 × 25 min/day (days)	No. of successful reaches	Relative increase of RNA neurons (%)	RNA composition of control neurons	RNA composition of test neurons
1	3	107	33	A 19.0 ± 0.4 G 24.9 ± 0.5 C 38.5 ± 0.8 U 17.6 ± 0.4	A 25.5 ± 3.0 G 36.1 ± 4.8 C 19.7 ± 10.7 U 28.7 ± 4.2
2	5	163	23	A 18.2 ± 0.4 G 25.5 ± 0.5 C 36.3 ± 0.7 U 20.0 ± 0.4	A 24.5 ± 3.2 G 35.7 ± 4.3 C 11.7 ± 7.9 U 28.1 ± 3.4
3	8	625	57	A 16.6 ± 0.3 G 26.8 ± 0.5 C 39.1 ± 0.8 U 17.5 ± 0.4	A 26.2 ± 2.7 G 34.9 ± 2.7 C 16.1 ± 6.5 U 22.8 ± 1.8
4	9	1041	105	A 18.2 ± 0.4 G 28.6 ± 0.6 C 33.6 ± 0.7 U 18.8 ± 0.4	A 21.0 ± 0.9 G 35.2 ± 1.6 C 24.0 ± 1.9 U 19.8 ± 0.9

it was found that goldfish forced to swim in a new way by a float attached to one fin had specific changes in their brain uracil-cytosine ratios (Shashoua, 1970). Several research workers have described special proteins found only in special areas of the brain in trained animals (e.g., Bogoch, 1968).

It is tempting to associate these changes with formation of a chemical memory code. Alternative and more prosaic explanations are available however. One theory of memory postulates synaptic growth (Cajal, 1909; Eccles, 1953; Barondes, 1965) as a result of use. Another explanation is that the RNA changes are just normal nonmemory-specific concomitants of neuron activity. It is well known that cells in many different organs increase their RNA content when they are stimulated appropriately (reviewed by Rose, 1970). For instance, stimulation of the kidney with aldosterone, of the thyroid with thyroid-stimulating hormone, and of the pancreas with pilocarpine all increase the RNA content of these organs. The brain is no exception. Increased brain activity produced, for instance by the convulsant drug strychnine, increases the RNA content of neurons. It should not be overlooked that all animal experiments involve some stress to the animal, at the minimum, some restraint and often an injection. It has been found that *one* intraperi-toneal injection of common salt solution will increase the RNA content of rat hippo-campal cells. An injection of amphetamine or nicotine, both of which are known to increase the activity of hippocampal cells, will produce rather greater RNA increases.

A very striking illustration of the changes in nuclear RNA of neurons after sensory stimulation comes from studies of catfish exposed to different odors (Rappoport and Daginawala, 1968). It was found that each odor could increase the whole brain nuclear RNA and produce a different base ratio change. In split-brain preparations the changes were confined to the half brain which received the stimulation. Natural foods such as shrimp caused the appearance of a pattern different from the pattern set up by artificial dissolved substances such as amylacetate. It must be concluded that changes in total RNA and composition of RNA cannot at present be associated with anything more than activity of the brain cells under study.

2. RNA and tissue injections

Another dramatic approach was also based on the hypothesis that long-term memory involved the establishment of a specific RNA. It was suggested that this RNA could perhaps be extracted and implanted in another animal which would now show signs of an improved performance due to this transfer of learned material. These ideas arose from experiments with flatworms (the planarian *Dugesia*). Very exciting claims were made for these experiments. After the flatworms were trained they could be cut in half. When allowed to regenerate, the half generated from the tail had learned as much as the half which regenerated from the head, and even more excitingly, if trained animals were fed to untrained animals, the untrained animals now learned more quickly than naive noncannibals. Incubation of the "trained" material with enzymes destroying RNA before feeding seemed to prevent the effect. The experiments appear to be repeatable but great argument rages as to the reasons for the results and whether the planarians actually learned anything (reviewed by Jacobson *et al.*, 1966; Corning and Riccio, 1970).

Some idea of the difficulties can be gathered from consideration of an actual experiment. For instance, in the experiments of Hartrey and her colleagues (Hartrey *et al.*, 1964; Fig. 3.3) flatworms were exposed to a light lasting three seconds which was combined with a shock making the animals contract for the last second of the three. After about 150 trials, the animal contracted to the light alone, which was taken as evidence for the formation of an association between light and shock by the animals—a form of learning known as a "conditioned reflex." One complication was that some 15 to 20 per cent of the animals contracted without any encouragement when exposed to a light. Further complications appeared when the animals become cannibals. It was found that flatworms allowed to eat trained animals *or* animals previously handled *or* just exposed to light all showed about the same reduction in training time. Only 60 to 70 trials were needed to train these cannibals

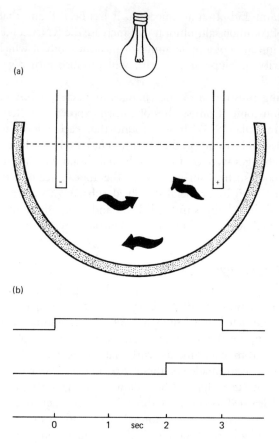

Fig. 3.3 Learning in flatworms. (a) The experimental apparatus. Flatworms were placed in a U-shaped trough where they could be subjected to light, or an electric shock produced by a brief current applied between the wires (+ and −). (b) The light shock sequence. Upper trace indicates 3-sec duration of light. Middle trace indicates 1-sec duration of shock. Lower trace gives time in seconds. A positive response was a contraction of the animal. The light shock sequence was applied only if the animal under observation was gliding toward the cathodal wire (− in a). Training was complete if the animal contracted in 23 of 25 consecutive trials. (Based on A. L. Hartrey, P. Keith-Lee, and W. D. Morton, *Science, 146,* 274–275, 1964.)

compared with 150 trials needed for noncannibals. Simply feeding the flatworms destined to be eaten or giving them an electric shock also made the cannibals more effective learners (about 90 trials needed).

These experiments indicate that flatworms can learn, but show that cannibalism does not necessarily speed learning by virtue of the consumption of a memory trace. It is not known as yet what it is that speeds learning in these experiments.

Other studies have revolved round the injection of RNA into the animal body, sometimes in the form of yeast. The rationale for these studies is that if animals' RNA is a memory substrate, then possibly memory might be improved by increasing the pool of RNA in the body. It is tacitly assumed in such studies that all RNA is equivalent. In fact, in species more highly developed than planarians, RNA is conjugated uniquely in unique genotypes. One of the most dramatic studies involved human subjects from an old peoples' home who were injected intravenously with RNA extracts in physiological saline. Great improvement in memory was found (Cameron et al., 1963) but there was no control group of patients. It could well have been that the memory-improving function of RNA injection was just due to a general stimulating effect.

A cogent objection to all such studies is that the brain, unlike other organs, is not easily accessible to substances circulating in the blood (blood-brain barrier). Even such relatively small molecules as sucrose and insulin penetrate extremely slowly into the brain (Davson, 1967). It would seem improbable that RNA or its breakdown products could penetrate into the brain, and, in fact, after intravenous injection of rabbits and mice with C^{14}-tagged RNA, this material did not penetrate into the cerebrospinal fluid or brain (Eist and Seal, 1965; Enesco, 1966). It is possible that the stimulant effect of yeast is due to a small molecular weight contaminant which does get into the nervous system.

A similar criticism may be made of experiments with mammals which followed the flatworm type. In the prototype experiment, RNA was extracted from the brain of rats which had been trained to approach a food cup when a click was sounded. This material was injected into the peritoneal cavity of untrained rats. It was found that these injected rats learned the association between a click and food more rapidly than uninjected controls. Many investigators have not been able to replicate such experiments (see Question 3.5). Part of the difficulty may be that injections of brain homogenates, whether from trained or naive animals, tend to decrease the activity of animals and also to decrease their food intake, presumably because of immune reactions to the homogenates. It is known that some types of learning are facilitated by depression of activity. More importantly, it has recently been found that it is the soluble material (that is, the supernatant) from homogenized, centrifuged, "trained" brain rather than RNA (Ungar et al., 1968) which facilitates learning in naive rats. Indeed it has been reported that the active material is a simple, twelve-amino acid compound which has been isolated and synthesized as well (Ungar et al., 1972). How this compound acts is at present unknown.

In another series of experiments, advantage has been taken of the ability of some animals to tolerate transplants of organs into their body cavities. The brain of a trained salamander was implanted into the abdominal cavity of a "naive" animal (Peitsch and Schneider, 1969). It was then found that there was an improvement in the rate of learning of the animal with the implanted brain. The improvement, however, was the same whether a trained or an untrained brain was implanted, and a "presumably naive" implanted leg gave the best results of all. These findings seem incompatible with transfer of a memory and give no encouragement to those who advocate eating brains. Again it seems possible that some chemical signal is being transferred by the implantation, but the signal seems relatively nonspecific. It might, for instance, only improve performance by making animals more attentive to the learning situation.

Despite these results, attempts to link RNA and memory continue. One line of investigation which has received considerable publicity involves the drug magnesium pemoline, which is thought to facilitate RNA production in the brain (Glasky and Simon, 1966). Initial studies made in rats (Plotnikoff, 1966), as a result of which it was claimed the drug facilitated the learning of the avoidance of shock, have been subjected to considerable criticism. It appears that any effect of the drug on learning is doubtful. Studies of rats, mice, dogs, cats, monkeys, and men indicate that the drug is a mild stimulant of the central nervous system rather than a substance having any specific action on memory (Talland and McGuire, 1967; Orzach et al., 1968; Plotnikoff et al., 1969).

3. Protein and RNA synthesis

It might be predicted from both chemical and synaptic theories of memory that RNA and protein synthesis would be needed for memory storage. Extensive experiments with drugs which inhibit protein synthesis in vivo and in vitro, such as puromycin, acetoxycycloheximide (ACX), and cycloheximide, and with drugs which inhibit RNA synthesis in vivo and in vitro (such as actinomycin D) have lead to three results.

(a) Invertebrate nervous system preparations in vitro continue to generate action potentials and synaptic potentials and exhibit changes in synaptic efficacy, such as post-tetanic potentiation, for long periods in the presence of the drugs (Schwartz et al., 1971), indicating that the electrical activity thought to be important in short-term memory is not immediately dependent on RNA and protein synthesis.

(b) Learning occurs in mice and goldfish even if the inhibitory drugs are injected before training so that protein or RNA synthesis is presumably greatly inhibited (reviewed by Agranoff, 1967; Barondes, 1969). For example, the existence of a cycloheximide-induced 96 per cent inhibition of protein synthesis does not block learning in mice (Andry and Luttges, 1972). If learning involves prolonged training, however, some impairment of the rate of learning is detectable (Squire et al., 1973).

(c) Animals treated with inhibitory drugs at the time of learning apparently "forget" the new knowledge sometime later.

The length of time appears to be drug and species dependent. In mice treated with cycloheximide or ACX it was six hours. In mice treated with puromycin it was three hours. Goldfish treated with ACX were found to show some impairment of memory six hours later, but four days were needed for marked amnesia. Mice treated with actinomycin D showed amnesia one day after training (reviewed by Barondes, 1969).

It may be concluded that learning can occur despite marked inhibition of protein and RNA synthesis. It is doubtful, however, if (c) indicates that long-term memories directly depend on protein and RNA synthesis. To accept this position means also postulating that short-term memory lasts three to twenty-four hours, which is not in accord with the human evidence (see Section IA-2). There are also certain facets of the experimental results that suggest that inhibition of RNA and protein synthesis is not directly connected with memory loss. First, there is not a good correlation between the extent of protein synthesis inhibition (Agronoff *et al.*, 1966) or RNA synthesis inhibition (Squire and Barondes, 1970) and the degree of amnesia. Similarly, electroconvulsive therapy, if it causes convulsions in mice, inhibits protein synthesis (some 28 per cent) and also impairs memory of a previously learned task. The amnesia is more profound than that caused by the drugs, yet the degree of protein synthesis inhibition is much smaller (Dawson and McGaugh, 1969; Cotman *et al.*, 1971).

Second, at least one of the drugs which was thought to cause amnesia in mice (puramycin) did not do so, for the apparent amnesia could be overcome upon saline injection into the forebrain (Flexner and Flexner, 1968). Presumably puramycin affects recall rather than memory formation. Third, in doses which markedly depress protein or RNA synthesis all the drugs are toxic, while electrical recording from the brains of drugged animals indicates abnormal activity which could be responsible for the amnesia (Barondes, 1969).

B. A synaptic change?

Why synapses? There are several reasons for considering a change in the properties of synapses as the long-term mechanism of memory storage. First, synapses are, so far as is known, the only part of the nervous system where neurons directly and rapidly influence each other.

We can remember past experiences very rapidly after prompting. Some animal experiments indeed suggest that electrical signs of this recall can be detected within 35 msec after stimulation. In these experiments, cats were trained to obtain food upon seeing a light flickering at one rate but to avoid a shock on seeing another frequency of flicker. The evoked potentials recorded from electrodes implanted in various parts of their brain during this procedure were characteristic for each task at each recording site. When a third rate of flickering was employed, midway between the previous two, sometimes the cats made the feeding response, sometimes the avoidance response. In each case, there was a characteristic pattern of recorded potential, resembling either the feeding or the avoidance type. Evidently the cat recalled the stored response pattern appropriate for its new response. The rate of recall was so rapid that it could only have been mediated by a pattern of nerve impulses in a characteristic pathway, that is, by the activation of a characteristic group of synapses (John *et al.*, 1969).

Second, drugs which affect the working of synapses do affect animal learning (McGaugh, 1973). For instance, strychnine, which in large doses causes convulsions, in small doses improves animal learning, if given within thirty minutes of training. Picrotoxin, another convulsant in large doses, has the same effect in small doses (McGaugh, 1966). The interesting fact is that both drugs have specific effects on synapses. Strychnine blocks one type of inhibitory synapse while picrotoxin blocks another type (Eccles, 1964).

Another type of drug experiment revolves around the transmitter molecule acetylcholine (ACh). This is the transmitter released by nerve impulses from axon terminals upon muscle. It is also released at some synapses in the central nervous system, although the exact location of all these synapses is not yet known. One probable site is the hippocampus. In the head of the hippocampus, the majority of cells can be excited by ACh (Steiner, 1968) while the synthesizing system for ACh has been found in the nerve terminals at these synapses (Lewis *et al.*, 1964). An enzyme, acetylcholinesterase, which destroys ACh is also present at these sites. It is not surprising then that drugs which block ACh action and drugs which poison acetylcholinesterase and thus cause ACh to accumulate can affect memory (Deutsch, 1971). In these experiments it was found that rats trained to escape shocks by running into the lighted arm of a Y maze apparently "forgot" if given injections of cholinesterase poisons at eight or fourteen days after training.

Both morphological and functional changes in synapses which could be responsible for long-term memory have been detected. Further, the problem of how modifiable synapses could be used to store information has been theoretically solved.

1. Changes of synaptic morphology

It has been found that the morphology and number of synapses in animal brains are not immutable. Cragg (1968, 1969), for instance, has made an electron microscopic examination of synapses in the visual pathway of dark-reared rats after exposure to light. Marked effects were found in the thalamic nucleus in the visual pathway (lateral geniculate) and in the visual cortex. In the lateral geniculate nucleus the axon terminals became 15 per cent smaller in diameter but their number increased by 34 per cent as compared with control dark-reared rats. Converse changes were found when diurnally-reared rats were put in the dark. Synaptic profiles became larger and fewer in number compared with controls. This investigation suggested then that changes in synaptic number and size could occur as a result of environmental changes.

A similar conclusion arises from a completely different kind of investigation carried on by Rosenweig and his collaborators at Berkeley (Bennett *et al.*, 1964). This team subjected rats to what they called "standard, enriched and impoverished environments" and after various periods of time looked at the rat's brain content of acetylcholinesterase. In the context of these experiments, "impoverished" meant solitary confinement with only food pellets and water. "Enriched" meant life in a large cage with about twelve other rats, with toys and thirty minutes a day exposure to a complex maze, the pattern of which was changed daily. Standard rats lived two to three in a cage but had no other experience. Genetic factors were excluded by using split litters, that is, rats from the same litter were subjected to different environments. Changes in brain content of acetylcholinesterase were found but the significance of this finding was, and is, obscure.

A breakthrough came when it was noticed that the weight of the rats' cortex differed according to the environment in which they had been reared. As Fig. 3.4 shows, a rat brain differs most obviously from the human in the prominence of

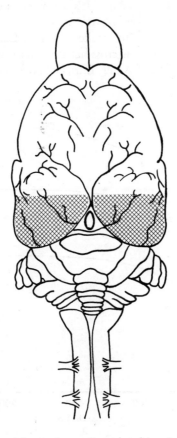

Fig. 3.4 A rat brain viewed from above. Cross-hatching indicates the areas which increased in size and weight in animals living in an "enriched" environment. (Based on the work of Rosenweig, Bennett and Diamond, *Scientific American,* February, 1972, 22–29.)

the olfactory bulbs and the smaller size and lack of folds of the cortex. The cross-hatching shows those areas in which there was the greatest weight gain. These areas include the occipital (visual) cortex and somatosensory cortex.

As Fig. 3.5 indicates, animals in the three environments gained cortex weight in a similar way and the weight reached a maximum dependent on the environment. As the broken lines indicate, a change in environment shifted an animal onto a new curve appropriate to the new environment. Changes in weight occur more rapidly in young animals, as shown by the shorter length of the broken lines between 150 and 100 days, but old animals (arrows 150 to 220 days) can change just the same (Reige, 1971).

The implications of these experiments are startling. But before concluding that they provide evidence for the old adage "It's never too late to learn," certain objections have to be answered. After all, the increases in weight in the enriched animal brains might just be due to intake of water. Careful examination of the structure of these brains (Fig. 3.4, cross-hatched area) showed that the changes were not due to just the intake of water. Enriched areas had more cells. As neurons

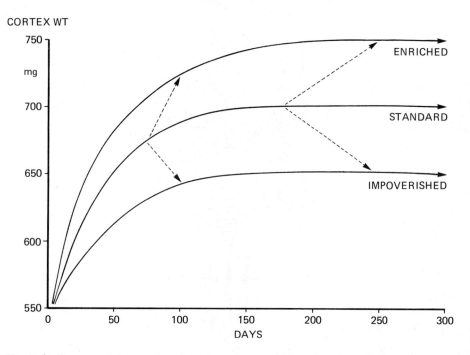

Fig. 3.5 Cortex weight as a function of age in rats subjected to three different environments (enriched, standard, and impoverished). Dashed lines indicate the change in weight which followed transference of a rat from one regime to the other in youth or maturity. (Based on the work of Reige, *Devel. Psychobiol., 42,* 157–167, 1971.)

do not divide, the increased number of cells must be glial supporting cells. This was interesting but not very informative. A greater degree of resolution was required, provided by the electron microscope.

As Fig. 3.6(a) shows, cortical neurons have long-branching dendrites which appear irregular in outline. The irregularity is, as Fig. 3.6(b) indicates, due to the spines which project from the dendrites and make synaptic contact with the axons of other neurons. Investigators using the light microscope have examined rats from the three environments and found a much greater branching of dendrites in rats from enriched environments, compared with control rats (Volkmar and Greenough, 1972). Others, using the electron microscope, find that rats in the enriched environments have an increased number of dendritic spines and synapses which have a larger area of synaptic contact (Fig. 3.6b, black borders); (Møllgaard *et al.,* 1971).

What is the significance of an enlarged synaptic contact? This question has so far only been investigated at frog nerve-muscle junctions. At such junctions the

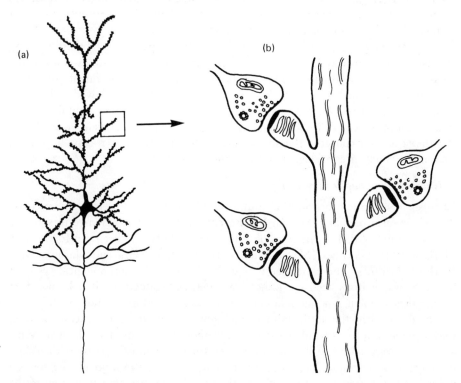

Fig. 3.6 A neuron, illustrating (a) its dendritic tree as seen in a light microscope and (b) the area inside the square in (a) as it might appear in an electron micrograph. The spine synapses in (b) correspond to the irregularities on the dendrites in (a).

nerve terminal is characterized by an accumulation of synaptic vesicles (Fig. 3.6b round profiles), each group being associated with membrane thickenings found at approximately micron intervals along the length of the terminal. These regions are thought to be the sites of transmitter release. Experiments of Kuno and his coworkers (1971) indicate that the length of a junction, and therefore the number of release sites, varies on different muscle fibres for reasons not at present fully understood. The amount of transmitter substance released is positively correlated with the length of a junction. It seems reasonable to conclude then that the enlargement of the synaptic contact on the dendritic spines of the neurons in the cortex of rats subjected to an enriched environment, may mean a more powerful synaptic linkage.

In parallel experiments it was shown that the rats with larger brains learned more quickly than controls and were more resistant to disturbances by such things as handling. They appeared brighter and tamer. The rats responded more adaptively to their environment. Rats from the poorest environment scored at the same level as their brothers from the enriched environment if the testing was continued for several days or if the problem was reversed, showing that there was no deficit of their basic brain mechanisms (Rosenweig et al., 1972).

Several questions must be answered before the implications of these exciting results can be transferred to human studies. Some of these questions concern the environment. Even enriched cages are hardly a natural environment. In recent experiments designed to answer this question, rats have been allowed to live outdoors and dig burrows. Such rats after some months had a greater brain weight than littermates kept in the enriched cage environment (Rosenweig et al., 1972). Another question concerns the species factor. Several types of rodent have been examined. What of cats, dogs, monkeys, and men?

2. Changes in synaptic function

Changes in synaptic function as a result of use have been considered in connection with short-term memory (Section V). Recently evidence for a change in synaptic function, which could be the basis of long-term memory, has been put forward by Mark and his colleagues (Marotte and Mark, 1970a, b; Mark and Marotte, 1972; Mark et al., 1972). The basic idea is that the existence of morphological synapses between two neurons need not indicate a functional connection. It is known that during development synaptic relationships are established much more widely than can be detected in the adult animal. The new idea is that these excess synapses may *survive* in a functionally ineffective but morphologically normal form. Mark and his colleagues find such synapses in experiments upon fish eye muscles. When their nerve is cut and a foreign nerve implanted in the eye muscles, the foreign nerve forms functional synapses, that is, the muscle contracts on stimulation of the foreign nerve. When the normal nerve regenerates into the muscle, it forms fresh functional synapses while the synapses formed by the foreign nerve become nonfunctional before any morphological change in them can be detected. Similar ineffective synapses have been described in the spinal cord of adult cats (Merrill and Wall, 1972). The present interest of such synapses is that they may become functional again as the result of some novel pattern of nervous activity. Cass *et al.* (1973) have observed such reactivation as the result of degeneration of neighboring nerve terminals, presumably resulting in derepression of the terminals of interest.

3. Synaptic changes and memory

Brindley (1967, 1969) has considered the possible classes of modifiable synapses and shown that it is possible to design nerve models which store information in such synapses (see Question 3.6). For rote learning tasks these models require only a small fraction of the number of the cells in the brain to carry out their task, and the number of inputs to each cell is well within the number actually found. It may be concluded that modifiable synapses are a plausible store for even a very complex memory.

REFERENCES

Agranoff, B. W., R. E. Davis, and J. J. Brink (1966) Chemical studies on memory fixation in goldfish. *Brain Res. 1*, 303–309.

Agranoff, B. W. (1967) Agents that block memory, in: *The Neurosciences: A Study Program*, G. C. Quarton, T. Melnechuk, and F. O. Schmitt, Eds., Rockefeller University Press, New York, pp. 756–764.

Andry, D. K. and M. W. Luttges (1972) Memory traces: experimental separation by cycloheximide and electro-convulsive shock. *Science, 178*, 518–519.

Baddeley, A. D. (1966) The influence of acoustic and semantic similarity on long-term memory for word sequences. *Quart. J. Exp. Psychol. 18*, 302–309.

Baddeley, A. D. and E. K. Warrington (1970) Amnesia and the distinction between long- and short-term memory. *J. Verb. Learn. Verb. Behav. 9*, 176–189.

Baker, J. J. W. and G. E. Allen (1968) *Matter, Energy and Life.* Addison-Wesley, Reading, Mass.

Barondes, S. H. (1965) Relationship of biological regulatory mechanisms to learning and memory. *Nature* (London), *205*, 18–21.

Barondes, S. H. (1970) Cerebral protein synthesis inhibitors block long-term memory. *Int. Rev. Neurobiol. 12*, 177–205.

Bennett, E. L., M. C. Diamond, D. Krech, and M. R. Rosenweig (1964) Chemical and anatomical plasticity of brain. *Science, 146*, 610–619.

Bickford, R. G., D. W. Mulder, H. W. Dodge, H. J. Svan, and H. P. Romes (1958) Changes in memory function produced by electrical stimulation of the temporal lobe in man. *Res. Publ. Ass. nerv. ment. Dis. 36*, 227–243.

Bliss, T. V. P. and T. Lømo (1973) Long-lasting potentiation of synaptic transmission in the dentate area of the anaesthetized rabbit following stimulation of the perforant path. *J. Physiol. 232*, 331–356.

Bogoch, S. (1968) *The Biochemistry of Memory with an Enquiry into the Function of the Brain Mucoids.* Oxford University Press, New York.

Bogoch, S. (1954) A preliminary study of postshock amnesia by amytal interview. *Am. J. Psychiat. 111*, 108–111.

Brindley, G. S. (1967) The classification of modifiable synapses and their use in models for conditioning. *Proc. R. Soc. B. 168*, 361–376.

Brindley, G. S. (1969) Nerve net models of plausible size that perform many simple learning tasks. *Proc. R. Soc. B. 174*, 173–191.

Cameron, D. E., S. Sved, L. Solyom, B. Wainrib, and H. Barik (1963) Effects of ribonucleic acid on memory defect in the aged. *Am. J. Psychiat. 120*, 320–325.

Cajal, S. R. (1909) *Histologie du système nerveux 2*, 886–890 Madrid, C.S.I.C.

Cass, D. T., T. J. Sutton, and R. F. Mark (1973) Competition between nerves for functional connections with axolotl muscles. *Nature* (London), *243*, 201–203.

Conrad, R. (1964) Acoustic confusions in immediate memory. *Brit. J. Psychol. 55*, 75–84.

Corning, W. C. and D. Riccio (1970) The planarian controversy, in *Molecular Approaches to Learning and Memory*, W. L. Byrne, Ed., pp. 107–149. Academic Press, New York.

Cotman, C. W., G. Banker, S. F. Zornetzer, and J. L. McGaugh (1971) Electroshock effects on brain protein synthesis: relation to brain seizures and retrograde amnesia. *Science, 173*, 454–456.

Cragg, B. G. (1968) Are there structural alterations in synapses related to functioning? *Proc. R. Soc. B. 171*, 319–323.

Cragg, B. G. (1969) The effects of vision and dark-rearing on the size and density of synapses in the lateral geniculate nucleus measured by electron microscopy. *Brain Res. 13*, 53–67.

Dale, H. C. A. and A. McGlaughlin (1970) Enhancing memory with redundant labels. *Nature* (London), *227*, 411–412.

Davson, H. (1967) The blood brain barrier, in *The Physiology of the Cerebrospinal Fluid*. Ch. 4, pp. 82–103. J. A. Churchill, London.

Dawson, R. G. and J. L. McGaugh (1969) Electroconvulsive shock effects on a reactivated memory trace: further examination. *Science, 166*, 525–527.

Deutsch, J. A. (1971) The cholinergic synapse and the site of memory. *Science, 174*, 788–794.

Douglas, R. J. and K. H. Pribram (1966) Learning and limbic lesions. *Neuropsychologica 4*, 197–220.

Eccles, J. C. (1953) *The Neurophysiological Basis of Mind.* Clarendon Press, Oxford.

Eccles, J. C. (1964) *The Physiology of Synapses.* Springer-Verlag, Berlin.

Eist, H. and U. S. Seal (1965) The permeability of the blood brain barrier and blood cerebrospinal fluid barrier to C^{14} tagged ribonucleic acid. *Amer. J. Psychiat. 122*, 584–586.

Enesco, H. E. (1966) Fate of ^{14}C-RNA injected into mice. *Exptl. Cell. Res. 42*, 640–645.

Flexner, L. B. and J. B. Flexner (1968) Intracerebral saline: effect on memory of trained mice treated with puromycin. *Science, 159*, 330–331.

Gage, P. W. and J. I. Hubbard (1966) An investigation of the post-tetanic potentiation of end-plate potentials at a mammalian neuromuscular junction. *J. Physiol. 184*, 353–375.

Glasky, A. J. and L. N. Simon (1966) Magnesium pemoline: enhancement of brain RNA polymerases. *Science, 151*, 702–703.

Haber, R. N. (1969) Eidetic images. *Sci. American 220* (4), 36–44.

Hartrey, A. L., P. Keith-Lee, and W. D. Morton (1964) Planaria: memory transfer through cannabalism re-examined. *Science, 146*, 274–275.

Hughes, R. A. (1969) Retrograde amnesia in rats produced by hippocampal injections of potassium chloride: gradient of effect and recovery. *J. Comp. Physiol. Psychol. 68*, 637–644.

Hyden, H. (1967) Biochemical changes accompanying learning, in *The Neurosciences*, pp. 765–771, G. C. Quarton, T. Melnechuk and F. O. Schmitt, Eds., Rockefeller University Press, New York.

Jacobson, A. L., C. Fried, and S. D. Horowitz (1966) Planarians and memory. *Nature* (London), *209*, 599–601.

Jarvik, M. E. (1970) The role of consolidation in memory, in *Molecular Approaches to Learning and Memory*, pp. 15–26, W. B. Byrne, Ed., Academic Press, New York.

John, E. R., M. Shimokochi, and F. Bartlett (1969) Neural readout from memory during generalization. *Science, 164*, 1534–1536.

Kimble, D. P. (1969) Possible inhibitory functions of the hippocampus. *Neuropsychologia 7*, 235–244.

Kuno, M., S. A. Turkanis, and J. N. Weakly (1971) Correlation between nerve terminal size and transmitter release at the neuromuscular junction of the frog. *J. Physiol. 213*, 545–556.

Lashley, K. S. (1950) In search of the engram. *S.E.B. Symposia, 4*, 454–482.

Lewis, P. R., C. C. D. Shute, and A. Silver (1964) Confirmation from choline acetylase analysis of a massive cholinergic innervation to the hippocampus. *J. Physiol. 172*, 9–10P.

Luria, A. R. (1968) *The Mind of a Mnemonist.* Basic Books, Inc., New York.

McGaugh, J. L. (1966) Time-dependent processes in memory storage. *Science, 153,* 1351–1358.

McGaugh, J. L. (1973) Drug facilitation of learning and memory. *Ann. Rev. Pharmacol. 13,* 229–241.

Mark, R. F. and L. R. Marotte (1972) The mechanism of selective reinnervation of fish eye muscles. III. Functional, electrophysiological and anatomical analysis of recovery from section of the IIIrd and IVth nerves. *Brain. Res. 46,* 131–148.

Mark, R. F., L. R. Marotte, and P. E. Mart (1972) The mechanism of selective reinnervation of fish eye muscles. IV. Identification of repressed synapses. *Brain Res. 46,* 149–157.

Mark, R. F. and M. E. Watts (1971) Drug inhibition of memory formation in chickens. I. Long-term memory. *Proc. R. Soc. Lond. B. 178,* 439–454.

Marotte, L. R. and R. F. Mark (1970a) The mechanism of selective reinnervation of fish eye muscles. I. Evidence from muscle function during recovery. *Brain Res. 19,* 41–51.

Marotte, L. R. and R. F. Mark (1970b) The mechanism of selective reinnervation of fish eye muscles. II. Evidence from electron microscopy of nerve endings. *Brain Res. 19,* 53–69.

Merrill, E. G. and P. D. Wall (1972) Factors forming the edge of a receptive field: the presence of relatively ineffective afferent terminals. *J. Physiol. 226,* 825–846.

Miller, G. A., J. S. Bruner, and L. Postman (1954) Familiarity of letter sequences and tachistoscopic identification. *J. Genet. Psychol. 50,* 129–139.

Milner, B. (1959) The memory defect in bilateral hippocampal lesions. *Psychiat. Res. Rep. 11,* 43–52.

Milner, B. (1965) Memory disturbance after bilateral hippocampal lesions, in *Cognitive Processes and the Brain,* P. Milner and S. Brickman, pp. 97–111, Van Nostrand Co., Princeton, New Jersey.

Møllgaard, K., M. C. Diamond, L. L. Bennett, M. Rosenweig, and B. Linder (1971) Quantitative synaptic changes with differential experience in rat brain. *Int. J. Neuroscience, 2,* 113–128.

Nathan, P. W. (1969) *The Nervous System.* Penguin Books, Harmondsworth, Middlesex, England.

Ojemann, R. G. (1966) Correlations between specific human brain lesions and memory changes. *Neurosciences Res. Prog. Bull. Supp. 4,* 1–70.

Olds, J., J. F. Disterhoft, M. Segal, C. L. Kornblith, and R. Hirsh (1972) Learning centers of rat brain mapped by measuring latencies of conditioned unit responses. *J. Neurophysiol. 35,* 202–219.

Orzack, M. H., C. L. Taylor, and C. Kornetsky (1968) A research report on the antifatigue effects of magnesium pemoline. *Psychopharmacologia 13,* 413–417.

Paivio, A. (1969) Mental imagery in associative learning and memory. *Psychol. Rev.* *76*, 241–263.

Penfield, W. (1958) *The Excitable Cortex in Conscious Man.* Liverpool University Press.

Pietsch, P. and C. W. Schneider (1969) Brain transplantation in salamanders: an approach to memory transfer. *Brain Res. 14*, 707–715.

Plotnikoff, N. (1966) Magnesium pemoline: enhancement of learning and memory of a conditioned avoidance response. *Science, 151*, 703–704.

Plotnikoff, N., F. Will, and W. Ditzler (1969) Stimulant activity of pemoline and magnesium hydroxide. *Arch. int. Pharmacodyn. Ther. 181*, 441–458.

Rappoport, D. A. and H. F. Daginawala (1968) Changes in nuclear DNA induced by olfaction in catfish. *J. Neurochem. 15*, 991–1006.

Reige, W. H. (1971) Environmental influences on brain and behavior of year-old rats. *Devel. Psychobiol. 4*, 157–167.

Rose, S. P. R. (1970) Neurochemical correlates of learning and environmental change, in *Short-term Changes in Neural Activity and Behavior*, pp. 517–551, G. Horne, and R. A. Hinde, Eds., Cambridge University Press.

Rosenweig, M. R., E. L. Bennett, and M. C. Diamond (1972) Brain changes in response to experience. *Sci. American 226* (2), 22–29.

Russell, W. R. (1959) *Brain, Memory, Learning.* Clarendon Press, Oxford.

Schwartz, J. H., V. F. Castellucci, and E. R. Kandel (1971) Functioning of identified neurons and synapses in abdominal ganglion of *Aplysia* in absence of protein synthesis. *J. Neurophysiol. 34*, 939–953.

Scoville, W. B. and B. Milner (1957) Loss of recent memory after bilateral hippocampal lesions. *J. Neuro. Neurosurg. Psychiat. 20*, 11–21.

Shallice, T. and E. Warrington (1970) Independent functioning of verbal memory stores: a neuropsychological study. *Quart. J. Exp. Psychol. 22*, 261–273.

Shashoua, V. E. (1970) RNA metabolism in goldfish brain during acquisition of new behavioral patterns. *Proc. Natl. Acad. Sci. U.S. 65*, 160–167.

Squire, L. R. and S. H. Barondes (1970) Actinomycin-D: Effects on memory at different times after training. *Nature* (London), *225*, 649–650.

Squire, L. R., G. A. Smith, and S. H. Barondes (1973) Cycloheximide affects memory within minutes after the onset of training. *Nature* (London), *242*, 201–202.

Steiner, F. A. (1968) Influence of microelectrophoretically applied acetylcholine on the responsiveness of hippocampal and lateral geniculate neurons. *Pflugers Arch. 303*, 173–180.

Talland, G. A. and M. T. McGuire (1967) Tests of learning and memory with Cylert. *Psychopharmacologia 10*, 445–451.

Terzian, H. and G. D. Ore (1955) Syndrome of Kluver & Bucy: reproduced in man by bilateral removal of the temporal lobes. *Neurology 5*, 373–380.

Thompson, R. (1969) Localization of the "visual memory system" in the white rat. *J. comp. Physiol. Psychol. 69*, Suppl. 2. 1–29.

Thompson, R. and R. E. Myers (1971) Brainstem mechanism underlying visually guided responses in the rhesus monkey. *J. comp. Physiol. Psychol. 74*, 479–512.

Ungar, G., D. M. Desiderio, and W. Parr (1972) Isolation, identification and synthesis of a specific-behaviour-inducing brain peptide. *Nature* (London), *238*, 198–202.

Ungar, G., L. Galvan, and R. H. Clark (1968) Chemical transfer of learned fear. *Nature* (London), *217,* 1259–1261.

Volkmar, F. R. and W. T. Greenough (1972) Rearing complexity affects branching of dendrites in the visual cortex of the rat. *Science*, *176*, 1445–1447.

Warrington, E. K. and L. Weiskrantz (1970) Amnesia syndrome: consolidation or retrieval? *Nature* (London), *228*, 628–630.

Watts, M. E. and R. F. Mark (1971) Drug inhibition of memory formation in chickens. II. Short-term memory. *Proc. R. Soc. B. 178*, 455–464.

Weinberg, H., W. Grey-Walter, and H. J. Crow (1970) Intracerebral events in humans related to real and imaginary stimuli. *Electroenceph. Clin. Neurophysiol. 29*, 1–9.

Weiskrantz, L. (1970) A long-term view of short-term memory in psychology, in *Short-term Changes in Neural Activity and Behaviour,* pp. 63–74, G. Horn and R. E. Hinde, Eds., Cambridge Univ. Press.

Whitty, C. W. M. and W. Lewin (1960) A Korsakoff syndrome in the post cingulectomy state. *Brain 83*, 648–653.

SUGGESTED FURTHER READING

Scientific American Reprints

Agranoff, B. W. *Memory and protein synthesis.* June, 1967, p. 115 (offprint 1077).

Atkinson, R. G. and R. M. Shiffrin. *The control of short-term memory.* August, 1971, p. 82 (offprint 538).

Boycott, B. *Learning in the Octopus.* March, 1965, p. 42 (offprint 1006).

Ceraso, J. *The interference theory of forgetting.* October, 1967, p. 117 (offprint 509).

Eccles, J. C. *The physiology of imagination.* September, 1958, p. 135 (offprint 65).

Gerrard, R. W. *What is memory?* September, 1953, p. 118 (offprint 11).

Haber, R. N. *How we remember what we see.* May, 1970, p. 104 (offprint 528).

Haitman, J. P. *How an instinct is learned.* December, 1969, p. 98 (offprint 1165).

Peterson, R. L. *Short-term memory.* July, 1966, p. 90 (offprint 499).

Pribram, K. H. *The neurophysiology of remembering.* January, 1969, p. 73 (offprint 520).

Rosenweig, M. R., E. L. Bennett and C. M. Diamond. *Brain changes in responses to experience.* February, 1972, p. 22 (offprint 541).

Underwood, B. J. *Forgetting.* March, 1964, p. 91 (offprint 482).

Books

The first three books are easy-to-read accounts of psychological aspects of memory.

Adams, J. A. (1967) *Human Memory.* McGraw-Hill, New York.

Hunter, I. M. L. (1964) *Memory.* Revised edition. Penguin Books, Harmondsworth, Middlesex, England.

Nathan, P. (1969) *The Nervous System.* Lippincott, Philadelphia (This book covers anatomy and clinical studies simply and well.)

Norman, D. A. (1969) *Memory and Attention.* John Wiley & Sons, New York.

QUESTIONS

More advanced students may want to try answering the following questions using the references as a starting point.

3.1 *How would you find out if someone had a photographic memory? Would this confer any advantage on them when studying?*

Haber, R. N. (1969) Eidetic images, *Sci. American, 220* (4), 36–44.

Pollen, D. A. and M. C. Trachtenberg (1972) Alpha rhythm and eye movement in eidetic imagery. *Nature* (London), *237,* 109–112.

Stromeyer, C. F. and J. Psotka (1970) The detailed texture of eidetic images. *Nature* (London), *225,* 346–349.
See also: *Nature, 225, 227* (1970) "Is there photographic memory?"

Kluver, H. (1926) *An Experimental Study of the Eidetic Type. Genetic Psychol. Bulletin 1,* No. 2, Worcester Mass.

Jaench, E. R. (1930) *Eidetic Imagery.* From 2nd ed. tr. by O. Oeser. Harcourt & Brace Co., New York.

3.2 *Is long term memory stored in a particular place or places in the brain?*

Lashley, K. S. (1950) In search of the engram. *S.E.B. Symposia 4,* 454–482.

Olds, J., J. F. Disterhoff, M. Segal, C. L. Kornblith, and R. Hirsh (1973) Learning centers of rat brain mapped by measuring latencies of conditioned unit responses. *J. Neurophysiol. 35,* 202–219.

Thompson, R. and R. E. Myers (1971) Brainstem mechanism underlying visually guided responses in the rhesus monkey. *J. comp. Physiol. Psychol. 74*, 479–512.

Thompson, R. (1969) Localization of the "visual memory system" in the white rat. *J. comp. Physiol. Psychol., 69*, Suppl. 2, 1–29.

Zangwell, O. L. (1961) Lashley's concept of cerebral mass action, in *Current Problems in Animal Behaviour*, pp. 56–89, W. H. Thorpe and O. L. Zangwell, Eds. Cambridge University Press.

3.3 *What physiological processes could account for short-term memory?*

Bliss, T. V. P. and A. R. Gardner-Medwin (1973) Long-lasting potentiation of synaptic transmission in the dentate area of the unanesthetized rabbit following stimulation of perforant path. *J. Physiol. 232*, 357–374.

Eccles, J. C. (1970) Synaptic mechanisms possibly concerned in learning and memory, Ch. 2 in *Facing Reality*, Springer-Verlag, New York.

Hughes, J. R. (1958) Post-tetanic potentiation. *Physiol. Rev. 38*, 91–113.

Watts, M. E. and R. M. Mark (1971) Drug inhibition of memory formation in chickens. II. Short-term memory. *Proc. R. Soc. London B. 178*, 455–464.

3.4 *What light can studies of an octopus throw on memory and learning?*

Sanders, G. D. (1970) Long-term memory of a tactile discrimination in *Octopus vulgaris*, and the effect of vertical lobe removal. *Brain Res. 20*, 59–73.

Sanders, G. D. (1970) Long-term tactile memory in *Octopus:* further experiments on the effect of vertical lobe removal. *Brain Res. 24*, 169–178.

Wells, M. J. and J. Z. Young (1969) The effect of splitting part of the brain or removal of the median frontal lobe on touch learning in *Octopus. J. Exptl. Biol. 50*, 515–526.

Young, J. Z. (1966) *The Memory Systems of the Brain*. Oxford University Press, London.

3.5 *Is there any good evidence that long-term memory can be transferred to naive animals by injection or implantation of tissue extracts from trained animals? If so, what is transferred?*

Albert, D. J. (1966) Memory in mammals: evidence for a system involving nuclear RNA. *Neuropsychologia 4*, 79–92.

Brindley, G. S. (1970) Chemical mnemology. *Nature* (London), *228*, 583.

Byrne, W. *et al.* (1966) Memory transfer. *Science, 153*, 658–659.

Frank, B., D. G. Stein, and J. Rosen (1970) Interanimal "memory" transfer: results from brain and liver homogenates. *Science, 169*, 399–402 and *178*, 522–523.

Rosenblatt, F. and R. G. Miller (1966) Behavioral assay procedures for the transfer of learned behavior by brain extracts. *Proc. Natn. Acad. Sci. U.S. 56*, 1424–1430 and 1683–1688.

Ungar, G. and E. J. Fjerdingstad (1971) Chemical nature of the transfer factors: RNA or protein, in *Biology of Memory*, pp. 137–143, G. Adam, Ed., Plenum Press, New York.

Ungar, G., L. Galvan, and R. H. Clark (1968) Chemical transfer of learned fear. *Nature* (London), *217*, 1259–1261.

Ungar, G., D. M. Desiderio, and W. Parr (1972) Isolation, identification and synthesis of a specific-behaviour-inducing brain peptide. *Nature* (London), *238*, 198–202.

3.6 *Devise a nerve net with modifiable synapses which will allow some simple learning (e.g. classical conditioning).*

Brindley, G. S. (1967) The classification of modifiable synapses and their use for conditioning. *Proc. R. Soc. B. 168*, 361–376.

Brindley, G. S. (1969) Nerve net models of plausible size that perform many simple learning tasks. *Proc. Roy. Soc. B. 174*, 173–191.

Brindley, G. S. (1974) The potentialities of different kinds of modifiable synapses. *J. theoret. Biol. 43,* 393–396.

Gardner-Medwin, A. R. (1969) Modifiable synapses necessary for learning. *Nature* (London), *223*, 916–919.

SLEEP, WAKEFULNESS, DREAMS, 4 AND VISIONS

For many centuries the experiences of dreamers and visionaries have been considered to be mental activity in the absence of body or brain activity. For example, the English Nobel prize-winning student of brain function, Charles Sherrington, in his prime at the beginning of this century, could say (Sherrington, 1940i):

> Sleep and his brother Death: there is the seeming resemblance between them that, to the naive observer, in both cases the "soul" has flown.

Sherrington here reflects the brain physiology of his time. In another passage from the same book, the brain is compared to a system of strings, the nerve fibres; and "knots" the nerve cells, with synapses upon them. In a most poetic passage Sherrington describes the brain and particularly the cerebral cortex (roof brain in this abstract) during sleep (Sherrington, 1940 ii):

> Suppose we choose the hour of deep sleep. Then only in some sparse and out of the way places are nodes flashing and trains of light-points running. Such places indicate local activity still in progress. At one such place we can watch the behaviour of a group of lights perhaps a myriad strong. They are pursuing a mystic and recurrent manoeuvre as if of some incantational dance. They are superintending the beating of the heart and the state of the arteries so that while we sleep the circulation of the blood is what should be. The great knotted head-piece of the whole sleeping system lies for the most part dark, and quite especially so the roof-brain. Occasionally at places in it lighted points flash or move but soon subside.

If this were all that was to be said, then clearly, if there is mental activity during sleep it must be largely divorced from brain activity.

A modern concept of sleep and of the awake conscious state is that both are the results of brain activity. The sleep state is perhaps the basic state from which we are aroused by external stimuli and to which we are returned by a cyclic brain

131

mechanism. Furthermore, brain activity, in sleep and while visions are being experienced, differs not in quantity but in quality from brain activity in the normal waking state. It seems likely indeed that dreams and visions arise *from* particular brain activity rather than in its absence.

I. OBJECTIVE SIGNS OF WAKEFULNESS AND SLEEP

When it became possible to measure the oxygen consumption of the human brain (by comparing oxygen levels in the blood going in and out of the brain and their rate of change), it was found that most forms of unconsciousness were accompanied by a fall in the oxygen consumption of the brain (Kety, 1950). For instance, the blood supply may fall to 60 per cent of normal during anesthesia and to about 50 per cent of normal in a diabetic coma. If brain cells are put out of action temporarily in sleep then the brain should require less oxygen in this condition too. When sleeping men were investigated in this way, however, the brain oxygen supply was found to be the same asleep and awake and the brain blood supply was greater in the sleeping state! Judged by this rough criterion then, the brain appeared as active asleep as awake (Mangold *et al.*, 1955).

Recordings from brain neurons showed that many areas of brain are actually more active asleep than in the waking state (Evarts, 1967). Recording of the EEG confirmed that brain cells were active but the activity in sleeping men was of a different type from that recorded from waking men. It was found that men could sleep in a laboratory with small metal plates taped to their skulls which allowed their EEG to be recorded. Wires from these electrodes went through the wall to a pen recorder in the next room so as not to disturb the sleeper. By this means the summed electrical activity of the brain recorded through the skull was traced out on paper from minute to minute.

In the waking alert state (as previously mentioned in Chapter 2, Fig. 2.7), the voltage changes recorded from the skull (EEG) are often very small with many irregular oscillations (desynchronized). In the recordings made over the temporo-parieto-occipital regions, however, a marked pattern of large voltage waves is often seen, known as the alpha rhythm. This consists of 30–50 μV waves (e.g., Fig. 4.1a, CTX) at a frequency of about 10/sec. Most prominent when the eyes are closed, the alpha rhythm disappears momentarily when they are opened. It also appears at times of boredom and inattention, even with both eyes open.

As one goes to sleep the alpha rhythm, characteristic of the drowsy state, disappears and is replaced by larger voltage waves of slower frequency (4 to 6/sec) which characterize stage 1 sleep (Dement and Kleitman, 1957a). As sleep becomes deeper (as judged by the difficulty of awakening sleepers), occasional bursts of fast waves (12 to 15/sec) called "sleep spindles" are seen, signalling stage 2 sleep. Stage 3 is intermediate between 2 and 4 and is characterized by the presence of high amplitude waves with a frequency of 1 to 2/sec. Records from stage 4 (Fig. 4.1b, CTX) shows predominantly large amplitude waves at 1 to 2/sec.

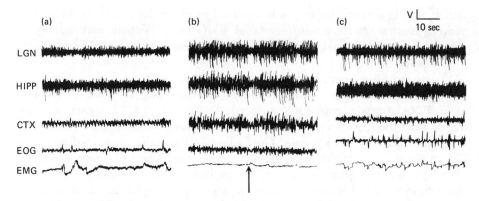

Fig. 4.1   The EEG criteria for waking (a), deep (b), and REM sleep (c). The records are from an adult cat, investigated in the author's laboratory. The top three traces in (a), (b), and (c) show records from lateral geniculate nucleus (LGN), hippocampus (HIPP) and cortex (CTX). The fourth record (EOG) shows eye muscle activity and the bottom record is from muscle (EMG). In the scale, V represents 100 μV for EOG. The arrow in (b) indicates a brief shift to Stage 1 sleep associated with muscle movements. Note the cortical desynchronization and the changes in LGN and HIPP.

Depth of sleep is greatest at stage 4 and shallowest in stage 1. Similar phenomena are seen in recordings from the skulls of brains of all mammals—even elephants have been used in studies of this type. The EEGs of the waking and sleeping stages are often summarized for research purposes as the synchronized (sleep) and desynchronized (awake) states.

Many other body changes occur at the same time as the changes in brain waves. For instance, the pupils of the eyes are constricted (miosis) but will constrict further in response to light. Two easily monitored changes are eye movements and muscle tone. Eye movements (Fig. 4.1a, EOG) can be easily measured by a recording electrode, often a small flat plate, attached to the head in the vicinity of the eyes, which detects the action potentials from eye muscles.

When people are awake their eyes are constantly moving (see Chapter 2, I-C.). As would be expected during sleep, eye movements are much reduced in amplitude and may even be absent (Fig. 4.1b, EOG). In Fig. 4.1(b) EOG, the trace shows small action potentials. These are of cortical origin and there are no large action potentials attributable to eye movement activity.

Muscle tone (Fig. 4.1a, EMG) is usually recorded by electrodes placed in large muscle groups in laboratory animals or over these muscle groups in men. In the waking state some of the fibres of muscles involved in maintenance of a particular posture are contracted all the time. The fibres take turns so that one group is active for only a short period and is then spelled by another group. As a result, muscles have a firm feeling and limbs, when passively moved, offer a resistance which is called "tone" by physicians. The muscle contractions are initiated by muscle action potentials which can be recorded by electrodes in or over the muscle and this is what the records in Fig. 4.1(a) EMG show. Without tonic activity in postural muscles, we could not stand. During sleep, as Fig. 4.1(b) EMG indicates, tone is reduced.

When records were made throughout the night at a laboratory at the University of Chicago (Aserinsky and Kleitman, 1957; Dement and Kleitman, 1957b; Dement, 1958), a new phenomenon appeared. As Fig. 4.1(c) CTX shows, at times during sleep the EEG from the cortex shows a desynchronized pattern resembling that recorded in the waking state. The finding indicated that the recording of the EEG alone is not a satisfactory indicator of sleep state. The EEG must be supplemented by recording muscle tone and/or eye movement. It is found that when a desynchronized EEG is recorded from sleeping men and animals, a great decrease in muscle tone can also be recorded (thin trace in Fig. 4.1c, EMG), although sudden jerks of limbs are common (wobbly baseline in Fig. 4.1c, EMG). Furthermore, large amplitude rapid (60–70/min) eye movements (REM) are recorded which have given the name "REM sleep" to this state of sleep (Fig. 4.1c, EOG). Most of the time the pupils are contracted, but sudden dilatation of the pupils (mydriasis) may accompany REM. In experiments on animals, a further parameter often studied is the EEG recorded from either the R or L lateral geniculate nucleus, the thalamic nuclei on the pathway from the retina to the cortex (Fig. 4.1, LGN). Well-marked large voltage waves are recorded there in REM sleep (Fig. 4.1c, LGN) and these waves indeed often signal the onset of sleep. The activity of hippocampal cells (Fig. 4.1a, HIPP) is also often recorded. Their EEG characteristics are often opposite to those of the cortex. For instance, when the cortex is showing synchronous large waves associated with sleep, low voltage fast waves can be recorded from hippocampal electrodes.

Closer examination has shown that the REM state is accompanied by a number of signs of excitement and stress. For instance, there is a marked variation in the pulse and blood pressure and irregularity in the respiration (Dement and Kleitman, 1957a, b; Snyder et al., 1964), accompanied by secretion of corticosteroids (Weizman et al., 1966; Mandell et al., 1966). Furthermore, a cycle of penile erections occurs, beginning with each REM period and ending at its end (Ohlmeyer and Bilmayer, 1947; Fisher et al., 1965), and testosterone secretion is increased at night in association with REM sleep (Evans et al., 1971).

It appears that we all spend some time every night in the two types of sleep, from here on called "slow wave" (SW) sleep and REM sleep. As Fig. 4.2 indicates, young adults normally spend some sixteen to eighteen hours awake. The remaining hours are divided between the SW and the REM states, with stage 4 coming early in the night and REM sleep becoming increasingly frequent as the night progresses. Normally, as Fig. 4.2 indicates, SW sleep precedes REM sleep and REM sleep precedes awakening.

Newborn animals whose central nervous system is not completely developed

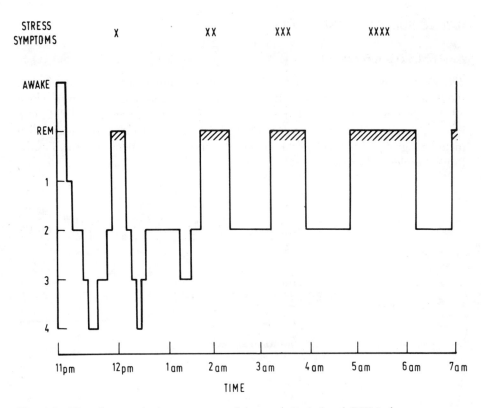

Fig. 4.2 The sleep cycle in a young adult man. Periods of REM sleep are cross-hatched. The stages of sleep (ordinate) are judged from EEG criteria. This particular cycle is idealized, showing only broad trends and omitting the brief cycling, for instance between REM and Stage 1, which is a normal feature of sleep. The subject is shown awaking from a REM period.

at birth show only alternations between waking and the REM state. SW sleep develops with maturation of the nervous system. Cats, rats, and rabbits show this pattern. In contrast, guinea pigs and lambs, which have well developed central nervous systems at birth, show alternation of waking and the SW and REM states. Human babies at birth spend some eighteen hours asleep of which 45 to 65 per cent is in the REM state. A two-year-old is still spending 40 per cent of his sleep time in REM sleep, but a five-year-old approaches the young adult figure of 20 per cent. For those over fifty, the period spent in REM sleep forms about 15 per cent of total sleep (Roffwarg *et al.*, 1966). The unique parameters of SW and REM sleep, compared with the waking state, indicate that sleep is a state of being that is distinct from the waking state. It certainly does not resemble the unconsciousness resulting from brain damage.

II. THE SLEEP-WAKING CYCLE

A. REM sleep mechanisms

The French investigator Jouvet (1967a) and his colleagues have found that in cats the neural mechanism triggering REM sleep survives lesions of the brain in which all the tissue above the pons is removed. The ability to demonstrate REM sleep is lost, however, when lesions are made in the pontine reticular formation, which includes a group of norepinephrine-containing and releasing neurons known as the locus coeruleus (Fig. 4.3).

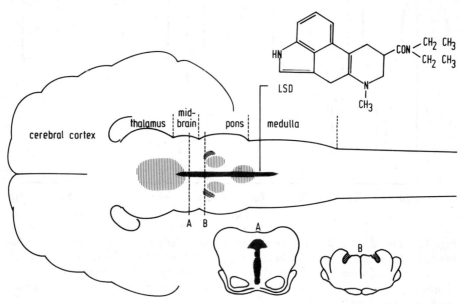

Fig. 4.3 A schematic drawing indicating brain areas important in the control of sleep. *A, B* indicate cross sections through the areas indicated by dashed lines. The midline raphe nucleus is shown in *A* and in black in the main drawing, while the bilateral locus coeruleus groups of neurons are similarly shown in *B*. Reticular formation nuclei are indicated by vertical shading. The formula for LSD is shown and the line indicates that this drug is thought to act on raphe system neurons. (From "The States of Sleep" by Michael Jouvet. Copyright © 1967 by *Scientific American*, Inc. All rights reserved.)

Studies of nervous system activity during REM sleep indicate that the brain is almost completely cut off from the outside world. Information reaches the brain with much more difficulty than usual and the motor pathways normally activated by the brain are depressed. It is as if the brain had locked itself up and was enjoying a private life of its own. The only signs of life are the eye movements and occasional muscle twitches. The mechanism responsible for all this is obviously complex.

Two distinct classes of events occur in REM sleep which have been termed "tonic" and "phasic." Tonic events are those (like loss of muscle tone and the low voltage, fast EEG) which persist throughout REM sleep. Phasic events are those which are rapid and discontinuous. The eye movements and muscle twitches of the REM state are obvious examples, but there are others, particularly the bursts of high voltage waves seen in the EEG when it is recorded from the visual cortex or the lateral geniculate nucleus (Fig. 4.1).

The phasic changes are brought about by the vestibular nuclei—groups of cells found on each side of the brainstem and normally concerned with the organs of balance (Pompeiano, 1967). These cells have connections with the neurons controlling the eye muscles and the neurons controlling the postural muscles. If you tilt your head sideways, your eyes rotate around their anterior-posterior axes so that you still see the world on a level plane. This reflex adjustment is an example of the action of the vestibular nuclei, activated by signals from the organs of balance, on the neurons controlling the eye muscles. In response to the stimuli from these controlling nerve cells, the muscles swivel the eyes to compensate for the head movement.

At the same time as these eye movements occur, there are changes in tone of the postural muscles, also brought about by nerve impulses from the vestibular nuclei to the neurons controlling these postural muscles. Both eye movements and postural movements are seen in REM sleep, but divorced from signals from the organ of balance and apparently brought into action by nerve impulses from pontine reticular neurons to the vestibular nuclei on both sides. It is in this way that rapid eye movements are produced during REM sleep. If the vestibular nuclei activated postural muscles in the same way, the muscle twitches would occur synchronously with the rapid eye movements, and in fact some twitches do occur in this way. Normally the muscles are limp in REM sleep. This is because the locus coeruleus by separate pathways inhibits the nerve cells controlling these muscles (Jouvet and Delorme, 1965). Similarly, nerve impulses pass to the midbrain reticular formation producing (presumably by norepinephrine release) the desynchronized EEG pattern. Activation of inhibitory connections (see Chapter 2, Attention) to the paths through which incoming sensory information goes to the cortex is responsible for the cutoff of sensory inflow (Hernandez-Peon et al., 1965). There is thus interaction between the tonic inhibitory influence, exerted from the locus coeruleus, and a phasic excitatory influence, exerted by way of the vestibular nucleus, which produces the observed REM state with a desynchronized EEG and postural hypotension together with intermittent muscle twitches and rapid eye movements.

B. The role of sensory stimulation

Men in isolation in a featureless prison cell, or an open boat under a cloudless sky, or floating blindfolded in a tank of water share a similar experience. Deprived of external stimulation they experience hallucinations and drift into a state between sleep and wakefulness. Clearly the human brain remains active though disordered where there is an extreme reduction in environmental stimuli (Lilly, 1956). There is ample evidence too (Heron, 1961) that men in a state of sensory deprivation are extremely suggestible. "Brainwashing" is apparently carried out by repeating material to be learned to the victim when he is in a state of sensory deprivation and fatigue.

The mechanisms by which external stimulation influences wakefulness (Arousal, Chapter 2, II), are well known. Lesions completely destroying the sensory pathways (Fig. 1.12) from spinal cord through thalamus to cortical sensory areas do not result in sleep or coma. During their passage through the brainstem, however, the axons concerned give off collateral branches to neurons in the reticular formation (Fig. 4.3) of the medulla, pons, and midbrain, whose axons in turn pass upward to the diencephalon and downward to the spinal cord. Stimulation of the reticular formation of sleeping animals in the midbrain and upper pons causes them to awaken with appropriate EEG signs (Fig. 4.1a) (Lindsley et al., 1949; Morruzzi and Magoun, 1949). Surgical interruption of the axons arising from these neurons cause an animal to become comatose with the EEG signs of sleep (Fig. 4.1b). It would be natural to think then that the reticular system when active produces the waking state and that when incoming stimulation is reduced to a minimal level, sleep results.

Clinical evidence certainly supports the controlling role of this region in sleep. A review of human lesions shows that injuries in the medulla and pons may result in coma, but the EEG is not that of sleep. Injection of sodium amytal into the vertebral artery of men depresses the function of the brainstem neurons, as can be shown by testing cranial nerve function. In these experiments, cranial nerves 3 to 8 and 10 and 12 showed signs of impaired function but no loss of consciousness occurred (Alema et al., 1966). Lesions of the upper midbrain and posterior diencephalon, however, invariably cause coma with EEG signs of SW sleep (Rossi, 1964), while lesions of this area are associated with the persistent sleepiness associated with some forms of encephalitis. As expected, cats whose brain is sectioned through the midbrain, the so-called "cerveau isolé" preparation, show EEG and ocular signs of sleep (Bremer, 1935) from which they can be temporarily awakened by stimulation of the midbrain reticular formation above the lesion.

A complementary set of experiments was the study of the effect of removal of cortex or thalamus upon the sleep-waking cycle. Cortical removal does affect the cycle—decorticate dogs go through six or more sleep-waking cycles in a day rather than the usual two, but the lesion does not affect the generation of a sleep-waking cycle (Kleitman and Camille, 1932). Similarly, removal of the thalamus does not affect the generation of a sleep-waking cycle (Naquet et al., 1966). The thalamus, however, does have some influence on sleep because electrical stimulation in the midline of the thalamus with low frequency shocks is known to induce sleep (Hess, 1944, 1954). If the stimulation is given by way of an implanted electrode to an otherwise mobile animal, the sleep appears quite natural, in the sense that the animal appears to look for a place to sleep and to lie down in the natural sleep position. Stimulation in the same place in man is reported to induce a feeling of tiredness with repeated yawning and loss of spontaneous speech and movement (Hassler, 1961). It seems probable that thalamic sleep, which can only be elicited in *sleepy* cats, occurs because this form of stimulation produces a tonic inhibition of the thalamic neurons of the specific sensory nuclei, thus cutting off the cortex from stimulation. In this way the animal is deprived of stimulation in a way similar to that of the isolated men mentioned earlier in this section.

The withdrawal of afferent input cannot be the sole cause of sleep, for it has been found that in the medulla and lower pons electrical stimulation may cause a synchronized EEG (sleep sign), while lesions in this area may cause insomnia. Indeed, an animal with the brain sectioned in the pons and the optic and olfactory nerves cut has a completely deafferented cerebrum, yet shows a desynchronized (waking) EEG, presumably because the balance of reticular input now favors waking. Jouvet and his colleagues (1967a) have shown that the neurons involved lie in the midline of the medulla and pons (the raphe nuclei, Fig. 4.3), and as the lesion experiments indicate, exert a tonic inhibitory influence on the neurons of the midbrain reticular system. Modern sleep theories revolve round the interaction of the two reticular systems or the action of these systems on hypothalamic neurons.

C. The cyclic mechanism

At the present time the mechanisms responsible for the alternation between sleep and waking are a matter of dispute (see Question 4.1). Three theories exist, each with its protagonists; they are:

- The neurophysiological
- The neurohumoral
- The humoral

1. *The neurophysiological theory*

According to the theory's leading protagonist (Morruzzi, 1972), the hypothalamus contains anteriorly neurons whose activity results in sleeping and posteriorly, adjacent to the midbrain, neurons whose activity results in wakefulness. These neurons are supposed to be capable of generating a sleep-wake cycle on their own by mutual interaction, but normally they are controlled by the ascending excitatory and inhibitory influence from the upper and lower brainstem.

The chief evidence for this theory is the finding that, if the *cerveau isolé* animal is maintained for a week or more, EEG signs appear, indicating a development of periods of wakefulness (Morruzzi, 1972, ii). Morruzzi (1972) interprets the development of the sleep-wake cycle as evidence for its generation above the lesion, that is, in the hypothalamus.

Support for the hypothesis comes from studies in which monkeys, rats, and dogs, after bilateral lesions of the caudal (posterior) hypothalamus, were initially sleepy, waking only when handled. Later the animals became less sleepy but always appeared drowsy. When the lesions were made in the rostral (anterior) hypothalamus of rats, the animals remained awake until they fell into a coma and died. Cats subjected to a similar lesion showed sleeplessness immediately after operation but recovered in four to eight weeks.

2. The neurohumoral theory

Jouvet (1972) suggests that brainstem neurons are responsible for the sleep-waking cycle. He points out that the axons of raphe system neurons (Fig. 4.3) terminate throughout the brainstem and cortex and suggests, firstly, that activity of these neurons provokes SW sleep by inhibiting the upper brainstem excitatory influence and, secondly, that by axon collaterals they prime the pontine neurons to initiate REM sleep.

Recent advances in the knowledge of the chemistry of the raphe nuclei and locus coeruleus (Fig. 4.3) has enabled ingenious experiments to be done to test Jouvet's hypothesis. It appears that the neurons in the raphe nucleus contain serotonin (5-hydroxy-tryptamine), a very active pharmacological agent, which is perhaps the transmitter substance released from the axons of these cells. The locus coeruleus nerve cells, as has been mentioned, contain a related chemical, norepinephrine which presumably they release as a transmitter. If serotonin production was impaired, and specific drugs are now known which do this, we would expect the raphe cells to be unable to affect either the locus coeruleus or the cells responsible for keeping the cortex awake. In conformity with these ideas, after administration of such drugs to cats, the animals showed an abrupt decrease in SW and REM sleep and for 30 to 60 hours almost total insomnia, that is, wakefulness. The normal pattern of sleep was not reestablished for 200 hours, by which time presumably the drug block had been overcome. Injection of substances which can be made into serotonin by neurons and which bypass the metabolic block caused by the poisons restored natural sleep. The reduction in the serotonin concentration in nerve terminals caused by drugs and the decrease in SW sleep go in parallel. If the raphe neurons are destroyed, almost total insomnia results. Partial lesions have a less pronounced effect. In monkeys deprived of serotonin, only SW sleep is affected and the animals cycle between REM sleep and wakefulness.

Interference with norepinephrine metabolism selectively suppresses REM sleep, presumably by interfering with the neurons of the locus coeruleus. A connection between REM and SW sleep is also shown by some of these chemical studies. Interference with serotonin production in cats, for instance, suppresses both REM and SW sleep. REM sleep does not reappear until the animal is spending at least 15 per cent of its time in SW sleep.

The fact that cats, dogs, and monkeys with midbrain sections still show a sleep-wake cycle in the part of the brain above the lesion, according to Jouvet

(1972), is because blood-borne transmitters (norepinephrine and serotonin), acting on higher centers, mimic the action of the sectioned axons.

At the present time it is not known how raphe neurons are able to suppress periodically the excitatory activity of the cells of the midbrain reticular formation. Perhaps the humoral theory provides the key.

3. *The humoral theory*

It is known that a low-molecular-weight peptide accumulates in the fluid bathing the brain and spinal cord of animals (dogs, goats, rabbits, cats) kept awake for a long time or stimulated in Hess's thalamic sleep center (Pappenheimer *et al.,* 1967; Fencl *et al.,* 1971; Jouvet, 1972; Schoenenberger *et al.,* 1972). Extracts from such fluids, when added to the cerebrospinal fluid of awake animals, cause these animals to take up a natural sleep posture and sleep with appropriate EEG signs. The site of action of the substance is presently unknown and the fact that Siamese twins sharing the same blood circulation can sleep independently (Alekseyeva, 1958) makes it unlikely that sleep depends solely on such a substance.

III. MENTAL ACTIVITY DURING SLEEP

It is common knowledge that the solutions to life's problems often come "if one sleeps on them." Many famous stories are told of new scientific insights gained seemingly in dreams. The discoverer of the benzene ring, one of the most important forms that carbon atoms take, was the German organic chemist Kekule. Dozing in front of his fire, he dreamt that he saw a chain of carbon atoms in snake-like motion before his eyes. Suddenly the chain coiled and one snake took the tail of another in its mouth, forming a ring. In a flash he awoke, realizing that this was the structure of the organic molecule (benzene) needed to explain his experimental findings. Another famous story concerns a biologist, Otto Loewi, whose problem was the mode of action of nerve fibres on the heart. In these experiments, as Fig. 4.4 shows, the heart and attached nerves (Fig. 4.4a) were taken out of the frog's body, a glass tube put into the heart, and the heart filled with a salt solution through this tube (Fig. 4.4b). This salt solution supplied inorganic ions needed for the continued spontaneous beating. Loewi dreamed that he was stimulating the nerve known as the "vagus" (Fig. 4.4c) and the heart, as usually occurs when this nerve is stimulated, slowed its beat, recorded by a lever writing on a smoked drum (Fig. 4.4d). In his dream, however, he now took the fluid from the beating heart and kept it, replacing it with fresh fluid. When the heart had recovered its normal rate of beat, the fresh fluid was replaced with the saved fluid nearby. The heart slowed again. Clearly the stimulation of the nerve had liberated something into the bathing fluid which could slow the heart. Loewi awoke in the middle of the night and made some notes of the experiment which the next morning proved illegible. On the next night he had the same dream; this time he arose (at 3 a.m.) and tried the experiment, which went just as in his dream (Dale, 1963).

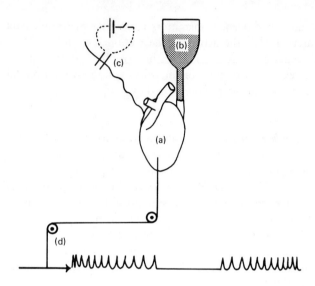

Fig. 4.4 Loewi's experiment. An isolated frog heart (a) is shown with its attached right vagus nerve (c). The heart is perfused with a salt solution (b). A lever and pulley system records the heart contractions on a smoked drum (d). The record in (d) illustrates the effects of stimulating the vagus nerve. The contractions of the heart come at increasingly longer intervals and finally stop, but they resume after stimulation stops.

Both stories are famous because great advances in knowledge flowed from the experimental insights arising from them. I can testify that not all such dreams are as important, and not all such dream experiments work as predicted! Still, the idea of mental activity during sleep is well documented and was a great block to the idea of a link between brain activity and mental activity in the days when the brain was thought to be inactive during sleep.

Judge the excitement, then, when it was reported that subjects awakened from REM sleep often reported that they had been dreaming (Aserinsky and Kleitman, 1955; Dement and Kleitman, 1957b). Apparently we all dream although we do not recall our dreams. It appears possible to improve recall. One technique is to practice writing down what you remember when you first wake up. As Fig. 4.2 shows, we nearly always awake from REM sleep.

It is attractive to suppose that the eye movements, limb twitches, and penile erections, together with the alternations of pulse and blood pressure and respiration which occur during REM state of sleep (see Question 4.4), are associated with the acting out of dreams. There is some evidence for this view (reviewed by Dement, 1967) largely drawn from correlation of the content of dreams and the observed signs. Dreams of course may be distressing and it is perhaps significant that angina pectoris, the pain associated with insufficient blood supply to the heart, may also occur at this time (Nowlin *et al.,* 1965) while sufferers from duodenal ulcer (Armstrong *et al.,* 1965) and migraine (Dexter and Weitzman, 1970), but not asthma (Kales *et al.,* 1968), tend to have exacerbations of their symptoms during periods of REM sleep. It has even been suggested that the direction and amplitude of the eye movements during REM sleep are correlated with dream content as reported by awakened sleepers. Careful testing, however, indicates this view is probably not sound (Moskowitz and Berger, 1969).

Mental activity also goes on during SW sleep. About 20 per cent of subjects awaking from this state say they have been "thinking" or even deny being asleep. Evidently the mental activity in this state is akin to everyday mental activity and lacks the hallucinatory aspect of dreaming. Incidentally, sufferers from nightmares and bedwetters awake from SW sleep, and sleepwalkers are in this stage of sleep (Broughton, 1968).

Learning during sleep. Since mental activity occurs during sleep it is natural to ask whether it is possible to influence this activity by external stimuli. It has been found that even during deep sleep (stage 4) subjects will show EEG signs of awakening if they hear sounds which are meaningful for them, e.g., if a mother hears her babies or a man hears his wife's name (Oswald, 1962).

The question can be taken further by investigating whether learning of not so significant material can be achieved during sleep. Some mail order firms supply "sleep-learning kits." Usually this consists of a pillow speaker, tape recorder, and a supply of tapes containing the material to be learned. Great benefits are promised if the subject will play the tape and go to sleep while it is still playing. It is suggested that much of what is heard will be remembered (sleep learning or hypnopedia). Research into the stage of sleep during which learning is possible indicates that only when the EEG shows alpha waves, i.e., stage 1 (Fig. 4.2), does learning occur. There is no good evidence for sleep learning when the EEG record shows slow waves or REM (Emmons and Simon, 1956; Simon and Emmons, 1956; Bruce *et al.,* 1970). It is possible that material presented during stage 1 sleep is remembered better than material presented at other times because of the sleep which follows (see Question 4.5).

IV. WHY SLEEP?

No sensible person needs to be persuaded of the need for sleep. In fact, sleep is a well-recognized treatment for sufferers from psychotic disorders and more recently coronary thrombosis. It could be asked however, "Can we do without one or the other of the two sleep components?" It appears that both SW and REM are needed, for people and animals deprived of one or the other for long periods tend to partially make up the loss in subsequent sleep periods. Analyzing many such experiments, Jouvet (1972) calculates that the duration of SW sleep is proportional to the logarithm of the duration of waking, while the duration of REM sleep is directly proportional to the duration of waking. There is some evidence that stage 4 of SW sleep, when people are hardest to awaken, is the most beneficial part of SW sleep (see Question 4.6). We all know people who sleep less than the average without ill effect. Indeed, two Australians have been described who are apparently quite healthy despite regularly taking only three hours of sleep in twenty-four. It appears that such people go into SW sleep rapidly and alternate between stage 4 SW and REM sleep without spending much time in the lighter states of SW sleep (Jones and Oswald, 1968).

Nothing definite is known about the functions of SW sleep despite the fact that it appears vital to life. Presumably it has a restorative function. This old idea has recently received some support from the finding that the amount of growth hormone in human plasma reaches a peak during the first period of SW sleep of a night. Smaller peaks may occur during later deep SW sleep phases. Growth hormone is important in building up body proteins, so this new evidence suggests repair is actually going on (Takahashi et al., 1968; Sassin et al., 1969).

The function of REM sleep is equally obscure (see Question 4.3). REM sleep is not vital to life. Dement (1960) selectively deprived men of REM sleep by awaking them immediately after the EEG signs were detected. An increase in attempts at REM sleep and an increase in the time spent in REM sleep on later undisturbed nights were the only significant changes. It has been possible to deprive animals, such as cats, of REM sleep for much longer periods than was possible in human studies. Cats or rats avoid cold water and remain either standing or crouched when placed on a small space such as the top of a bucket (the island) surrounded by water (Vimont et al., 1966). During the REM state the neck muscles relax completely and the animal's head begins to fall. It can be arranged that when the head falls, it will touch water. Touching the water wakes the animal and stops the REM sleep. The animals rapidly acquire a conditioned reflex so that they wake up as soon as their neck begins to drop.

Cats deprived of REM sleep for seventy days showed an enhancement of motivational behavior, in particular their sex drive. Male cats persisted in trying to mount other male cats. Upon recovery from REM deprivation this abnormal behavior disappeared. Interestingly, this hypersexuality could be brought on much more rapidly if the animals were deprived of phasic activity by being awakened whenever spikes appeared in the EEG record from the lateral geniculate. This finding suggests that deprivation of phasic rather than tonic events is the important effect of REM sleep deprivation (Vimont et al., 1966). There is some suggestion that deprivation of REM sleep increases the excitability of the nervous system; the threshold for electroshock seizures is lowered for instance (Cohen and Dement, 1965).

The evidence that our brain is replaying distressing events (as dreams) during REM sleep has been mentioned and there is of course evidence that this may be creative and enable better integration of our personalities. Indeed it is found that the more extreme the intellectual retardation of mental patients the less time they spend in REM sleep (Feinberg, 1968). Conversely, as people with brain damage gradually recover, the proportion of time they spend in REM sleep increases (Greenberg and Dewan, 1969).

Such an explanation is not completely satisfactory because we cannot be sure that animals such as monkeys or cats dream, although it is said that cats purr during REM sleep. Moreover, dreaming cannot be the only function of REM sleep, for signs of REM sleep occur in decorticate men and other animals (Jouvet, 1967).

A plausible hypothesis is that brain activity in REM sleep has a function in brain maturation (Roffwarg et al., 1966). It has been known for many years that human and animal brains are not fully developed at birth but go on growing and developing appropriate connections for some time afterward. Recently it has been found that while the potentiality for full development is present (in the genes), its expression demands appropriate activity in the brain pathways. Brain activity during REM sleep might be important in this regard and it is certainly true that babies spend more time in REM sleep than adults.

A particular application of the maturation theory has been put forward by Berger (1969), who suggests that the chief function of REM sleep in infants is the establishment of conjugate eye movements. This is the mechanism by which both eyes are moved together (conjugate movement) and focused on the same spot. There is experimental evidence that this ability deteriorates in a few hours if the eyes are closed (Wallach and Karsh, 1963). It is natural to suppose therefore that eye movement in REM sleep prevents this loss of function and indeed it has been found that depth perception is better when a subject wakes in the morning than it was when tested before he went to bed. In this connection, it is of some interest that eye movements in REM sleep in infants are conjugate while their eye movements during wakefulness are partly uncoordinated (Prechtl et al., 1967).

Men who are congenitally blind, or have been blind for thirty years or so, do not have rapid eye movements during sleep although they show the other signs of REM sleep (Berger et al., 1962). Berger suggests that it is an indication of the disuse of the mechanism when it is no longer needed.

V. VISIONS

The normal conditions of life of most Western students are not appropriate for inducing visions. We are not half starved or toxic with sores, nor do we fast every year in Lent as our ancestors did. We may have experienced the delirium of fever but the visions of starvation are fortunately not our lot. These sorts of visions arise because of disturbance of brain function. The content of a vision is of course unique, for each of us has laid down, in his or her brain, a unique record. Deprivation of sensory stimulation is another way of disturbing brain function. It was noted previously (Section II-B, this chapter) that men in a featureless, noiseless room felt sleepy and were prone to hallucinations (Lilly, 1956; Heron, 1961).

Many other ways of affecting brain function are known. Most of these will lead to the seeing of visions if the period between the onset of the effect and unconsciousness is sufficiently prolonged. For instance, a blow on the head will produce some disturbance of consciousness, the seeing of stars, etc., before one lapses into unconsciousness. Other ways of becoming unconscious are less painful and take longer so that one has time to appreciate the disorder of consciousness. For instance, as doctors know, volatile anesthetics like ether or nitrous oxide bring about a state of excitability before any loss of consciousness. In the late nineteenth century, ether parties were common in England and indeed they are still common in South America. People sit around sniffing ether, which apparently gives them an intense euphoric sensation. A normally phlegmatic friend told me that on one of these occasions the main effect he noticed was that he felt himself grinning but could not stop. Glue and gasoline sniffing are other ways of producing disturbances of consciousness. What is happening is that the integrity of the brain is being disturbed; part of the brain is being disabled by whatever agent we are using. Some of these agents, it may be remarked, are extremely toxic. Glue sniffing, for instance, will lead to death of brain cells very quickly. Other agents, such as alcohol and hallucinogenic drugs, are not so immediately toxic. Each particular drug then which causes disturbances of consciousness will, if taken in large enough doses, cause loss of consciousness.

In Eastern countries, the way to see visions has not been through deprivation, disease, or brain damage but through the use of drugs, known from time immemorial, such as hashish. Today, in its weaker form (marihuana), hashish, it seems, is known and available to every high school student. Chemists have synthesized drugs more powerful than hashish, for instance, lysergic acid diethylamide (LSD). Visions of heaven and hell are now available cheaply to every man and no longer the privilege of seers and mystics. As one writer on the effect of these drugs has said (Cohen, 1965), "the drugs allow unusual manifestations of human mental function which are ordinarily inaccessible. The ability to produce them chemically clarifies some obscure and puzzling experiences found in the religious, historical, and mystical literature."

The different types of experiences produced by taking different drugs arise because each drug has an affinity for certain groups of nerve cells. Ideally it should be possible to associate the drug experience with the site of drug action and the function of the affected nerve cells. This position is being approached currently with many drugs and will be illustrated for marihuana and LSD.

A. Marihuana

The source of marihuana is a tall annual weed, *Cannabis sativa*, which sometimes reaches a height of fifteen feet. It will grow in almost any waste or fertile area over a wide climatic range. There are both male and female plants, the male being taller than the female. Differentiation of the two sexes is important because the chemical compound responsible for the euphoric effect of marihuana is found primarily in a sticky golden yellow resin with a minty fragrance that covers the female flowers and adjacent leaves (Farnsworth, 1968). Hashish is made from this resin. It is taken by mouth. The product used in the Western world (marihuana) is contaminated with considerable leaf material which makes it much weaker. It is usually smoked. Cigarettes containing marihuana are referred to as "reefers," "muggers," "greeters," or "gates." Because much of marihuana comes in across the border from Mexico, it is often referred to as "Acapulco gold" by its users. A number of pharmacologically active compounds have been isolated from the resin of *Cannabis* (Gill *et al.,* 1970), $\triangle^9$-tetrahydrocannabinol ($\triangle^9$THC, Fig. 4.5a), is the major active euphoric principle in *C. sativa* resin (Isbell *et al.,* 1967; Mechoulam, 1970).

$\triangle^9$THC is three times as effective smoked as it is swallowed. Threshold doses of 2 mg smoked and 5 mg taken orally produced euphoria. Marked changes in body image, disorders of time sense, and hallucinations occurred with 15 mg smoked or 25 mg orally ingested marihuana (Isbell *et al.,* 1967). Some somatic signs can be detected, most prominently an increase in pulse rate (Renault *et al.,* 1971) and reddening of the conjunctivae. Dryness of the mouth and throat also appears a constant symptom, but pupil size does not increase (Weil *et al.,* 1968).

The effects of marihuana are thus largely private to the user (see Question 4.7), and presumably because of the small amounts of the active principle in some

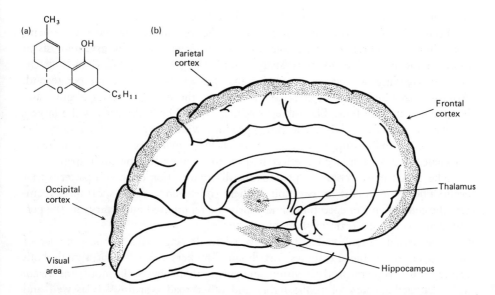

Fig. 4.5 The active principle of marihuana ($\triangle^9$-tetrahydrocannabinol, a) is shown together with the brain areas (b, stippled) in which it is localized 15 minutes after injection. (Based on the account of McIsaac, *et al., Nature 230,* 593–594, 1971.)

cigarettes, rather variable. Reports of feelings of detachment, floating, a mild euphoria, and an enhancement of visual and auditory perception are common. Visual images are bright and outlines stand separately apart. Thoughts appear more lucid. These changes begin about fifteen minutes after smoking begins, peak at about three hours and may last up to twelve hours.

Certain deficiencies in marihuana smokers have been detected in experimental situations (see Question 4.8). For instance, experienced marihuana users commonly report a difficulty in talking to others when "high." Apparently they feel they may not be making sense and they report they are forgetting what the other person is saying and may be saying crazy things. Very few nonusers, however, can actually detect any difficulty in a user's speech. Here is a description of the phenomenon from a twenty-five-year-old male lawyer (Weil and Zinberg, 1969):

> I very much agree with the idea that marihuana does something to memory when you're trying to talk normally. For one thing, I've noticed that conversations in groups where everyone has been smoking marihuana are peculiar in a specific way that supports this hypothesis. Very often, the last statement made by a member of the group is totally ignored, as if everyone has just forgotten it, and the next remark refers to something said a minute or so earlier—also I found myself that if I am distracted or interrupted in any way while talking when I am high, I forget what I was saying and have to wait a minute or so in order to get it back. Most people I know have had the same experience.

The interference reported seems to be with short-term memory.

Both direct and indirect evidence supports the conclusion that short-term memory is impaired. Direct evidence comes from experiments used by psychologists to examine the immediate memory span (Tinklenberg et al., 1970). Such tests involve the reading of series of random digits at the steady rate of one per second. After each reading the subject is asked to repeat the list. The series is gradually lengthened until he fails. The subject's span (forward or backward) is the largest number of digits that he or she can reproduce without error on two successive trials. For normal adults it is seven. Subjects who took any dose of marihuana sufficient to cause a subjective effect had an impairment of the digit span.

The deficit may account in part for the disorganization of speech patterns that occurs under marihuana intoxication. If there is deficiency in the short-term memory, the components of speech become poorly interconnected and over time the person is apt to lose his train of thought.

Considerable attention has been devoted to driving skills in the presence of marihuana. As Table 4.1 shows, marihuana smokers missed light signals both central and peripheral to their vision, suggesting that they would not be as aware as undrugged persons of traffic lights and other road warnings (Casswell and Marks, 1973).

In other studies, the effects of marihuana on driver performance have been

TABLE 4.1

Mean number of signals missed following cannabis administration for naive and experienced subjects.

Δ9-THC (mg)	Mean no. of misses, center light signal		Mean no. of misses, peripheral light signal	
	Naive	Experienced	Naive	Experienced
0	1.6	2.4	6.1	5.0
3.3	4.3	6.2	9.0	9.1
6.6	8.1	7.4	13.7	9.3
F values	9.25		4.19	
P values	<0.001		<0.01	

The results were tested using two-way analysis of variance. F values are for drug-level effect. Between groups effects were nonsignificant for both central and peripheral signals. (With permission from Casswell and Marks, *Nature (London)*, *241*, 60–61, 1973.)

examined in experienced smokers (Crancer *et al.,* 1969). Subjects experiencing a marihuana "high" made substantially more speedometer errors than under control conditions, but there were no significant differences in accelerator, brake, signals, steering, and total errors. Impairment in this simulated driving did not seem to be a function of increased marihuana dosage or inexperience with the drug. Marihuana users of course often report alterations of time and space perception and presumably this leads to an altered sense of speed which generally results in driving more slowly (see Question 4.9).

Studies in which a radioactive label was chemically attached to the active principle (Fig. 4.5a) show that marihuana is preferentially concentrated in specific brain areas (Fig. 4.5b). The labelled compound was given to monkeys by intravenous injection. The animals were then killed at various later times. When their brains were examined for radioactivity, it was found that within fifteen minutes after injection there was a high concentration of radioactivity in the cerebral cortex. The areas particularly affected were the frontal, parietal, and occipital cortex, including the visual area and the lateral and medial geniculate nuclei of the thalamus (Fig. 4.5b). The hippocampal nuclei were also well labelled. The experimenters (McIsaac *et al.,* 1971) noticed that at the time the geniculate area had a high level of radioactivity, other animals not yet sacrificed showed signs of defects in visual perception, as well as behavior suggestive of hallucination.

The accumulations in the cortex and hippocampus seem unique effects of marihuana. The neurons of the hippocampus are involved in recall of recent events (Chapter 3) while neurons of the frontal cortex are possibly involved in evaluation of the effects of one's actions (Chapter 2). Simultaneous defects in function of these two areas could then account for the time distortion reported by marihuana takers.

B. Lysergic acid diethylamide (LSD)

This compound (Fig. 4.3) is the prototype synthetic hallucinogen. Patients tolerant to LSD are not cross-tolerant to $\triangle^9$THC, indicating the two drugs act at different sites (Isbell and Tasinski, 1969). LSD was discovered by a Swiss chemist, Albert Hofman, in 1943, while investigating substances analogous to mescaline, the most active substance in the plant hallucinogen, peyote. He later wrote of the strange experience which led him to its discovery (Hofman, 1968, pp. 184–186). It appears that one Friday afternoon, as well as experiencing a lack of concentration which afflicts most of us at that time, he felt giddy and, more alarming, noticed that the shape of his laboratory assistants kept changing. Naturally enough he went home to bed, but instead of sleep he experienced fantastic dreams of intense color. Like a good Swiss, however, he recovered in time for dinner. Next day he awoke feeling tired but otherwise normal. Returning to the laboratory, he looked at the substance he had been synthesizing and decided he must have absorbed through his skin a small amount of a substance entered in his lab book as "LSD-25," an abbreviation for lysergic acid diethylamide, plus the date. He therefore took by mouth 0.25 mg, which he supposed to be a minimally small dose. He did not know the substance was a thousand times stronger than mescaline (160 times stronger than marihuana, Isbell and Jasinski, 1969), and he had actually taken several times the maximum dose. Before long he felt extreme sensations of unease, felt he was two people (depersonalization), had a pronounced disruption of his time sense, and was beset by strange visions. He was driven home where a series of fantastic hallucinations beset him, with some nausea. He felt sure that he had gone out of his mind, and that he would never be able to report his discovery. To his surprise, however, he was his usual self the next day.

It is now known that the minimal effective dose in humans is about 20 μg, that is, as small as 0.5 μg/kg, and the first effects occur within forty minutes (Hofman, 1968). The initial effects are not psychic but somatic—indicative of autonomic nervous system stimulation. Dilation of pupils, a slight increase in pulse rate, and rise in blood pressure occur, as well as a rise in blood sugar. Less commonly there is a parasympathetic stimulation indicated by salivation, nausea, and, rarely, vomiting. These effects fade as the psychic changes occur. The sequence of psychic events following usual doses of LSD can be summarized by saying that during the first four and a half hours there is an internal TV show marked by shifts of bodily sensations and perceptions. This is followed by another four to five hour period in which the subjective sense of change is less marked; many subjects feel detached and have the conviction that they are magically in control of the world or that the eyes of the world are upon them. After twelve to twenty-four hours there may be some let-down and slight fatigue. There is no craving to relieve this and no true physiological withdrawal. The LSD state has been much described and appears to be a multipotential state in the sense that a variety of outcomes are possible. These include inspirational insights, psychoses, exalted states, and perhaps behavioral or value changes, which have led to its therapeutic use by some psychiatrists.

Marked changes in the quality of visual and auditory perceptions are usually reported. For instance, Jane Dunlap (1961, pp. 152 and 155) listened to music under the influence of LSD and reported:

> I noticed that the familiar *Second Symphony* of Brahms then being played had taken on exaggerated and overwhelming beauty. Soon the music seemed to lift me with infinite tenderness into the air where I floated bodiless and weightless, moving gently in rhythm and rising and falling with each crescendo and diminuendo.

> Never before had I been so aware of every component of sound or the magnificence of the whole. As visions shifted continuously with breath-taking speed and thoughts pelted my brain, the music constantly filled me with a sort of exploding force impossible to describe. At the same time it was the stabilizing influence which maintained my sanity as wave after wave of soul-shattering emotions engulfed me.

LSD has long been known to block effects of a potent chemical, serotonin, upon smooth muscle. This discovery (Amin *et al.*, 1954), at first a pharmacological curiosity, now seems relevant to the mind-changing effects of LSD (see Question 4.10). Most, if not all, of the serotonin of the brain is contained in the somata and processes of the cells of the raphe in the brainstem (Fig. 4.3) which is important in the control of slow-wave sleep. If cells in the raphe are destroyed, virtually all the serotonin disappears in areas of the forebrain quite distinct from where the lesions are placed. Presumably this is because processes of the destroyed raphe cells once projected to the forebrain. In the presence of LSD the amount of serotonin in the raphe cells is increased (Rosecrans *et al.*, 1967). There are many possible mechanisms that could account for this LSD-induced change in serotonin metabolism. One explanation, for which there is evidence, is that LSD alters the rate of firing of raphe neurons. Cells in the cat dorsal raphe nucleus are spontaneously active. Minute doses of LSD (e.g. 10–20 μg/kg) given intravenously can slow or even stop the firing of these cells, the effects lasting for ten minutes after a single injection (Aghajanian *et al.*, 1968, 1970).

Most of the effects of LSD can be accounted for in terms of its action in the brainstem (presumably on the raphe nucleus). These areas can be compared to the boss's secretary in a big business. Unimportant to the outside world, not particularly well paid, she is the barrier which must be passed before the boss can be influenced. The brainstem particularly is the secretary to the boss cortex. Normally, like a secretary, the brainstem acts as a filter, scanner and blocker, in this case of the stream of information coming from all over the body to the brain. This is the process of selective attention and is also operative in sleep. LSD disrupts this system, as Seymour Kety (1970, p. 114), a well-known researcher into this system has reported:

> Abnormal phenomena emerge as an excessive increase in the span of awareness and the profiles of sensory events are also altered so that insignificant things become enormously significant and pregnant with inexpressible depths of meaning. The proprioceptive sensory input is no longer scanned and filtered properly and strange alien feelings in the body may arise together with many complex sensory disturbances that may be due to similar vestibular disturbances. Creative artists and mathematicians as well as students of Yoga have developed means of slipping in and out of these states.

Spiders as well as men show behavior disorders after taking LSD. The LSD-treated spider makes a characteristically abnormal web (Witt *et al.,* 1968).

Not much is known about changes produced by chronic LSD ingestion. One very peculiar finding which appears to be significant is that the threshold for hearing is definitely lower in chronic LSD takers than in nondrugged controlled subjects. No significant changes are found in taste and smell thresholds. Furthermore, the threshold for auditory discomfort is higher than normal in the LSD takers so that people commonly taking LSD have more acute hearing yet can tolerate louder sounds (Meyer 1969, p. 15).

Chromosome breakage after taking LSD has received considerable publicity. Theoretically, such breakages, if they occurred in the germ cells, could lead to conception of individuals with mutations of a harmful sort. Most of these would presumably abort spontaneously, but others might survive with crippling deformities. There is also an association between excessive chromosome breakage (such as occurs after radiation damage) and leukemia, and this possibility would arise for individuals with broken chromosomes rather than for their offspring.

Some caution is needed however in interpreting the importance of chromosome breakage. After the report that adding LSD to cultures of blood cells in a test tube markedly increased the number of such cells with broken or deformed chromosomes (Cohen *et al.,* 1967) and that LSD users had chromosome abnormalities in their white blood cells (Irwin and Egozcue, 1967), it was found that people with virus diseases, such as influenza, had transitory episodes of chromosome breakages in their blood cells (Meyer, 1969, p. 37). This cast doubt on the importance of chromosomal breakage per se. Support, however, was given by experiments in which a single dose of 5.0 μg/kg LSD was given to female rats on the fourth day of pregnancy. This dose produced abortions or stillbirths in three of five rats (Alexander *et al.,* 1967). A much smaller dose (0.08 μg/kg) was given to hamsters on the eighth day of pregnancy, and the embryos were examined on the twelfth day. While controls (saline injected) showed no major congenital abnormalities, of 105 LSD treated animals 7 per cent had a dead foetus, 7 per cent had a foetus with gross abnormalities, 8 per cent had resorbed their foetus, and 7 per cent had runts (Geber, 1967). Similar effects were reported in mice embryos (Auerbach and Rugowski, 1967) after their mother was injected with LSD. Human LSD-taking has been going on now for some twenty years and recently there has been some evidence of an increased incidence of congenital defects in the babies of LSD and marihuana users (reviewed in Maugh, 1973).

VI. MENTAL DISORDERS FOLLOWING DRUG-TAKING

Beside the pleasant and/or exciting effects of hallucinogens must be set a variety of unpleasant effects which depend on the drug, the dose, and the setting. All hallucinogens, if taken in high enough dosage, will affect motor and cognitive function, the exact dosage of course varying from person to person. In general, for marihuana a performance impairment is found for doses above 15–30mg taken orally or 4–10 mg smoked.

A potent drug such as LSD is more likely to give rise to unpleasant consequences. Freedman (1967, 1970) has distinguished six chief hazards:

1. The "bad trip" is a panic state occurring during the 8 to 14 hours of drug experience. It is easy to understand how such a panic can arise, for normally we are not surprised by what we see and we feel in control of our affairs. In the drug state, our perceptions are more than surprising—they are alarming, strange, and therefore threatening. The drug taker feels a lack of any ability to regulate this flood of new experiences. Indeed he or she seems to be a passive observer in an actively encroaching world. In such circumstances a "split" in the stream of consciousness is common. There are then, it seems, two selves—a passive observer and an active participator. Many young people sometimes have this type of sensation without drugs. Indeed, a double self is a common phenomenon of early adult life and can be achieved easily.

2. Confusion which can be mild or severe may occur during the drug state and may be followed by depression when the normal world is found to be not so stimulating as the drug state.

3. Paranoid states may occur during a bad trip or soon afterward because of the divorce from reality which occurs.

4. Psychosis may be precipitated. Indeed LSD was used to induce what were thought to be models of schizophrenia. People with preexistent personality disorders are more prone to development of a psychosis following ingestion.

5. Even a good trip may be followed by bad consequences—usually a dropping out of society and loss of will or desire to get on with the business of life. Victims of this syndrome are found to be persisting in the magical thinking of the drug state.

6. Recurrent states (flashbacks) occur in which the drug user feels as if he were back in the drug state *without* taking the drug. The cause is at present unknown.

VII. STATE-DEPENDENT LEARNING

Animals trained in a drugged state may remember their training better if tested in a comparable drugged state than in a nondrugged state. Similarly, learning acquired in a nondrugged state transfers better to the same state than to a drugged state. These effects have been demonstrated with sedatives such as barbiturates, alcohol, and marihuana as well (Overton, 1964, 1966; Goodwin et al., 1969; Hill et al., 1973). All these agents were expected to impair performance of learned responses. However, the observation that performances were actually improved in a drugged state, provided learning was in the same state, suggests that learning is state-dependent; that is, it depends, for optimal expression, on restoration of the original condition in which learning was acquired. In a recent investigation of this effect in man, forty-eight medical students participated in a rote memory task (Goodwin et al., 1969). Their learning was much better when the subjects were intoxicated with alcohol during both the initial and the recall session than when they were intoxicated only during the learning sessions. It is well known that alcoholics report hiding liquor or money while drinking with no recall of the event when sober. If intoxicated again they can go straight to the place.

It may be deduced that the "stoned" student will not do so well when he sobers up for examination. Nor, if he stays "stoned," is he likely to do well either; he may remember the material well enough, but with an inability to maintain a train of thought and a deficient time sense, he would be gravely handicapped.

The memory deficit associated with the change of state probably reflects impairment of retrieval rather than difficulty in registering and retaining the material; a subject who learns material while intoxicated and has difficulty recalling it when sober can be shown to differ from a subject who has never learned the material. This can be determined in tests in which the subject is retrained to some set criterion, for example, 90 per cent correct. Subjects who learned material while intoxicated take fewer trials to reach criterion than do completely naive subjects (Goodwin et al., 1969).

The phenomenon of state-dependence should be kept in mind when evaluating reports that some drug or other affects learning (Chapter 3). Clearly, if the subject was tested in the nondrugged state and then again when drugged, any effect of the drug on learning may be confounded with the state-dependent changes.

REFERENCES

Aghajanian, G. K., W. E. Foote, and M. H. Sheard (1968) Lysergic acid diethylamide: sensitive neuronal units in the midbrain raphe. Science, 161, 706–708.

Aghajanian, G. K., A. W. Graham, and M. H. Sheard (1970) Serotonin-containing neurons in brain: depression of firing by monamine oxidase inhibitors. Science, 169, 1100–1102.

Alekseyeva, T. T. (1958) Correlation of nervous and humoral factors in the development of sleep in nondisjointed twins (in Russian), *Zh. Vyssh. Nerv. Deyat. Pavlova 8*, 835–844.

Alèma, G., L. Perria, G. Rosadini, G. F. Rossi, and J. Zattoni (1966) Functional inactivation of the human brainstem related to the level of consciousness. *J. Neurosurg. 24*, 629–639.

Alexander, G. J., E. B. Miles, R. B. Alexander, and G. M. Gold (1967) LSD: injection early in pregnancy produces abnormalities in offspring of rats. *Science, 157*, 459–460.

Amin, A. H., T. B. B. Crawford, and J. H. Gaddum (1954) The distribution of substance P and 5-hydroxytryptamine in the central nervous system of the dog. *J. Physiol. 126*, 596–618.

Armstrong, R. H., D. Burnap, A. Jacobson, A. Kales, S. Ward, and J. Golden (1965) Dreams and gastric secretion in duodenal ulcer patients. *New Physician 14*, 241–243.

Aserinsky, E. and N. Kleitman (1955) Two types of ocular motility occurring in sleep. *J. appl. Physiol. 8*, 1–10.

Auerbach, R. and J. A. Rugowski (1967) Lysergic acid diethylamide: effect on embryos. *Science, 157*, 1325–1326.

Berger, R. J. (1969) Oculomotor control: a possible function of REM sleep. *Psychol. Rev. 76*, 144–164.

Berger, R. J., P. Olley, and I. Oswald (1962) The EEG, eye movements and dreams of the blind. *Q. J. Exptl. Psychol. 14*, 183–186.

Bremer, F. (1935) *Cerveau "isolé" et physiologie du sommeil. C. R. Soc. Biol.* (Paris) *118*, 1235–1241.

Broughton, R. J. (1968) Sleep disorders: disorders of arousal? *Science, 159*, 1070–1078.

Bruce, D. J., C. R. Evans, P. B. C. Fenwick, and V. Spencer (1970) Effect of presenting novel verbal material during slow-wave sleep. *Nature* (London), *225*, 873–874.

Casswell, S. and D. Marks (1973) Cannabis-induced impairment of performance of a divided attention task. *Nature* (London), *241*, 60–61.

Cohen, H. B. and W. C. Dement (1965) Sleep: changes in threshold to electroconvulsive shock in rats after deprivation of "paradoxical" phase. *Science, 150*, 1318–1319.

Cohen, M. M., M. J. Marmello and N. Back (1967) Chromosomal damage in human leukocytes induced by lysergic acid diethylamide. *Science, 155*, 1417–1419.

Cohen, S. (1965) *Drugs of Hallucination,* p. 125, Granada Publishing Corp.

Crancer, A., Jr., J. M. Dille, J. C. Delay, J. E. Wallace, and M. D. Haykin (1969) Comparison of the effects of marihuana and alcohol on simulated driving performance. *Science, 164*, 851–854.

Dale, H. H. (1963) In memoriam Otto Loewi, *Ergebnisse der Physiol. 52*, 1–19.

Dement, W. (1958) The occurrence of low voltage, fast, electroencephalogram patterns during behavioral sleep in the cat. *Electroenceph. clin. Neurophysiol. 10*, 291–296.

Dement, W. (1960) The effect of dream deprivation. *Science, 131*, 1705–1707.

Dement, W. (1967) Possible physiological determinants of a possible dream intensity cycle. *Exp. Neurol. 19*, supp. 4, 38–55.

Dement, W. and N. Kleitman (1957a) Cyclic variations in EEG during sleep and their relation to eye movements, bodily motility, and dreaming. *Electroenceph. clin. Neurophysiol. 9*, 673–690.

Dement, W. and N. Kleitman (1957b) The relation of eye movements during sleep to dream activity: an objective method for the study of dreaming. *J. Exp. Psychol. 53*, 339–346.

Dexter, J. D. and E. D. Weitzman (1970) The relationship of nocturnal headaches to sleep stage patterns. *Neurology 20*, 513–518.

Dunlap, J. (1961) *Exploring Inner Space*. Victor Gollancz, Ltd., London.

Emmons, H. and C. W. Simon (1956) The non-recall of material presented during sleep. *Amer. J. Psychol. 69*, 76–81.

Evans, J. I., A. W. Maclean, A. A. A. Ismail, and D. Love (1971) Concentrations of plasma testosterone in normal men during sleep. *Nature* (London), *229*, 261–262.

Evarts, E. V. (1967) Unit activity in sleep and wakefulness, pp. 545–556, in *The Neurosciences*, G. C. Quarton, T. Melnechuk, F. O. Schmitt, Eds., Rockefeller University Press, N.Y.

Farnsworth, N. R. (1968) Hallucinogenic plants. *Science, 162*, 1086–1092.

Feinberg, I. (1968) Eye movement activity during sleep and intellectual function in mental retardation. *Science, 159*, 1256.

Fencl, V., G. Koski, and J. R. Pappenheimer (1971) Factors in cerebrospinal fluid from goats that affect sleep and activity in rats. *J. Physiol. 216*, 565–589.

Fisher, C., J. Gross, and J. Zuch (1965) Cycle of penile erection synchronous with dreaming (REM) sleep. *Arch. Gen. Psychiat. 12*, 29–45.

Freedman, D. X. (1967) On the use and abuse of LSD. *Arch. Gen. Psychiat. 18*, 330–347.

Freedman, D. X. (1970) Drug dependence and its treatment. *Postgrad. Med. 47*, 150–154.

Geber, W. F. (1967) Congenital malformations induced by mescaline, lysergic acid diethylamide, and bromolysergic acid in the hamster. *Science, 158*, 265–267.

Gill, E. W., W. D. M. Paton, and R. G. Pertwee (1970) Preliminary experiments on the chemistry and pharmacology of *cannabis*. *Nature* (London), *228*, 134–136.

Goodwin, D. W., B. Powell, D. Bremer, H. Hoine, and J. Stern (1969) Alcohol and recall: state-dependent effects in man. *Science, 163*, 1358–1360.

Greenberg, R. and E. M. Dewan (1969) Aphasia and rapid eye movement sleep. *Nature* (London), *223*, 183–184.

Hassler, R. (1961) *Motorische und sensible Effekte umschriebener Reizungen und Auschaltungen im menschlichen Zwischenhirn. Dtsch. Z. Nervenheilk 183,* 148–171.

Hernández-Péon, R., J. J. O'Flaherty, and A. L. Mazzuchelli-O'Flaherty (1965) Modification of tactile-evoked potentials at the spinal trigeminal sensory nucleus during wakefulness and sleep. *Exp. Neurol. 13,* 40–57.

Heron, W. (1961) Cognitive and physiological effects of perceptual isolation, in *Sensory Deprivation,* pp. 6–33, P. Solomon *et al.,* Eds., Harvard University Press, Cambridge, Mass.

Hess, W. R. (1944) *Das Schrafsyndrom als Folge dienzephaler Reizung. Helv. Physiol. Pharmacol. Acta 2,* 305–344.

Hess, W. R. (1954) The diencephalic sleep centre, in *Brain Mechanisms and Consciousness,* pp. 117–136, J. F. Delafreznaye, Ed., Oxford, Blackwell Scientific Publications.

Hill, S. Y., R. Schwin, B. Powell, and D. W. Goodwin (1973) State-dependent effects of marihuana on human memory. *Nature* (London), *243,* 241–242.

Hofman, A. (1968) Psychotomimetic agents; in *Drugs Affecting the Central Nervous System,* Vol. 2, pp. 169–236, A. Burger, Ed., Marcel Dekker, Inc., New York.

Irwin, S. and J. Egozcue (1967) Chomosomal abnormalities in leukocytes from LSD—25 users. *Science, 157,* 313–314.

Isbell, H. and D. R. Jasinski (1969) A comparison of LSD-25 with (-)-Δ^9- Trans-tetrahydrocannabinol (THC) and attempted cross tolerance between LSD and THC. *Psychopharmacologia (Berl). 14,* 115–123.

Isbell, H., C. W. Gorodetsky, D. Jasinski, U. Claussen, F. W. Spulek, and F. Korte (1967) Effects of (-)-Δ^9-trans-tetrahydrocannabinol in man. *Psychopharmacologia (Berl). 11,* 184–188.

Jones, H. S. and I. Oswald (1968) Two cases of healthy insomnia. *Electroenceph. clin. Neurophysiol. 24,* 378–380.

Jouvet, M. (1967a) Neurophysiology of the states of sleep. *Physiol. Rev. 47,* 117–177.

Jouvet, M. (1967b) The states of sleep. *Sci. American, 216*(2), 62–72.

Jouvet, M. (1972) The role of monoamines and acetylcholine-containing neurons in the regulation of the sleep-waking cycle. *Ergebnisse der Physiologie 64,* 166–307.

Jouvet, M. and J. Delorme (1965) *Locus coeruleus et sommeil paradoxal. Compt. Rend. Soc. Biol. 159,* 895–899.

Kales, A., G. D. Beall, C. F. Bagor, A. Jacobson, and J. D. Kales (1968) Sleep studies in asthmatic adults: relationship of attacks to sleep stage and time of night. *J. Allergy 41,* 164–173.

Kety, S. (1950) Circulation and metabolism of the human brain in health and disease. *Am. J. Med. 8,* 205–217.

Kety, S. (1970) In: The model of action of psychotomimetic drugs. *Neuroscience Res. Proc. Bull. 8*(1), 114.

Kleitman, N. and N. Camille (1932) Studies on the physiology of sleep. VI. The behavior of decorticated dogs. *Am. J. Physiol. 100*, 474–480.

Lilly, J. C. (1956) Mental effects of reduction of ordinary levels of physical stimuli on intact healthy persons. *Psychiat. Res. Rep. 5*, 1–9.

Lindsley, D. B., J. W. Bowden, and H. W. Magoun (1949) Effect upon the EEG of acute injury to the brainstem activating system. *Electroenceph. clin. Neurophysiol. 1*, 475–486.

McIsaac, W. M., G. E. Fritchie, J. E. Idanpaan-Heikkila, B. G. Ho, and L. F. Englert (1971) Distribution of marihuana in monkey brain and concomitant behavioural effects. *Nature* (London) *230*, 593–594.

Mandell, M. P., A. J. Mandell, R. T. Rubin, P. Brill, J. Rodnick, R. Sheff, and B. Chaffey (1966) Activation of the pituitary adrenal axis during rapid eye movement sleep in man. *Life Sci. 5*, 583–587.

Mangold, R., L. Solokoff, E. Connor, J. Kleinerman, P. G. Therman, and S. Kety (1955) The effects of sleep and lack of sleep on the cerebral circulation and metabolism of normal young men. *J. Clin. Invest. 34*, 1092–1100.

Maugh, T. H. (1973) LSD and the drug culture: new evidence of hazard. *Science, 179*, 1221–1222.

Mechoulam, R. (1970) Marihuana chemistry. *Science, 168*, 1159–1166.

Meyer, E. (1969) Adverse reactions to hallucinogenic drugs, with background papers. U.S. Dept. of Health, Education and Welfare, *Public Health Services Publication No. 1810.*

Morruzzi, G. (1972) The sleep-waking cycle (i, p. 59; ii, p. 16; iii, p. 83) *Ergebnisse der Physiologie 64*, 1–165.

Morruzzi, G. and H. W. Magoun (1949) Brainstem reticular formation and activation of the EEG. *Electroenceph. clin. Neurophysiol. 1*, 455–474.

Moskowitz, E. and R. J. Berger (1969) Rapid eye movements and dream imagery: are they related? *Nature* (London) *224*, 613–614.

Naquet, R., M. Denavit and D. Albe-Fessard (1966) *Comparison entre le rôle du subthalamus et celui des différentes structures bulbomés-encéphaliques dans le maintien de la vigilance. Electroenceph. clin. Neurophysiol. 20*, 149–164.

Nowlin, J. B., W. G. Troyer, W. S. Collins, G. Silverman, C. R. Nichols, H. D. McIntosh, E. H. Estes, and M. D. Bogdonoff (1965) The association of nocturnal angina pectoris with dreaming. *Ann. Int. Med. 63*, 1040–1046.

Ohmeyer, P. and H. Brilmayer (1947) *Periodische Vorgange im Schlaf. Pfluger Arch. ges. Physiol. 249*, 50–55.

Oswald, I. (1962) *Sleeping and Waking.* Elsevier Publishing Company, New York.

Overton, D. A. (1964) State dependent or "dissociated" learning produced with pentobarbital. *J. comp. Physiol. Psychol. 57*, 3–12.

Overton, D. A. (1966) State-dependent learning produced by depressant and atropine-like drugs. *Psychopharmacologia 10*, 6–31.

Pappenheimer, J. R., R. B. Miller, and C. A. Goodrich (1967) Sleep-promoting effects of cerebrospinal fluid from sleep-derived goats. *Proc. Nat. Acad. Sci.* (U.S.) *58*, 513–517.

Pompeiano, O. (1967) The neurophysiological mechanisms of the postural and motor events during desynchronized sleep. *Proc. Ass. Res. nerv. ment. Dis. 45*, 351–423.

Prechtl, H. F. R. and H. G. Lenard (1967) A study of eye movements in sleeping newborn infants. *Brain Res. 5*, 477–493.

Renault, P. F., C. R. Schuster, R. Heinrich, and D. X. Freedman (1971) Marihuana: standardized smoke administration and dose effect curves on heart rate in humans. *Science, 174*, 589–591.

Roffwarg, H. P., J. N. Muzio, and W. C. Dement (1966) Ontogenetic development of the human sleep-dream cycle. *Science, 152*, 604–619.

Rosecrans, J. A., R. A. Lovell, and D. X. Freedman (1967) Effects of lysergic acid diethylamide on the metabolism of brain 5-hydroxytryptamine. *Biochem. Pharmacol. 16*, 2011–2021.

Rossi, G. F. (1964) Hypothesis on the neural basis of consciousness, consideration based on some experimental work. *Acta Neurochir. 12*, 187–197.

Sassin, J. F., D. C. Parker, J. W. Mace, R. W. Gotlin, L. C. Johnson, and L. G. Rossman (1969) Human growth hormone release; relation to slow-wave sleep and sleep-waking cycles. *Science, 165*, 513–515.

Schoenenberger, G. A., L. B. Cueni, M. Monnier, and A. M. Hatt (1972) Humoral transmission of sleep. VII: Isolation and characterization of the "sleep inducing factor delta." *Pflugers Arch. 338*, 1–17.

Sherrington, C. S. (1940) *Man on His Nature* (i, p. 215, ii, p. 186), Penguin Books, Harmondsworth, Middlesex, England.

Simon, C. W. and H. Emmons (1956c) Responses to material presented during various levels of sleep. *J. Exp. Psychol. 51,* 89–97.

Snyder, F., J. A. Hobson, D. F. Morrison, and F. Goldfrank (1964) Changes in respiration, heart rate, and systolic blood pressure in human sleep. *J. Appl. Physiol. 19*, 417–422.

Takahashi, Y., D. M. Kipnis, and W. H. Daughaday (1968) Growth hormone secretion during sleep. *J. Clin. Invest. 47*, 2079–2090.

Tinklenberg, J. R., F. T. Melges, L. E. Hollister, and H. K. Gillespie (1970) Marijuana and immediate memory. *Nature* (London), *226*, 1171–1172.

Vern, B. A. and J. I. Hubbard (1971) Reinvestigation of the effects of gamma hydroxybutyrate on the sleep cycle of the unrestrained intact cat. *Electroenceph. clin. Neurophysiol. 31*, 573–580.

Vimont-Vicary, P., D. Jouvet-Mounier, and J. F. Delorme (1966) *Effets EEG et comportementaux des privations de sommeil paradoxal chez le chat. Electroenceph. clin. Neurophysiol. 20,* 439–449.

Wallach, H. and E. B. Karsh (1963) Why the modification of stereoscopic depth perception is so rapid. *Am. J. Psychol. 76,* 413–420.

Weil, A. T. and N. E. Zinberg (1969) Acute effects of marihuana on speech. *Nature* (London), *222,* 434–437.

Weil, A. T., N. E. Zinberg, and J. M. Nelsen (1968) Clinical and psychological effects of marihuana in man. *Science, 162,* 1234–1242.

Weizman, E. D., H. Schaumberg, and W. Fishbein (1966) Plasma 17–hydroxy corticosteroid levels during sleep in men. *J. Clin. Endocrinol. 26,* 121–127.

Witt, P. N., C. F. Read, and D. B. Peakall (1968) *A Spider's Web.* Springer-Verlag Inc., Berlin.

SUGGESTED FURTHER READING

Scientific American Reprints

Barron, F., M. E. Jarvic, and S. Bunnel, Jr. *The Hallucinogenic Drugs,* April, 1964, p. 29 (offprint 483).

Brazier, M. A. B. *The Analysis of Brain Waves.* June, 1962, p. 142 (offprint 125).

Grinspoon, L. *Marihuana.* December, 1969, p. 17 (offprint 524).

Jouvet, M. *The States of Sleep.* February, 1967, p. 62 (offprint 504).

Kleitman, N. *Sleep.* November, 1952, p. 34 (offprint 431). See also *Patterns of Dreaming.* November, 1960, p. 58 (offprint 460).

Books

On sleep and dreaming:

Hartman, E. (1967) *The Biology of Dreaming.* Charles C Thomas, Springfield, Illinois.

Kleitman, N. (1963) *Sleep and Wakefulness,* revised edition. University of Chicago Press, Chicago. (A compendium, not an evening's reading).

Nauta, W. J. H. and W. P. Koella (1966) *Sleep, Wakefulness, Dreams, and Memory. Neurosc. Res. Prog. Bull. 4,* 1–103.

Webb, W. B. (1968) *Sleep: An Experimental Approach.* Macmillan, New York.

Webb, W. B. (1973) *Sleep: An Active Process.* Scott, Foresman & Co. Glenview, Illinois.

On hallucinogens:

Cohen, S. (1965) *Drugs of Hallucination.* Secker and Warburg, London.

De Ropp, R. S. (1957) *Drugs and the Mind.* Grove Press, New York.

Huxley, A. *The Doors of Perception*. Also, *Heaven and Hell*. (Both books were originally published separately by Chatto & Windus but have been available in one volume from Penguin since 1959).

Joyce, C. R. B. and S. H. Curry (1970) *The Botany and Chemistry of Cannabis*. (Proceedings of conference organized by The Institute for the Study of Drug Dependence at the Ciba Foundation, 1969.) J. & A. Churchill, London.

Singer, A. J., Ed. (1972) *Marihuana: Chemistry, Pharmacology, and Patterns of Social Use. Annals N.Y. Acad. Sci. 191*, 1–268.

Smythies, J. R. (1970) *The Mode of Action of Psychosomatic Drugs. Neurosciences Res. Prog. Bull. 18*, No. 1.

Solomon, D., Ed. (1966) *The Marihuana Papers*. Granada Publishing Corp., London.

Marihuana and Health. U.S. Government Printing Office (1971). A report to Congress from the Secretary of Health, Education, and Welfare.

QUESTIONS

More advanced students may want to try answering the following questions using the references as a starting point.

On Sleep and Dreaming:

4.1 *Why do we alternate between sleep and wakefulness?*

Chu, N. S. and F. E. Bloom (1973) Norepinephrine containing neurons: changes in spontaneous discharge patterns during sleep and waking. *Science, 179*, 908–910.

Jouvet, M. (1972) The role of monoamines and acetylcholine containing neurons in the regulation of the sleep-waking cycle. *Ergebnisse der Physiologie, 64*, 166–307 (Section V).

Magoun, H. W. (1963) *The Waking Brain*. Charles C Thomas, Springfield, Illinois.

Morruzzi, G. (1972) The sleep-waking cycle. *Ergebnisse der Physiologie, 64*, 1–165. (Section V4).

Schoenberger, G. A., L. B. Cueni, M. Monnier, and A. M. Hatt (1972) Humoral transmission of sleep. VII: Isolation and characterization of the "sleep inducing factor delta." *Pflugers Arch. 338*, 1–17.

4.2 *What is the relationship between slow wave and REM sleep?*

Jouvet, M. (1969) Biogenic amines and the states of sleep. *Science, 163,* 32–41.

Jouvet, M. (1972) The role of monoamines and acetylcholine containing neurons in the regulation of the sleep-waking cycle. *Ergebnisse der Physiologie, 64*, 166–307 (Section IVA).

Wyatt, R. J., T. N. Chase, J. Scott, F. Snyder, and K. Engleman (1970) Effect of L-dopa on the sleep of man. *Nature* (London), *228*, 999–1001.

4.3 *What function does REM sleep serve?*

Allison, T. and H. Van Twyver (1970) Sleep in the moles *Scalopus aquaticus* and *Condylura cristata. Exp. Neurol. 27*, 564–578.

Berger, R. J. (1969) Oculomotor control: a possible function of REM sleep. *Psychol. Rev. 76*, 144–164.

Jouvet, M. (1972) The role of monoamines and acetylcholine containing neurons in the regulation of the sleep waking cycle. *Ergebnisse der Physiologie 64*, 166–307 (Section VIB).

Roffwarg, H., J. Muzio, and W. Dement (1966) The ontogenetic development of the human sleep-dream cycle. *Science, 152*, 604–619.

Tagney, J. (1973) Sleep patterns related to rearing rats in enriched and impoverished environment. *Brain Res. 53*, 353–361.

Tauber, E. S., J. Rojas-Ramirez, and R. Hernández-Peón (1968) Electrophysiological and behavioral correlates of wakefulness and sleep in the lizard *Ctenosaura pectinata. Electroenceph. clin. Neurophysiol. 24*, 424–433.

Wyatt, R., D. Kupfer, J. Scott, D. S. Robinson, and F. Snyder (1969) Longitudinal studies of the effect of monoamine oxidase inhibitors on sleep in man. *Psychopharmacologia 15*, 236–244.

4.4 *When do we dream and why?*

Dement, W. and N. Kleitman (1957a) Cyclic variations in EEG during sleep and their relation to eye movements, bodily motility, and dreaming. *Electroenceph. clin. Neurophysiol. 8*, 673–690.

Dement, W. and N. Kleitman (1957b) The relation of eye movements during sleep to dream activity: an objective method for the study of dreaming. *J. Exp. Psychol. 53*, 339–346.

Dement, W. (1958) The occurrence of low voltage, fast, electroencephalogram patterns during behavioral sleep in the cat. *Electroenceph. Clin. Neurophysiol. 10*, 291–296.

Dement, W. C. (1967) Possible physiological determinants of a possible dream intensity cycle. *Exp. Neurol. 19*, Suppl. 4, 38–55.

Hartman, E. (1967) *The Biology of Dreaming*. Charles C Thomas, Springfield, Illinois.

Jouvet, M. (1972) The role of monoamines and acetylcholine containing neurons in the regulation of the sleep-waking cycle. *Ergebnisse der Physiologie, 64*, 166–307 (Section VIB).

4.5 *Is it possible to learn while sleeping?*

Bruce, D. J. M., C. R. Evans, P. B. C. Fenwick, and V. Spencer (1970) Effect of presenting novel verbal material during slow-wave sleep. *Nature* (London), *225*, 873–874.

Emmons, W. H. and C. W. Simon (1956) The non-recall of material presented during sleep. *Amer. J. Psychol. 69*, 76–81.

Empson, J. A. C. and P. R. F. Clarke (1970) Rapid eye movements and remembering. *Nature* (London), *227*, 287–288.

Fowler, J. M., M. J. Sullivan, and B. R. Ekstrand (1973) Sleep and memory. *Science, 179*, 302–304.

Fox, B. H. and J. S. Robbin (1952) The retention of material presented during sleep. *J. Exp. Psychol. 43*, 75–79.

Lovatt, D. J. and P. Warr (1968) Recall after sleep. *Am. J. Psychol. 81*, 253–257.

Rubin, F., Ed. (1968) *Current Research in Hypnopaedia.* American Elsevier, New York.

Rubin, F. (1971) *Learning and Sleep.* Williams & Wilkins Co., Baltimore.

Simon, C. W. and W. H. Emmons (1956) Responses to material presented during various levels of sleep. *J. Exp. Psychol. 51*, 89–97.

Tani, K. and N. Yoshii (1970) Efficiency of verbal learning during sleep as related to the EEG pattern. *Brain Res. 17*, 277–285.

4.6 *Which sleep stage is more beneficial? How do hypnotic drugs affect sleep stages? What criteria would you use to rate the usefulness of a hypnotic drug?*

Carroll, D., S. A. Lewis, and I. Oswald (1960) Effect of barbiturates on dream content. *Nature* (London), *223*, 865–866.

Kales, A., T. A. Preston, T-L Tan, and C. Allen. (1970) Hypnotics and altered sleep-dream patterns. I: All night EEG studies of glutethimide, methylprylon and pentobarbital. *Arch. Gen. Psychiat. 23*, 211–218.

Kales, A., J. D. Kales, M. B. Scharf, and T-L Tan (1970) Hypnotics and all-night EEG studies of chloral hydrate, flurazepam and methaqualone. *Arch. Gen. Psychiat. 23*, 219–225.

Kales, A., C. Allen, M. B. Scharf, and J. D. Kales (1970) Hypnotic drugs and their effectiveness. All night studies of insomniac subjects. *Arch. Gen. Psychiat. 23*, 226–232.

Matsumoto, J., T. Nishisho, T. Suto, T. Sadahiro, and M. Miyoshi (1968) Influence of fatigue on sleep. *Nature* (London), *218*, 177–178.

Oswald, I. (1973) Drug research and human sleep. *Ann. Rev. Pharmacol. 13*, 243–252.

Webb, W. B. and H. W. Agnew, Jr. (1970) Sleep stage characteristics of long and short sleepers. *Science, 168*, 146–147.

On Hallucinogenic Drugs:

4.7 *"Look, Dad, we found this sticky stuff on a real high plant in the back lot and it had a real funny spider web on it too." In the light of the following references, what did the children find and why did the spider spin an unusual web?*

Farnsworth, N. R. (1968) Hallucinogenic plants. *Science, 162,* 1086–1091.

Mechoulam, R., A. Shani, H. Edery, and Y. Grunfeld (1970) Chemical basis of hashish activity. *Science, 169,* 611–612.

Schultes, R. E. (1969) Hallucinogens of plant origin. *Science, 163,* 245–254.

Witt, P. N., C. R. Reed, and D. B. Peakall (1968) *A Spider's Web.* Springer-Verlag, Inc., New York.

4.8 *Why should one* not *drive under the influence of marihuana?*

Casswell, S. and D. Marks (1973) Cannabis-induced impairment of performance of a divided attention task. *Nature* (London), *241,* 60–61.

Lemberger, L., S. D. Silberstein, J. Axelrod, and I. J. Kopin (1970) Marihuana: studies on the disposition and metabolism of Delta-9 tetrahydrocannabinol in man. *Science, 170,* 1320–1322.

Melges, F. T., J. R. Tinklenberg, L. E. Hollister, and H. K. Gillespie (1970) Marihuana and temporal disintegration. *Science, 168,* 1118–1120.

Tart, C. T. (1970) Marihuana intoxication: common experiences. *Nature* (London), *226,* 701–704.

Tinklenberg, J. R., F. T. Melges, L. E. Hollister, and H. K. Gillespie (1970) Marihuana and immediate memory. *Nature* (London), *226,* 1171–1172.

Zinberg, N. E. and A. T. Weil (1970) A comparison of marijuana users and non-users. *Nature* (London), *226,* 119–123.

4.9 *Compare driving performance in the presence of marihuana and alcohol.*

Crancer, A., J. M. Dille, J. C. Delay, J. E. Wallace, and M. D. Haykin (1969) Comparison of the effects of marihuana and alcohol on simulated driving performance. *Science, 164,* 851–854.

Ng, L. K. Y., F. Lamprecht, R. F. Williams, and I. J. Kopin (1973) Δ9- Tetrahydrocannabinol and ethanol: differential effects on sympathetic activity in differing environmental settings. *Science, 180,* 1368–1369.

Rafaelsen, O. J., P. Beck, J. Christiansen, H. Christup, J. Nyboe and L. Rafaelsen (1973) Cannabis and alcohol: effects on simulated car driving. *Science, 179,* 920–923.

4.10 *Find out what you can about the effects of, and the mechanism of action of, LSD.*

Aghajanian, G. K., W. E. Foote, and M. H. Sheard (1968) Lysergic acid diethylamide: sensitive neuronal units in the midbrain raphe. *Science, 161,* 706–708.

Aghajanian, G. K., A. W. Graham, and M. H. Sheard (1970) Serotonin-containing neurons in the brain: depression of firing by monoamine oxidase inhibitors. *Science, 169,* 1100–1102.

Freedman, D. X. (1969) The psychopharmacology of hallucinogenic agents. *Ann. Rev. Med. 20,* 409–418.

Geber, W. F. (1967) Congenital malformations induced by mescaline, lysergic acid diethylamide, and bromolysergic acid in the hamster. *Science, 158,* 265–267.

Hofmann, A. (1968) Psychotomimetic agents. In *Drugs effecting the central nervous system,* Vol. 2, pp. 169–236, A. Burger, Ed., Marcel Dekker Inc., New York.

Irwin, S. and J. Egozcue (1967) Chromosomal abnormalities in leukocytes from LSD-25 users. *Science, 157,* 313–314.

McKay, J. M., and G. Horn (1971) Effects of LSD on receptive fields of single cells in the lateral geniculate nucleus of the cat. *Nature* (London), *229,* 347–348.

Maugh, T. H. (1973) LSD and the drug culture: new evidence of hazard. *Science, 179,* 1221–1222.

5 BRAIN AND MIND

I. THE BRAIN-MIND LINK

The state of consciousness is difficult to define. Clearly it presupposes knowledge of the external world as this world is created by perception, together with knowledge of the past (memory), with which is bound up learning from experience, and an ability to anticipate the future. Again consciousness is, from our own experience, a variable quantity. It is regularly lost in sleep and is affected by drugs such as alcohol and narcotics. Consciousness also varies through dimensions of growth and development. Clearly the consciousness of a child differs from that of an adult.

Certain aspects of consciousness may give rise to behavior which can be observed and measured. These aspects include:

(a) Self awareness—knowledge of the self as distinct from other selves.

(b) Anticipation of the future—the forward projection of the self in time. Behavior suggesting this aspect of consciousness includes the making and use of tools, the formation of hunting gangs, and ultimately the anticipation of death, the end of all life. Funeral customs and grieving for the dead then are often considered as strong evidence for the presence of a conscious mind.

(c) The possession of ethical values. This includes empathy—sympathy for another based upon the use of the mind to, as it were, put one's self in the place of another and thus understand and share his or her feelings. This quality can be recognized in men by their caring for their fellows in distress and other selfless (altruistic) gestures.

(d) The ability to manipulate abstract ideas.

(e) The ability to pay attention and to shift attention from one object to another.

It can be seen that consciousness, like mind, is a collective term. The variety of abilities and capabilities which compose consciousness can, however, be individually assessed and measured.

In previous chapters the influence of functional and morphological brain changes upon mental phenomena has been described. A man's personality is, among other things, a function of his hormonal balance (Chapter 1) and the integrity of his frontal lobes (Chapter 2). What he perceives is contingent on his ability to pay attention, and both perception and attention in turn depend on nerve impulses acting at brainstem, thalamic and cortical stations (Chapter 2). Circumscribed brain lesions can produce bizarre defects of perception (Chapter 2). Emotional behavior and emotional states can be influenced selectively by lesions of, or stimulation of, the structures on the medial aspects of both hemispheres—the "limbic" lobes (Chapter 2). The ability to recall and remember depends upon the integrity of the temporal lobes of the cortex and the hippocampal neurons contained within these lobes (Chapter 3), while being awake or asleep depends on the activity of brainstem neurons (Chapter 4). Visions are associated with brain disorders (Chapter 4).

These examples of dependence of mental events upon brain structure and function can be classified as examples of psychoneural parallelism. It is generally agreed that this parallelism always exists. Profound problems arise at this point. If mind and body do not have any qualities in common then they cannot interact. As the English philosopher Joad (1943, p. 40) wrote, "A paving stone can crush a butterfly because the butterfly, like itself, possesses mass and substance; but how can it effect a wish?"

Several answers to this problem have been put forward. It has been argued that the problem is not a real one because mental events are states of the nervous system. Globus (1973, p. 1130) formulates one view of this position, which may be termed *monism,* as follows:

> Since the causes of behavior can be ascertained empirically to be states of the nervous system, it can be argued that the postulated mental events which also are held to cause behavior can be identified with states of the nervous system.

Alternatively, it has been argued that the problem is not a real one because material things exist only as the ideas of finite minds constituting the real but immaterial physical world. This position was formulated by the British philosopher Berkeley, part of whose argument has been dealt with in Chapter 2. He postulated that because our seeing, touching, or hearing, etc., result in perceptions dependent on the working of our brains, and therefore at one remove from the objects seen, touched, or heard, we therefore cannot "know" of the existence of material things. Thus far all investigators of the nervous system agree with Berkeley. Berkeley argues further however that material objects do not exist separate from mental constructs. The flavor of Berkeley's thoughts may be gathered from his *Principles of Human Knowledge* (reprinted in Calkins, 1929, pp. 136–37).

> But, say you, surely there is nothing easier than for me to imagine trees, for instance, in a park, or books existing in a closet, and nobody by to perceive them. I answer,

you may so, there is no difficulty in it. But what is all this, I beseech you, more than framing in your mind certain ideas which you call *books* and *trees,* and at the same time omitting to frame the idea of any one that may perceive them? But do not you yourself perceive or think of them all the while? This therefore is nothing to the purpose: it only shews you have the power of imagining, or forming ideas in your mind; but it does not shew that you can conceive it possible the objects of your thought may exist without the mind. To make out this, it is necessary that you conceive them existing unconceived or unthought of; which is a manifest repugnancy. When we do our utmost to conceive the existence of external bodies, we are all the while only contemplating our own ideas. But the mind, taking no notice of itself, is deluded to think it can and does conceive bodies existing unthought of, or without the mind, though at the same time they are apprehended by, or exist in, itself. A little attention will discover to any one the truth and evidence of what is here said, and make it unnecessary to insist on any other proofs against the existence of material substance.

Finally, it has been argued that mind and body are separate (*dualism*), and either have qualities in common, enabling them to interact, or do not have any qualities in common and do not interact. In the latter case, it has been contended that psychoneural parallelism is an example of divine intervention causing events in mind and body to go on in strict synchronization.

No final determination has been reached on these questions. The various answers are being explored today by science fiction writers as well as by philosophers. Berkeley's conclusions, while eminently defensible, are alien to the tenor of the preceding chapters of this book and will not be further explored. Holders of other viewpoints may be separated by their answers to the question, "Is brain activity sufficient for mental activity?"

A. Is brain activity sufficient for mental activity?—the dualist answer

Dualists answer no to the question posed in the title of this and the following section (see Question 5.2). Those dualists who contend that minds interact with brains usually add that only a man's brain is developed enough to make liaison with "mind." Eccles (1970, Chapter VI, pp. 10–11), for instance, writes:

> We must remain agnostic with regard to the consciousness or self-awareness of animals. Such statements of a progressive emergence of conscious mind during evolution are not supported by any scientific evidence, but merely are statements made within the framework of a faith that evolutionary theory, as it now is, will at least in principle explain fully the origin and development of all living forms including ourselves.

Modern dualists regard as the only evidence for their beliefs their knowledge of their own minds, which they say they obtain by observation. This process, first described by Locke in 1690 and termed "introspection," has been unpopular with psychologists for some time because of its private nature. Introspection is of course basic to psychoanalysis and an essential part of research into perception and disorders of perception. It may be queried, however, whether the process gives one the assurance that one is dealing with a separate mind and body. The psychologist Hebb (1969) has tackled this point by analyzing the content of introspection. He pointed out that all one obtains by introspection is sensations and images. For instance, if asked, "What are 6 and 2 added together?" the figures "6" and "2" and the answer "8" pop into one's mind; one does not find addition signs or rules for addition or indeed anything other than the figures and the answer. Hebb makes the point that sensations and images are part of the brain mechanism of looking at the external world. Images are internal representations of parts of this world. Furthermore, as Hebb (1969) points out, it has been shown that:

> Images are not, as it were, a picture gallery of the sort around which the mind may wander at will observing the pictures. No, as first shown by Binet of intelligence-testing fame, images are organized as a rigid sequence of perceptions. For instance, having learned a poem by heart, try and remember the last word of each line from the bottom to top. You will find you will have to repeat the poem from the beginning in sequence to find the words, unless you practice the trick.

Hebb makes the general point too that images must be considered always as derived from sensory input to the brain, that is they are based on (learned) perceptions. After a limb amputation, a man may sometimes report he feels sensation in the absent limb, due to excitation of nerves to the limb above the site of amputation. These are actually perceptions: the central connections produce the same sensation as when the limb was present. Images of one's holiday site or absent friends may be produced by stimulation of appropriate parts of the brain, from one's memory; that is, what were once perceptions may now be recalled as images.

Hebb concludes that introspection is an hallucination which provides no evidence for the mind's self-contemplation (Hebb, 1969). "I found that introspection included some imagery of looking into the interior of my skull from a point at the back of my head. Unfortunately, this seemed so ridiculous that I rapidly became unable to introspect any longer." It may be added that hallucinations themselves are everyday events; we all have dreams and daydreams.

1. *Minds apart from brains*

If mind and brain are separate entities, it is proper to ask if there is any evidence for the existence of minds apart from brains. Minds in the absence of brains conjure up thoughts of superhuman powers, of ghosts and of the spirits of the dead, all of which are unknown to science. Members of the Society for Psychical Research of England, however, have been investigating such matters since 1882 and many curious findings will be found in their journal, *The Proceedings of the S.P.R.* Communication with the spirits of the dead has been investigated and claims of such communications have *not* been verified to the satisfaction of independent observers.

Ghosts, too, seem rarely to encounter scientists (see Question 5.3). Critical investigations of some famous cases (for example, "the haunting of Borley Rectory") have shown no ghost but plenty of credulous people, together with faking of the evidence by interested parties (Dingwall *et al.,* 1956). Nearly one hundred years ago the noted physicist Sir William Crookes was much interested in psychical phenomena and conducted a series of seances at which mediums allegedly induced the appearance of other worldly beings with human bodies who walked and talked before many well-known people. There is no doubt that fraud occurred on at least some of these occasions; in any case the phenomena were clearly not bodiless minds—they had palpable bodies and clothes, indeed even locks of their hair are preserved (Medhurst and Goldney, 1964). Today mediums claiming such powers are unknown. Despite the rash of science fiction novels which may suggest otherwise, it appears that minds are not found apart from brains.

2. Mind-brain interaction—A dualist viewpoint

One seemingly plausible suggestion made by Eccles (1953, p. 276–78) is that if minds have the power to move material objects (psychokinesis), this power could be exerted on the junctions between neurons (synapses), making them more or less effective and thus influencing brain working.

It is known that the neurons in the brain are continually active due to their multitude of synapses. As their membrane potential is always close to the level at which nerve impulses would be generated, Eccles presumed that even a small psychokinetic action could be effective if applied at the right time and place. The mind as it were, tipped the balance in the desired direction. There is at present no evidence for or against these actions in the brain. It should be added that of course "mind power" is not necessarily a dualistic prop. Monists could equally claim that such powers had their origin in as yet unexplained brain actions. What is the evidence for such powers?

Evidence for mind power. Telepathy (the ability to communicate with another mind at a distance), clairvoyance (the ability to see objects beyond the range of vision), and precognition or prophecy (the ability to know and communicate future events) have been part of folklore for many generations but have only recently been investigated by scientists.

Evidence for the existence of these abilities, together with psychokinesis, has been presented, most prominently by J. B. Rhine (1937, 1948) in the United States and S. G. Soal (1956) in England (see Question 5.4). In the experiments of Rhine and his colleagues, subjects were able to predict the fall of dice and it was on the basis of this ability that psychokinesis was claimed, as it was thought that dice were pushed in the desired direction as they fell by psychokinesis. Clairvoyance was demonstrated by having subjects, hidden from an experimenter, say which one of a possible five symbols was on a card the experimenter was indicating. In a proportion of cases it was found that subjects could describe the symbol correctly many more times than would be expected from chance alone. All the experiments were of this type. There are no reports, however, of the fortunate possessors of telepathy, clairvoyance, or precognition making fortunes on the stock exchange or in real estate speculation.

Most scientists now regard the existence of "mind power" as far from proven and indeed rather unlikely. This change in opinion can be dated to the period between 1955 and 1960 in which very critical reviews of both Rhine's and Soal's experiments were published by Price (1955) in the United States and Hensel (1960) in England. Price pointed out that the precepts of extrasensory perception are not within the conceptual framework of science as we know it. It is therefore in the category of a miracle to which the strictest criteria of proof must be applied. For instance, Price quoted the philosopher Hume in *An Enquiry Concerning Human Understanding* (1748, Section 10):

A miracle is a violation of the laws of nature; and as a firm and unalterable experience has established these laws, the proof against a miracle, from the very nature of the fact, is as entire as any argument from experience can possibly be imagined. Why is it more than probable, that all men must die; that lead cannot, of itself, remain suspended in the air; that fire consumes wood, and is extinguished by water; unless it be, that these events are found agreeable to the laws of nature, and there is required a violation of these laws, or in other words, a miracle to prevent them? ... The plain consequence is (and it is a general maxim worthy of our attention), "That no testimony is sufficient to establish a miracle, unless the testimony be of such kind, that its falsehood would be more miraculous, than the fact, which it endeavours to establish; and even in that case there is a mutual destruction of arguments, and the superior only gives us an assurance suitable to that degree of force, which remains, after deducting the inferior." When anyone tells me, that he saw a dead man restored to life, I immediately consider with myself, whether it be more probable, that this person should either deceive or be deceived, or that the fact, which he relates, should really have happened. I weigh the one miracle against the other; and according to the superiority which I discover, I pronounce my decision, and always reject the greater miracle. If the falsehood of his testimony would be more miraculous than the event which he relates; then, and not till then, can he pretend to command my belief or opinion.

More briefly, Tom Paine in *The Age of Reason* asked "Is it more probable that nature should go out of her course or that a man should tell a lie?" (1794, Pt. 1, p. 86).

Against this argument it must be pointed out that any new and unexpected finding might be subjected to the same criticism. More serious is the imputation, in the quotation from Paine, that Rhine's results might be the result of fraud. Price indeed contended that fraud had not been excluded in the conduct of the

Rhine experiments, while Hensel similarly contested the experiments of Dr. Soal in England. In reply, Dr. Soal (1960) admitted the main reason why present-day faith in extrasensory perception is at a low ebb. He suggests that "successful" subjects, those who demonstrate extrasensory perception, are hard to find, particularly at universities. Indeed, Soal felt that subjects should be looked for in rural areas or that young children should be tested. Clearly Soal felt that sophistication or education in some way destroyed extrasensory perception.

Perhaps the best comment on the present status of extrasensory perception (ESP) is found in the following extract from a presidential address to The Society of Psychical Research made by Dr. C. J. West, himself an investigator of psychical phenomena (West, 1965):

> The history of ESP research has run a curious course. Many times during the life span of this Society it has seemed that a decisive "breakthrough" in research has occurred and that swift developments both theoretical and practical must soon follow. Each time these hopes have been shattered by the failure of subsequent work to confirm or reproduce the original findings, at least not in their original form. . . . The simplest explanations of these turns of events is, that in each instance the early work was methodically faulty and that subsequent experiments yielded nothing because improved technique had eliminated spurious effects. . . . It is also a plausible argument that the present dearth of mediums, incapable of producing material suggestive of the presence of ESP, is a direct consequence of the more rigorous approach of present-day investigations. . . . The real difficulty [is] that so far experimenters have never been able to establish any consistent characteristics of the ESP phenomena they have studied.

It is only fair to add that West felt that even with the admitted difficulties, there was still something to be investigated.

It should be added that coincidence appears a sufficient explanation for many happenings in everyday life which might be thought to involve extrasensory perception. For instance, Dr. Alvarez, a physics professor, reported in 1965 that while reading the local (San Francisco) paper on May 16, 1965, he noted a reference to the anthropologist Carleton S. Coon. This reminded him of another Carleton Coon and of his partner, Joe Sanders, who had played with him in a dance band in Chicago thirty years before, when Dr. Alvarez had been an undergraduate at the University of Chicago. Less than 5 minutes later, Dr. Alvarez noticed an obituary notice for Joe Sanders, which referred to his association with Carleton Coon. These two recollections of a person, one involving a death notice after thirty years, might popularly have been attributed to extrasensory perception. A more prosaic explanation was given by Dr. Alvarez. He took a thirty-year period and assumed that an average person would know the names of three thousand different people who might die within the period (probably an overestimate). He further assumed that the subject would learn of the death of each of these persons at some time in the thirty years. The question then arises, how probable is it that in the five minutes preceding the learning of the death an unrelated recollection will take place. This probability, if the subject thinks of these persons once in thirty years, becomes the ratio of five minutes to thirty years, which is about 3×10^{-7}. If the subject thinks of the person once a year, then the probability rises to $30 \times 3 \times 10^{-7}$, or about 10^{-5}.

The probability then that a person will have such an experience when learning of the death of any one of the three thousand is about $3000 \times 3 \times 10^{-7}$ or about 10^{-3} in a thirty-year period, or 3.10^{-5} a year. Given the approximately 10^8 adults in the United States, 3000 ($3.10^{-5} \times 10^8$) experiences of this sort should occur every year, or about ten per day.

Essentially then, as another commentator pointed out, the statistically improbable can also, given a sufficient number of cases, be the frequently observed.

B. Is brain activity sufficient for mental activity?—the monist answer

Monists are at present the majority party, and some idea of their beliefs may be gained from the following quotation from Mountcastle, the foremost investigator of psychoneural parallelism in sensory systems (p. 1315, 1968):

> So far as the public behavior of man is concerned, there is nothing that could not be duplicated by a mechanical device, nor is there anything inherent in the structure or function of brains that is outside the limits of the physical world; nothing which, in principle, could not be duplicated by an automaton, provided it were made of organic molecules and not electronic devices, for brains are a triumph of the organization of the former, not the latter. The nub of the matter is the problem of consciousness, for surely if humans are conscious, the monistic position dictates that such a complete automaton would itself also be a conscious agent. Such a proposition is difficult for many to accept.

The psychologist Hebb is even more forthright (1949, p. xiii):

> Modern psychology takes completely for granted that behavior and neural function are perfectly correlated, that one is completely caused by the other. There is no separate soul or life-force to stick a finger into the brain now and then and make neural cells do what they would not otherwise. Actually, of course, this is a working assumption only, as long as there are unexplained aspects of behavior.

The problem monists have to explain is how the events we describe as mental can arise from the working of brains. Clearly this question is unanswerable at present at the level of mechanism. It is possible, however, to take cognizance of the fact that, as all animals, including man, have evolved from primitive one-celled organisms, obviously nervous systems must have likewise evolved. Anatomists have long recognized this evolution and the differential development of brains according to an animal's way of life and its place in the evolutionary hierarchy. It would be reasonable to suppose that conscious mind has also emerged during evolution as a function of brains.

Monists vary among themselves in their willingness to impute mind to various classes of animals (see Question 5.5). The palaeontologist De Chardin (1956), for instance, recently argued in favor of the view that mind is present in all life forms but, due to progressive evolution, the mind of man is of a different and higher character than that of animals.

The answer to these problems must obviously come from a study of animals; as they cannot talk their mental abilities must be deduced from their behavior. Students of animal behavior in Darwin's time were optimistic about their ability to deduce the existence of mind in animals by observation. Darwin (1872), for instance, in his book *The Emotions in Man and in Animals* showed that the facial expressions and posture of men and monkeys expressing emotions such as grief, fear, and rage were very much alike. Darwin's friend and disciple Romanes (1904) in his classic *Animal Intelligence* recounted the anecdotes he had collected about animals from amoeba to chimpanzees. Each anecdote was thought to illustrate "intelligent" behavior, which Romanes used as a criterion of mind. Careful readers of Romanes' book will find that he placed animals in much the same rank as present-day scientists. Today, however, we do not share his enthusiasm for single-celled organisms.

After this early period, there was a reaction and it became fashionable to explain animal behavior without invoking mental activity at all. One result is that the behavior of single-celled animals, which lack a nervous system, is thought of as a simple mechanism, in the same way as the behavior of a single cell in a multicelled organism is explained, without any need to involve mind. For instance, the movement of the ciliated protozoan, *Paramecium,* can be completely explained in simple mechanistic terms (see Question 5.6).

Those aspects of behavior suggesting a state of consciousness can be examined in animals for evidence suggesting consciousness. It is only in recent years that the life of animals has been observed closely enough to enable any judgments to be made on such matters. For some years it was embarrassingly true that laboratory tests were not refined enough to distinguish between the abilities of a wide range of mammals while field studies had not reached much further than the anecdotal stage.

1. *Self-awareness*

One of the most amusing games one can play with a kitten at the exploratory stage is to confront it with a mirror. The variety of responses include rapid pounces on the reflection and hunts behind the mirror for the presumed intruder. Finally the kitten appears to show a distaste for the whole game. There is never any sign that it realizes that it is looking at itself. Far different, however, is the effect of a mirror on our closer relatives, the great apes. When a mirror was placed in front of the cage of four young preadolescent chimpanzees, after an initial reaction as to another chimp, the animals began to use the mirror for many purposes, such as grooming themselves, picking material from their teeth, making faces, and blow-ing bubbles. Indeed their social behavior markedly declined as they played with their new toy. All this was observed by a peeping-Tom, a psychologist observing the animals through a small hole in the wall of the room in which the chimps' cage sat (Gallup, 1970). Some experimental evidence that the animals recognized themselves was given by applying a red dye to their eyebrow ridges and eartops. When exposed to the mirror the chimps touched the marked areas four to ten times but only once without the mirror.

The mirror test seems to distinguish rather sharply between the capacities of animals. Stump-tailed macaques, rhesus monkeys, and cynomolgus monkeys showed virtually no evidence of self-recognition. Indeed, considerable intellect is probably necessary for self-recognition. It is known that some mentally retarded children are apparently not aware of themselves in a mirror.

2. Anticipation of the future

Two classic signs of anticipatory behavior are the use of tools and the formation of hunting groups. Both types of behavior were found by Jane Goodall (Van La-wick-Goodall, 1967) who observed chimpanzee behavior in the natural state for four years in a game reserve in Tanzania. The commonest use of tools was the fashioning of "rods" to probe termite nests. The insects bite the rods and are with-drawn with the rod and eaten. "Sponges" are manufactured by chewing leaves and are used to soak up water from small pools which the chimps cannot get their lips to. Chimps have also been seen to use leaves to clean themselves of mud or blood or to clean up the mess left after carrying a bunch of overripe bananas.

Several chimps working together were also observed to hunt and kill baboons. In one such incident, one animal walked toward a tree in which there was a baboon without appearing to notice it. Ten feet from the tree, it stopped. Whatever signal it gave is not known, but immediately several other chimps stood up, two males moved to the base of the tree, and three others moved to cut off likely escape routes. Yet another, the youngest, began to move toward the baboon very slowly and carefully. Unfortunately for the hunting party, the baboon noticed the young chimp stalking him, took fright, ran off and after a chase got away.

3. Possession of ethical values

If we look for evidence that animals show some understanding of the state of other members of the species, again there are indications that mammals and birds ex-hibit such behavior. Thorpe (1966), an ethologist, has reviewed a wide variety of behavior in animals suggestive of elaborate self-awareness and something like ethical values. One animal showing such behavior is the dolphin. For instance, John Lilly, an American scientist who worked with dolphins, reports that these animals utter a particular cry when unable to come to the surface to breathe. This cry attracts other dolphins who, when they find the signalling dolphin, place their heads under its head and raise it so it can breathe. This done, there is an inter-change of noises and the helping dolphins then take appropriate action, depending on the circumstances, rather than making a stereotyped response (Lilly, 1963).

Behavior suggestive of altruism has also been demonstrated in laboratory animals (reviewed by Ebling, 1969). In one experiment for instance, rats could get food by pressing either a heavy or a light weight bar. In time, they all preferred the light bar. A relay was now attached to the light bar so that each time it was pressed, a second rat, in sight of the first, was shocked. Rats now pushed the heavy bar more often, particularly if they had themselves been shocked. In fact, 80 per cent of previously shocked rats pressed the heavy bar. Twenty per cent of the rats pressed the heavy bar even without being previously placed in the shocked position. Russian studies suggest that altruism may be an animal characteristic which is more strongly developed in some members of a species than others. In the Russian experiments on rats and dogs, which were basically similar in design to the American experiments mentioned, two groups of the animals could be distinguished. One group spared their suffering colleagues without needing experience of that situation themselves; of the other group, who had themselves suffered, only 60 per cent could be trained to spare their suffering colleagues. Similar findings have been reported by Delgado and his colleagues at Yale, working with monkeys.

4. Manipulation of abstract ideas

Chimpanzees can locate food buried in sand outside their cages after a sixteen-and-a-half hour delay (Kohler, 1925). Presumably the animals have some internal representation of the food which enables them to find it after this delay. More systematic exploration of this idea has been carried out with a wide range of animals. Hunter (1913), for instance, found that animals could be trained to choose the lighted one of three otherwise similar doorways (Fig. 5.1a). Having learned this task, the animals were now restrained until the light went off (Fig. 5.1b), and their ability to choose the right doorway at various later times was tested. It was found that rats could remember for only ten to forty seconds and then only if they were able to orient themselves by forward movements or scratching on a certain spot. If they were turned round, they could no longer choose correctly. Dogs,

(a)   (b)

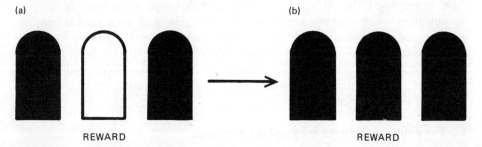

REWARD   REWARD

Fig. 5.1 The delayed response test. (a) shows three doorways, one of which is lighted. An animal is trained to choose this doorway. Then all the doorways are darkened (b) and the ability of the animal to choose the previously lighted doorway is tested.

which could delay for five minutes, similarly showed a need for bodily orientation. Raccoons, however, did better; they could delay for up to twenty-five seconds, and turning them around did not prevent them choosing the right door. Interestingly, a suitably water variant of the delayed reaction test applied to octopuses shows them to be also capable of ten to twenty second delay with no sensitivity to postural disturbance (Dilly, 1963). Rhesus monkeys can wait twenty-four hours to look under a cup under which they have seen a banana hidden. Furthermore they showed signs of anger if the experimenter who put the bananas under the cup had later exchanged the bananas for lettuce (Tinkelpaugh, 1928).

There is also evidence that animals have some concept of number, an ability which in children requires thought. Logler (1959), for instance, was able to show that a gray parrot (*Psittacus enthacus*) could recognize that a number of light flashes was the signal for the same number of irregularly distributed baits to be taken from food trays. Changes in the time between flashes did not impair this ability. The same bird also learned to perform the same program with notes from a flute (which could change in pitch). The bird did not learn to combine the number of flute notes and light flashes. It did, however, without mistake open a lid with two or one spots on it following two or one light stimuli or two *or* one acoustic stimuli—that is, the action depended on the number of stimuli rather than their nature.

5. *Ability to pay attention and to shift attention*

Assuming that an animal is selecting one of a number of possible stimuli in making some behavioral response, how is attention to be assessed? It cannot be assumed that because the animal has the appropriate general posture, facial expression, and head and eye orientation that it is necessarily attending. As was pointed out in Chapter 2, similar criteria do not guarantee human attention. A method acceptable at present is to require the animal to perform some response before it can view the stimulus to be discriminated (reviewed by Weinberger, 1971). For instance, it has been shown that monkeys will open a window in order to see various objects or parts of a laboratory (Butler, 1953). Rats similarly will put their heads through a hole. Interestingly, they keep their heads in the hole longer when viewing complex stimuli than when viewing simple stimuli. The results of such studies may be summarized in the statement that a wide spectrum of animals, probably including all mammals, can pay attention and shift their attention. It will be appreciated that because of the possibility that behavioral changes may occur without consciousness, this is a much less satisfactory criterion of consciousness than those mentioned in preceding sections.

C. The difference between man and other animals

The closest relatives of man in an evolutionary sense appear to behave in a manner suggesting a rudimentary form of consciousness. Animals lower in the scale appear to differ only quantitatively. It is natural to ask whether there is instead, or in addition, some difference in kind between man and other animals.

While there is some similarity between human and monkey behavior, a great difference appears when a developing child and a developing chimpanzee are compared. Psychologists have reared chimps with their own children and found that up to the age of one or two years, the human and chimpanzee babies differ little. Both manage much the same sorts of puzzles and tests. The chimp is, if anything, more dextrous in mastering mazes and piling up blocks. One difference is apparent however—the human baby babbles continuously, the chimp is silent. In time, the human child begins to talk, the chimpanzee does not (see Question 5.7). Intense training enabled one chimpanzee to learn four words which were used as signals to gain desired ends when all other signals failed (Kellogg, 1968). The chimp never gave any indication of appreciating the symbolic value of language. Even a child has to learn this slowly. "Tables" to a child means first, *this* table *here*. Only after months can the word be applied to *all tables everywhere*.

The point is emphasized in a story told by Thorndike (1911, p. 149), an experimental psychologist, who reported that one of his cats used to climb up the front of his cage whenever he said, "I must feed the cat." The cat climbed up in the same way if, instead, he said, "Today is Tuesday," or, "My name is Thorndike." When I read this, I was irresistibly reminded of the time when I worked with a Japanese colleague who, in retrospect, had not mastered as much English as I gave him credit for at the time. He used to manage a movie camera while I directed another part of the experiment, saying "Camera on, please" when the film was about to be taken. One day when the experiment was going poorly, I said, "Let's have lunch," whereupon my colleague turned the camera on.

Only man is known to talk. It is claimed by Lilly that dolphins have their own language and may be trained to imitate human speech (Lilly and Miller, 1961; Lilly, 1965). This claim awaits confirmation (see Question 5.8). The ability to talk of course enables symbolic speech, i.e., discussion of objects and activities not present to the senses, thus allowing a great advance in reasoning and problem solving. It is probable that animals of species closely related to our own are capable of symbolic thought but lack the nervous and muscular mechanism for expressing their thoughts as speech. Recently for instance, a chimpanzee has been taught the American sign language (the language used by the deaf in North America). The experiment is still proceeding, but already the twenty-two-month old chimp can generalize (Gardner and Gardner, 1969). For instance, knowing the symbol for "cup" as applied to one particular cup, it recognizes other cups; again, it distinguishes itself (I—me) from not-self (you). Another ape has been taught a form of language by the use of pieces of plastic backed with metal which stick to a magnetized slate (Premack, 1971). This animal has a seventy to ninety "word" vocabulary and can form and understand simple noun-verb-noun sentences.

Studies of the development of children, most noticeably by Piaget, a Swiss psychologist and zoologist, have given some further insight into differences between man and other animals (Almy *et al.*, 1966). For instance, by the age of eight to nine months, children will make a limited search for objects they cannot see. This is taken to indicate that the children have a mental image of these objects. The parallel with the delayed response tests of animals is obvious. By the time children are one and a half to two years old there is evidence that they have some internal representation (presumably pictorial) of their actions as well, and there is also evidence of mental combinations of these internalized actions to form new action patterns. At this stage children's play is an extension of their thoughts so that play is spoken of as the thought of the child. Children of this age still cannot speak, however, and the behavior exhibited is not more than can be achieved by the higher apes. These are important points, for it follows that *thought develops as internalized action,* and is not dependent on first learning to speak.

The thought of young children then is presumably akin to that of subhuman animals. With the learning of a language, children acquire verbal signs for their internalized actions. As adults we can all alternate pictorial and verbal modes of thought, all stemming from this early period of our lives. Evidence from other sources supports the concept of thought as internalized action and the further concept that with development thought is severed from immediate action and can be a pictorial or verbal representation of the immediate or the past or of an imaginary scene.

Learning to talk is all-important in this further development. If children do not learn to talk (as in the cases reported in the last century of children brought up with animals), then the level of thinking does not advance beyond a pictorial representation.

It is easy to see how verbal thought takes over from pictorial thought. Even in adults the process can be detected. For instance, the physiologist Jacobson (1931, 1973), who monitored tongue movements, found that the movement which occurred when his subjects *said* a certain word reoccurred on a microscale when they *thought* the word. After thinking for a few minutes without speech, however, his subjects' tongues relaxed and made no more movements. Even more interestingly, records were made from finger muscles of deaf mutes who had been trained to use their fingers in communication. When these people thought, signs of subthreshold activity were found in the muscles controlling their fingers.

Fig. 5.2 (a) Areas in which brain stimulation induces utterance of sounds (vocalization) or aphasic interference with speech. The vocalization area in the frontal cortex and that within the longitudinal fissure are found in both hemispheres. The three areas—frontal, parietal, and temporal—in which stimulation produces temporary aphasia are marked "aphasic arrest." They are found only in the dominant hemisphere. (With permission from *Cerebral Context of Man* by W. Penfield and T. Rasmussen. Copyright © 1950 by Macmillan Co., New York.) (b) Primary language areas of the human brain in the left hemisphere. Broca's area, which is adjacent to the region

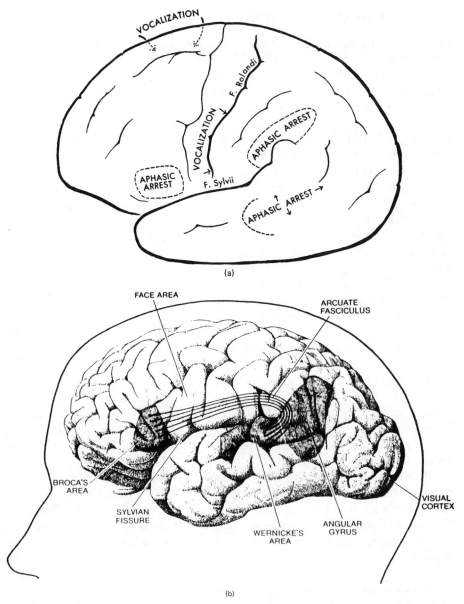

(a)

(b)

of the motor cortex that controls the movement of the muscles of the lips, the jaw, the tongue, the soft palate, and the vocal cords apparently incorporates programs for the coordination of these muscles in speech. Wernicke's area lies between the temporal area, which is the primary receiver of auditory stimuli, and the angular gyrus, which acts as a way station between the auditory and the visual regions. (With permission from "Language and the Brain" by Norman Geschwind. Copyright © 1972 by *Scientific American,* Inc. All rights reserved.)

II. THE CEREBRAL HEMISPHERES AND MIND

In the preceding section (I-C.) it was concluded that the difference between man and other animals lay in man's ability to speak. It has long been known that this ability depends on the integrity of only one of the two cerebral hemispheres, the dominant hemisphere. In most people the neurons of the left hemisphere control speech. The left hemisphere also controls the right hand, but cerebral dominance is not necessarily paralleled by appropriate handedness. The majority of left-handed people and almost all right-handed people have their speech faculty controlled by neurons in their left hemisphere. As Fig. 5.2(a) indicates, stimulation of areas in the frontal, temporal, and parietal lobes of the left cerebral hemisphere of a conscious man will stop speech (Penfield and Rasmussen, 1950). The area in the frontal lobe is known as Broca's area (Fig. 5.2b), after the clinician who first showed that damage to this particular area of brain results in a disturbance of speech; an aphasia. Neurons here apparently control the coordination of muscles in speech. Patients with damage to this region have difficulty in speaking (motor aphasia) but speech of others and writing is still understood. In the parietal and temporal lobes (Fig. 5.2b) we find Wernicke's area, again named for a clinician. Patients with damage here have sensory aphasia—they can utter jargon but do not apparently understand spoken or written language. Wernicke's and Broca's areas are joined by the arcuate fasciculus (Fig. 5.2b), a bundle of nerve fibres. When this is damaged, patients have abnormal speech; they can comprehend the speech of others but cannot repeat it.

This functional specialization of the left cerebral hemisphere is matched by anatomical specialization: Wernicke's area in the left parietal lobe is significantly larger than the corresponding area in the right lobe, in adults (Geschwind and Levitsky, 1968) and also in the newborn, suggesting that the human infant is born with a preprogrammed capacity to process speech sounds (Witelson and Pallie, 1973).

If, as suggested in section I-C, thought develops beyond the pictorial level as a consequence of an ability to speak, one might justifiably wonder whether such thought, or even consciousness itself, was dependent on activity of the dominant hemisphere. Such problems can be resolved by examining the performance of men and other animals after disconnection of the two cerebral hemispheres (*split brain* studies).

A. Consciousness and the dominant hemisphere

Disconnection is quite a big undertaking. As Fig. 5.3 indicates, the two cerebral hemispheres are connected by a large bundle of nerve fibres, the corpus callosum, and two small bundles, the anterior and hippocampal commissures (not shown in Fig. 5.3), together with the bilateral connections from the eyes. As Fig. 5.3 further indicates, the axons of half of the ganglion cells in each retina cross to the opposite

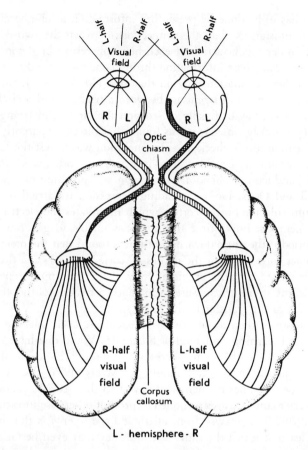

Fig. 5.3 Split-brain preparation seen in dorsal view. Normally, fibres from the nasal half of each retina cross over at the optic chiasm and are relayed to the visual cortex of the opposite hemisphere. Cutting the chiasm restricts the visual information entering each hemisphere to that from the external half of the retina on its own side. When the corpus callosum is also cut, no visual information at all can pass from one side of the brain to the other. (Modified from Sperry, *Science, 133*, 1749–57. Copyright 1961 by the American Association for the Advancement of Science.)

thalamus and are relayed to the cortex. The other half pass to the thalamus and are relayed to the cortex on the same side. Each ear is also connected to both hemi-spheres.

Surprisingly, the first studies of split-brain men (Akelaitis, 1944) indicated that little or no change in their abilities occurred as a result of surgery. However, as later tests of one man in this series has shown (Goldstein and Joynt, 1969), changes were present—the testing was at fault. Testing of split-brain men or any other creatures has to be done by presenting information to one hemisphere only. Under these circumstances if *all* the connections between the two cerebral hemispheres are cut, independent action of each hemisphere can be demonstrated. For instance, sectioned cats given information through one visual field only were found to have learned the information only on that side (Myers, 1956). In such experiments, a cat was taught to differentiate between a triangle and a circle (e.g., Fig. 5.4). If this eye was now artificially closed and the circle and triangle shown to the other eye (previously closed), it was found that the cat apparently knew nothing of the problem at all. A check on this conclusion was to test the learning abilities of animals with intact nervous systems in which one cortex was temporarily put out of action by inducing a phenomenon known as "spreading depression" in this cortex (Russell and Ochs, 1963). Spreading depression is carried out by putting strong potassium chloride on the cortex, which inactivates the electrical signalling system of the neurons. For a time this cortex is unable to generate any signals. During this period if the animal learns a task it is found that the memory is stored only in the intact cortex. When the depressed cortex recovers (as the chemical is absorbed), it is ignorant of the problem. Now, if the training is repeated, the ignorant cortex learns after one exposure. Apparently activation of the stored learning on one side leads to the transfer to the other side.

Exciting questions then arose. To what extent are such phenomena as attention, memory, and learning unilateral or bilateral? Would one have two minds if the connections between the hemispheres were absent? Experiments have now been made on split-brain cat and monkeys (Myers, 1956; Sperry, 1958), and there have also been studies of men who have had their corpus callosum and anterior and posterior commissures sectioned to prevent otherwise intractable epilepsy (Gazzaniga, 1970). The answer from all these experiments is that both sides of the brain can learn at much the same rate and they may even be taught opposing tasks. Through one eye a cat could be taught to choose a triangle in preference to a circle; through the other eye it could be taught the reverse discrimination. Gazzaniga and his colleagues have found that split-brain monkeys can apparently deal with nearly twice as much information as normal animals. In this test a

(a)   (b)   (c)

REWARD   REWARD   REWARD

Fig. 5.4 Discrimination reversal. An animal is trained to recognize a circle on either the right (a) or left (b) side of a pair, formed by a circle and a triangle. Now (c), it is trained to recognize a triangle. The measure of the animal's ability is how many trials are required to switch its choice from the circle to the triangle. The test may then be repeated, switching back to the circle as the preferred symbol.

monkey was trained to pull a knob which lighted eight of sixteen panels. The task was to punch the lit panels (which turned them off) and no others, starting at the bottom. Brain-bisected men can also carry out two tasks (each presented to one hemisphere by way of the corresponding eye) as fast as a normal man can do one (Gazzaniga, 1967). In some circumstances then, the possession of a split brain leads to increased efficiency (but see Question 5.9).

It is clear from these experiments that some cerebral mechanisms are bilateral. What of consciousness? Split-brain men given information through the left eye can speak about the matter. Information presented through the right eye remains private to the right hemisphere, which cannot communicate in this way. Men appear not to know of information presented to their nonspeech controlling hemisphere. Consciousness then is apparently linked to the speech controlling dominant hemisphere.

B. The role of the minor hemisphere

Is the minor hemisphere conscious? Certainly some aspects of consciousness are displayed here—attention, memory, the ability to perform complex intellectual tasks. The abilities of the minor hemisphere are summarized in Fig. 5.5. The minor hemisphere generally cannot control speech or writing, but a few simple or emotional words can be expressed in response to stimuli private to the minor hemisphere. If the minor hemisphere is shown pornographic pictures by means of the associated eye, it is found that a feeble grin chases over the face of the split-brained man. Apparently empathy can be demonstrated in these circumstances (Gazzaniga and Sperry, 1967). Moreover, the minor hemisphere can be shown by nonverbal means to understand spoken or written words. Matching tests can be performed, for instance, in which a patient is shown a word through his right visual field and uses his left hand to pick out the matching object from a tray. It should be noted that in such tests the dominant hemisphere is ignorant of the whole transaction (Gazzaniga and Sperry, 1967).

More recent investigations indicate that there is a fundamental difference in the way the two hemispheres process information. The dominant hemisphere codes verbally and performs poorly if this coding is difficult (Fig. 5.6, R-hand). The minor hemisphere, in contrast, appears to appreciate shapes as a whole (Fig. 5.6 L-hand). A face which is difficult to describe in words is recognized by the minor hemisphere. Indeed, prosopagnosia, the aphasia in which familiar faces cannot be recognized, is usually the result of a minor hemisphere lesion.

Levi-Agnesti and Sperry (1968) have suggested that the specialization of the hemisphere has developed because of a basic incompatibility between language functions on one hand, and synthetic perception factors on the other. It is plain that in man the minor hemisphere displays abilities which suggest a pictorial form of thought and a level of functioning which is superior to the abilities of the hemispheres of other animals.

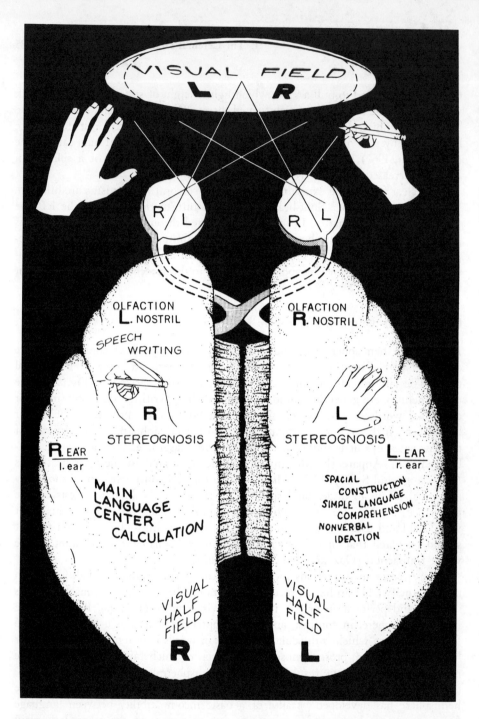

Fig. 5.5 The separate functions of the right and left hemispheres, as shown by separate testing after section of forebrain commissures. (With permission from R. W. Sperry, *Proc. Ass. Nerv. Ment. Dis., 48*, 123–138, 1970.)

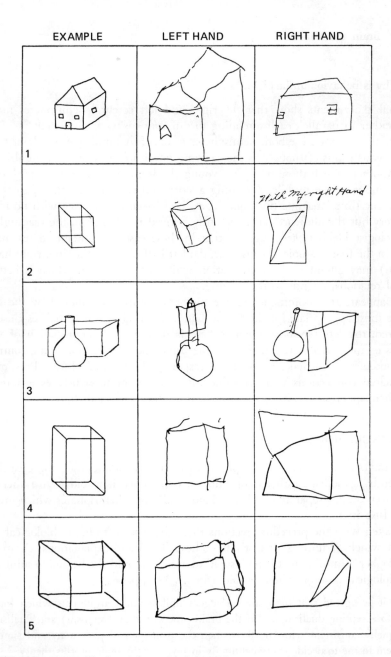

| EXAMPLE | LEFT HAND | RIGHT HAND |

With my right Hand

Fig. 5.6 Drawing with the right and left hand by a man with a complete transsection of the corpus callosum and anterior commissure. The patient had always been right-handed and had never written or drawn with the left hand, so far as he or his family could recall. As the figure shows, when he copied five sample figures that suggested spatial perspective, his performance with the left hand was consistently better than with the right hand. (With permission from M. S. Gazzaniga, J. E. Bogen, and R. W. Sperry, *Brain, 88*, Part 2, 221–236, 1965.)

C. Why is behavior unitary?

Animal experiments show that the right and left cerebral hemispheres may be used either in parallel, each attending to different tasks, or alternately.

Do normal men use both hemispheres at once? A familiar example of two simultaneous trains of thought is the carrying on of a conversation while driving a car. Another, which those who have young children will have experienced, occurs when one is in the middle of reading a story and suddenly thinks of something else; some time later one finds oneself at the bottom of the page with no idea of the story but the audience has apparently noticed no change in the reading! The psychologist Hebb (1969) suggests that in these cases both hemispheres may be used. In the first example, for instance, the left half of the brain (in a right-handed person) may attend to the conversation while the right half, which is better at spatial relations, attends to the driving.

It appears that dominance of the motor apparatus is achieved by the hemisphere most appropriate for the task at hand. If verbal or conceptual responses are required, the left (speaking) hemisphere is dominant. If appreciation of visual shapes or memories is required, then the minor hemisphere may take control of the musculature to make a nonverbal response (Levy *et al.,* 1972). Presumably, the shared connections with hypothalamic and midbrain structures ensure that both hemispheres can give expression to the same emotional state.

III. CONCLUSIONS

The results of investigations of split-brain men and monkeys are more easily explained by a monistic rather than a dualist hypothesis: it would seem rather ludicrous to postulate separate minds for major and minor hemispheres which mysteriously fuse in man.

Taken with the preceding sections then, there seem to be no biological arguments which require a dualist's hypothesis for their explanations. A modern philosopher, summing up the philosophical position, could also be said to summarize the biological position when he said (Smart, 1959, p. 56):

> If it be agreed that there are no cogent philosophical arguments which force us into accepting dualism, and if the brain process theory (monism) and dualism are equally consistent with the facts, then the principles of parsimony and simplicity seem to me to decide overwhelmingly in favor of the brain-process theory.

How mental activity results from brain activity remains obscure. The majority view is that this property of the brain will prove explicable in terms of the regularities of physics and chemistry when applied to biological systems. A variant view (emergence) is that as biological systems become more organized, new properties emerge (such as mind), not predictable from the properties of the separate parts of the combination (see, e.g., Polyani, 1968). It must be remarked that in the laboratory most scientists act as if this view were true. To take a simple example, if we want to study the properties of common salt, sodium chloride, we investigate the salt rather than the constituent sodium or chloride. However, we have confidence (justified by recent advances in understanding of crystal structures) that the properties of sodium chloride will ultimately prove explicable in terms of its constituent sodium and chloride atoms. The history of biology demonstrates a long series of phenomena once thought to be examples of unique, emerging properties which have proved explicable in terms of concepts applicable to simpler systems. In a word, complexities and peculiarities of matter in living systems may lead to the observed phenomenon appearing unique. Investigation has always shown that a mechanism using concepts which are common to other systems and to the properties of matter as they are studied in the inorganic state can be found.

It seems possible that the relationship between mind and brain is of this type. While mental activity at present indeed appears to be of a different nature from other processes studied by scientists, the subject matter of this book is in a sense a catalogue of the inroads experimental scientists are making on this once mysterious territory. Neither dualism nor emergence seem necessary concepts. Undoubtedly, the mechanisms as yet unravelled will be so complex as to satisfy the pride of those who wish to think of man as a unique being, as well as satisfying those who see man as one, albeit the most destructive and dangerous, of the creations in the evolutionary process.

REFERENCES

Akelaitis A. J. (1944) A study of gnosis, praxis, and language following section of the corpus callosum and anterior commissure. *J. Neurosurg. 1,* 94–102.

Almy, M., E. Chittendon, and P. Miller (1966) *Young children's thinking.* Teachers College Press, Teachers College, Columbia University, New York.

Alvarez, L. W. (1965) A pseudo-experience in parapsychology. *Science 148,* 1541.

Berkeley, G. (1685–1753) *Essays and Principles, Dialogues, with selections from Other Writings* (1929) M. W. Calkins, Ed., Charles Scribner's Sons, New York.

Butler, R. A. (1953) Discrimination learning by rhesus monkeys to visual exploration motivation. *J. Comp. Physiol. Psychol. 46,* 95–98.

Darwin, C. (1872) *The Expression of the Emotions in Man and Animals.* John Murray, London.

De Chardin, P. T. (1956) *"L'apparition de l'homme,"* tr. by J. M. Cohen (1965) as *The Appearance of Man;* Ch. XVII. The singularities of the human species. Harper & Row, New York.

Dilly, P. N. (1963) Delayed responses in *Octopus. J. exp. Biol. 40,* 393–401.

Dingwall, E. J., K. M. Goldney, and T. H. Hall (1956). The haunting of Borley Rectory: a critical survey of the evidence. *S.P.R. Proc. 51,* 1–181.

Ebling, F. J. (1969) Introduction XIII-XXIX in *Biology and Ethics,* F. J. Ebling, Ed., Academic Press, London and New York.

Eccles, J. C. (1953) *The Neurophysiological Basis of Mind.* Clarendon Press, Oxford.

Eccles, J. C. (1970) *Facing Reality.* Springer-Verlag, New York.

Gallup, G. G. Jr. (1970) Chimpanzees: self-recognition. *Science, 167,* 86–87.

Gardner, R. A. and B. T. Gardner (1969) Teaching sign language to a chimpanzee. *Science, 165,* 664–672.

Gazzaniga, M. S. (1967) The split brain in man. *Sci. American 217,* (2) 29–30.

Gazzaniga, M. S. (1970) *The bisected brain.* Appleton-Century Crofts, New York.

Gazzaniga, M. S., J. E. Bogen, and R. W. Sperry (1965) Observations on visual perception after disconnection of the cerebral hemispheres in man. *Brain 88:* Part 2, 221–236.

Gazzaniga, M. S. and R. W. Sperry (1967) Language after section of the cerebral commissures. *Brain 90,* Pt. 1, 131–148.

Geschwind, N. (1972) Language and the brain. *Sci. American 226,* No. 4, 76–83.

Geschwind, N. and W. Levitsky (1968) Human Brain: left-right asymmetries in the temporal speech region. *Science, 161,* 186–187.

Globus, G. G. (1973) Unexpected symmetries in the world knot. *Science, 180,* 1129–1136.

Goldstein, M. N. and R. J. Joynt (1969) Long-term follow-up of a callosal-sectioned patient. *Arch. Neurol. 20,* 96–102.

Hansel, C. E. M. (1960) A critical review of experiments with Mr. Basil Shackleton and Mrs. Gloria Stewart as sensitives. *S. P. R. Proc. 53,* 1–42.

Hebb, D. O. (1949) The organization of behavior. John Wiley & Sons, New York.

Hebb. D. O. (1969) The Mind's Eye. *Psychology Today 2,* No. 12, p. 54.

Hume, D. (1748) Concerning miracles, Ch. 10 from An Enquiry Concerning Human Understanding. In *Essays moral, political and literary* (1875) Vol. II, ed. T. H. Green and T. H. Grose. Longmans, Green & Co., London.

Hunter, W. S. (1913) The delayed reaction in animals and children. *Behav. Monog. ii* no 1.

Jacobson, E. (1931) Electrical measurements of neuromuscular states during mental activities. VII: Imagination, recollection, and abstract thinking involving the speech musculature. *Am. J. Physiol. 97,* 200–209.

Jacobson, E. (1973) Electrophysiology of mental activities and introduction to the psychological process of thinking. In: *The Psychophysiology of Thinking,* F. J. McGuigan and R. A. Schoonover, Eds., pp. 3–31, Academic Press, New York.

Joad, C. E. M. (1943) *A Guide to Modern Thought,* revised edition, 1948, Pan Books; London.

Kellogg, W. N. (1968) Communication and language in the home-raised chimpanzee. *Science, 162,* 423–427.

Kohler, W. (1925). *The Mentality of Apes.* Routledge & Kegan-Paul, London.

Lawick-Goodall, J. (1967) *My Friends the Wild Chimpanzees.* National Geographic Society, Washington, D.C.

Levi-Agresti, J. and R. W. Sperry (1968) Differential perceptual capacities in major and minor hemispheres. *Proc. Nat. Acad. Sci. (US) 61,* 1151.

Levy, J., C. Trevarthen, and R. W. Sperry (1972) Perception of bilateral chimeric figures following hemispheric deconnexion. *Brain, 95,* 61–78.

Lilly, J. C. (1963) Distress call of the bottlenose dolphin : stimuli and evoked behavioral responses. *Science, 139,* 116–118.

Lilly, J. C. (1965) Vocal mimicry in Tursiops: ability to match numbers and durations of human vocal bursts. *Science, 147,* 300–301.

Lilly, J. C. and A. M. Miller (1961). Vocal exchanges between dolphins. *Science, 134,* 1873–1876.

Lögler, P. (1959) *Versuche zur Kage der Zahl-vermogens an einem Grau Papagai. Z. Tierpsychol. 16,* 179–217.

Medhurst, R. G. & Goldney, K. M. (1964) William Crookes and the physical phenomena of mediumship. *S.P.R. Proc. 54,* 25–157.

Mountcastle, V. B. (1968) Sleep, wakefulness, and the conscious state: intrinsic regulatory mechanisms. In *Medical Physiology,* 12th Ed., V. B. Mountcastle, Ed., Ch. 60, pp. 1315–1342, C. V. Mosby Co., St. Louis.

Myers, R. E. (1956) Function of corpus callosum in interocular transfer. *Brain 79,* 358–363.

Paine, T. (1794) *Age of Reason.* Reprinted by John Wiley & Sons.

Penfield W. and T. Rasmussen (1950) *The cerebral cortex of man.* Macmillan Co., New York.

Polyani, M. (1968) Life's irreducible structure. *Science, 160,* 1308–1312.

Premack, D. (1971) Language in the chimpanzee. *Science, 172,* 808–822.

Price, G. R. (1955) Science and the supernatural. *Science, 122,* 359–367.

Price, G. (1956) Where is the definitive experiment? *Science, 123,* 17–18.

Rhine, J. B. (1937) *New Frontiers of the Mind.* Republished by Penguin Books, London (1950).

Rhine, J. B. (1948) *The Reach of the Mind.* Faber & Faber, London.

Romanes, G. J. (1904). *Animal Intelligence*. The International Scientific Series, Vol. XLI. London: Kegan-Paul, Trench, Trubner & Co., Ltd.

Russell, I. S. and S. Ochs (1963) Localisation of a memory trace in one cortical hemisphere and transfer to the other hemisphere. *Brain 86*, 37–54.

Smart, J. J. C. (1959) Sensations and brain processes. *Phil. Rev. 68*, 141–156.

Soal, S. G. (1956) On "science and the supernatural" *Science, 123*, 9–11.

Soal, S. G. (1960) A reply to Mr. Hansel. *S. P. R. Proc. 53*, 43–82.

Sperry, R. W. (1958) Corpus callosum and interhemisphere transfer in the monkey *(Macacca mulatta)*. *Anat. Rec. 131*, 297.

Sperry, R. W. (1961) Cerebral organization and behavior. *Science, 133*, 1749–1757.

Sperry, R. W. (1970) Perception in the absence of the neocortical commissures. *Proc. Ass. Res. nerv. ment. Dis. 48*, 123–138.

Thorndike, E. L. (1911) *Animal Intelligence: Experimental Studies*. Macmillan Co., New York.

Thorpe, W. H. (1966) Ethology and consciousness, pp. 470–505. In *Brain and Conscious Experience*. J. C. Eccles, Ed., Springer Verlag, Berlin.

Tinklepaugh, O. L. (1928) An experimental study of representative factors in monkeys. *J. Comp. Psychol. 8*, 197–286.

Weinberger, N. M. (1971) Attentive processes. In *Psychobiology*, J. L. McGaugh, Ed., pp. 129–198, Academic Press, New York.

West, D. J. (1965) ESP, the next step. *S. P. R. Proc. 54*, 185–202.

Witelson, S. F. and W. Pallie (1973) Left hemisphere specialization for language in the newborn. Neuroanatomical evidence of asymmetry. *Brain, 96*, 641–646.

SUGGESTED FURTHER READING

Scientific American Reprints

Animal Intelligence:

Bitterman, M. E. *The evolution of intelligence*. January, 1965, p. 92 (offprint 490).

Premack, A. J. and D. Premack *Teaching language to an ape*. October, 1972, p. 80 (offprint 540).

Rensch, B. *The intelligence of elephants*. February, 1957, p. 44 (offprint 421).

Stettner, L. J. and K. A. Matyniak. *The brain of birds*. June, 1968, p. 64 (offprint 515).

Warden, C. J. *Animal intelligence*. June, 1951, p. 64 (offprint 424).

Split Brain:

Gazzaniga, M. S. *The split brain in man*. August, 1967, p. 24 (offprint 508).

Geschwind, W. *Language and the brain*. April, 1972, p. 76 (offprint 1246).

Sperry, R. W. *The great cerebral commissure*. January, 1964, p. 42 (offprint 174).

Kimura, D. *The asymmetry of the human brain*. March, 1973, p. 70 (offprint 554).

Easily Read Reviews and Books

Animal language and behavior:

Neuroscience Research Bulletin 9 (5) Are apes capable of language? 1971

Lawick-Goodall, J. (1967) *My friends the wild chimpanzees*. National Geographic Society, Washington, D.C.

Lilly, M. A. (1961) *Man and Dolphin*. Doubleday & Co. Inc., Garden City, New York.

Lilly, M. A. (1967) *The Mind of the Dolphin*. Doubleday & Co. Inc., Garden City, New York.

Riopelle, A. J. (1967) *Animal Problem Solving* (selected readings). Penguin Books Ltd., Baltimore.

Extrasensory perception:

Price, G. R. (1955) Science and the supernatural. *Science, 122,* 359–367.

Rhine, J. B. (1937) *New Frontiers of the Mind*. Republished by Penguin Books Ltd., London.

Rhine, J. G. (1948) *The Reach of the Mind*. Faber & Faber, London.

More difficult but well worth reading:

Darwin, C. (1872) *The Expression of the Emotions in Man and Animals*. John Murray, London.

Gazzaniga, M. S. (1970) *The Bisected Brain*. Appleton-Century Crofts, New York.

Sherrington, C. S. (1940) *Man on His Nature*. Penguin Books, Harmondsworth, Middlesex, England.

QUESTIONS

More advanced students may want to try answering the following questions using the references as a starting point:

5.1 *What is the relationship between mental states and brain states?*

Eccles, J. C. (1970) *Facing Reality*. Springer-Verlag, New York.

Feigl, H. (1967) *The "Mental" and the Physical*. University of Minnesota Press, Minneapolis.

Globus, G. G. (1973) Unexpected symmetries in the world knot? *Science, 180,* 1129–1136.

5.2 *Compare and contrast the views of Eccles and Mountcastle on the nature of mind.*

Eccles, J. C. (1970) Evolution and the conscious self. Ch. 4 in *Facing Reality*. Springer-Verlag, New York.

Mountcastle, V. B. (1968) Sleep, wakefulness and the conscious state: intrinsic regulatory mechanisms, in *Medical Physiology,* 12th Ed., V. B. Mountcastle, Ed., Ch. 60, pp. 1315–1342. C. V. Mosby Co., St. Louis.

5.3 *Comment on the evidence for disembodied spirits in the light of the following references.*

Broad, C. D. (1964) Cromwell Varley's electrical tests with Florence Cook. Some notes and queries. *Society for Psychical Research Proc. 54,* 148–172.

Dingwell, E. J., K. M. Goldney, and T. H. Hall (1956) The haunting of Borley Rectory: A critical survey of the evidence. *Society of Psychical Research Proc. 51,* 1–181.

Medhurst, R. G. and K. M. Goldney (1964) Williams Crookes and the physical phenomena of mediumship. *Society for Psychical Research Proc. 54,* 24–157.

Stephenson, C. J. (1966) Further comments on Cromwell Varley's electrical test on Florence Cook. *Society for Psychical Research Proc. 54,* 363–417.

5.4 *Comment on the evidence for extrasensory perception in the light of either of the following two sets of references:*

Nicol, J. F. (1950) Some difficulties in the way of scientific recognition of extrasensory perception, in *Extrasensory Perception,* pp. 24–37 G. E. M. Wostenholme and E. C. P. Millar, Eds., (Ciba Foundation Symposium), J. & A. Churchill Ltd., London.

Price, G. R. (1955) Science and the supernatural. *Science, 122,* 359–367.

Price, G. R. (1956) Where is the definitive experiment? *Science, 123,* 17–18.

or

Hansel, C. E. M. (1960) A critical review of experiments with Mr. Basil Shackleton and Mrs. Gloria Steward as sensitives. *Society for Psychical Research Proc. 53,* 1–42.

Soal, S. G. (1960) A reply to Mr. Hansel. *Society for Psychical Research Proc. 53,* 43–82.

Scott, C. and P. Haskell (1973) Normal explanation of the Soal-Goldney experiments in extrasensory perception. *Nature (London), 245,* 52–54.

5.5 *Compare and contrast the views of Mountcastle and De Chardin on the nature of mind.*

De Chardin, P. T. (1956) *L'apparition de l'homme,* translated by J. M. Cohen (1963) as *The Appearance of Man;* see especially Ch. 17, The singularities of the human species. Harper & Row, New York.

Mountcastle, V. B. (1968) Sleep, wakefulness, and the conscious state: intrinsic regulatory mechanisms, in *Medical Physiology,* 12th Ed., V. B. Mountcastle, Ed., Ch. 60, pp. 1277–1314, C. V. Mosby Co., St. Louis.

5.6 *What is the evidence for the view that the movement of Paramecium can be explained in mechanistic terms?*

Eckert, R. and Y. Naitoh (1970) Passive electrical properties of *Paramecium* and properties of ciliary coordination. *J. Gen. Physiol. 55,* 467–483.

Eckert, R. (1972) Bioelectric control of ciliary activity. *Science, 176,* 473–481.

Kung, C. and Y. Naitoh (1973) Calcium-induced ciliary reversal in the extracted models of "Pawn," a behavioral mutant of *Paramecium. Science, 179,* 195–196.

Satow, Y. and C. Kung (1974) Genetic dissection of active electrogenesis in Paramecium aurelia. *Nature (London)* 247, 69–71.

5.7 *Why can't chimpanzees talk?*

Fouts, R. S. (1973) Acquisition and testing of gestural signs in four young chimpanzees. *Science, 180,* 978–980.

Gardner, R. A. and B. T. Gardner (1969) Teaching sign language to a chimpanzee. *Science, 165,* 664–672.

Geschwind, N. (1970) The organization of language and the brain. *Science, 170,* 940–944.

Kellogg, W. N. (1968) Communication and language in the home-raised chimpanzee. *Science, 162,* 423–427.

Lenneberg, E. H. (1969) On explaining language. *Science, 164,* 635–643.

Premack, D. (1971) Language in the chimpanzee? *Science, 172,* 808–822.

5.8 *Can any other animal "talk" besides man?*

Lilly, J. C. (1963) Distress call of the bottlenose dolphin: stimuli and evoked behavioral responses. *Science, 139,* 116–118.

Lilly, J. C. (1963) Cortical brain size and language. *Perspectives in Biol. Med. 6,* 246–255.

Lilly, J. C. (1965) Vocal mimicry in *Tursiops:* ability to match numbers and durations of human vocal bursts. *Science, 147,* 300–301.

Lilly, J. C. (1967) *The Mind of the Dolphin*. Doubleday & Co., Inc., Garden City, New York.

Lilly, J. C. and A. M. Miller (1961) Vocal exchanges between dolphins. *Science, 134,* 1873–1876.

5.9 Is it better to have a split brain?

Dimond, S. and G. Beaumont (1971) Use of two cerebral hemispheres to increase brain capacity. *Nature (London) 232,* 270–271.

Sechzer, J. A. (1970) Prolonged learning and split-brain cats. *Science, 169,* 889–892.

Sperry, R. W. (1967) Split-brain approach to learning problems, pp. 714–722, in *The Neurosciences,* R. Melnechuk and F. O. Schmidt, Eds., Rockefeller University Press, New York.

Sperry, R. W. (1970) Perception in the absence of the neocortical commissures. *Proc. Ass. Res. nerv. ment. Dis. 48,* 123–138.

INDEX

INDEX

INDEX